Praise for *My Heart Is in the Earth*

Wayne Greenhaw has been one of the South's finest wordsmiths for a long time. In this perceptive collection we find him at the top of his game.

—Paul Hemphill

Few authors have written about Mexico as well as Mr. Greenhaw. I should know. I've lived in, run businesses, and written about Mexico for twenty years. My Heart Is in the Earth is a superb collection of stories about Mexico and Alabama written by a man who understands the nuances of each . . . His description of San Miguel de Allende and the "writers'" colony there in the 1950s is priceless. . . . The Jack Kerouac anecdotes are some of the best anywhere. . . . Students of Mexico will learn a lot here . . .

—"Mexico" Mike Nelson

A marvelous book. I love its gossipy overtones. When Frida Kahlo's leg was amputated, she wanted it sent to actress Dolores Del Rio who was having an affair with her husband Diego Rivera at the time.

—Ron Butler

For Wayne Greenhaw, writing and life are synonymous. From his childhood days in rural Alabama to his days spent south of the border in Mexico, he relates stories of his experiences, finding an Alabama/Mexico connection in some of the most unlikely places. . . . His cast of characters reads like a Who's Who of the Famous, from Governor George Wallace, a personal friend of his daddy, to William Spratling, an Alabama native son, who single-handedly revolutionized the silver and pottery-making industry of Mexico. . . . Each character gives Greenhaw's tales a special twist that makes life in both Alabama and Mexico easily understood.

—Bob Brooke

Wayne Greenhaw's generous heart is clearly in this scrupulously objective anthology of essays.

—David Lida

Also by Wayne Greenhaw

NONFICTION

Alabama: A State of Mind, Community Communications
and the Business Council of Alabama, 2000

Alabama on My Mind: A Collection, Sycamore Press, 1986

Alabama: Portrait of a State, Black Belt Press, 1998

Elephants in the Cottonfields: Ronald Reagan and the New Republican South, Macmillan, 1981

Flying High: Inside Big-Time Drug Smuggling, Dodd Mead, 1984

The Making of a Hero: Lt. William L. Calley and the My Lai Massacre, Touchstone, 1971

Montgomery: Center Stage in the South, Windsor Publications, 1990

Montgomery: The Biography of a City, The Advertiser Company, 1993

Watch Out for George Wallace, Prentice-Hall, 1976

NOVELS

Beyond the Night, Black Belt Press, 1999

The Golfer, J. B. Lippincott, 1968, also Sycamore Press, 1991

Hard Travelin', Touchstone, 1971

King of Country, Black Belt Press, 1994

DRAMA

Rose: A Southern Lady, a one-actress play

The Spirit Tree, a play in two acts

SHORT STORIES

Tombigbee and Other Stories, Sycamore Press, 1991

My Heart Is in the Earth

By
Wayne Greenhaw

MY HEART
IS IN THE EARTH

True Stories of Alabama and Mexico

By

Wayne Greenhaw

RIVER CITY PUBLISHING

Montgomery, Alabama

Copyright © 2001 by Wayne Greenhaw. Published in the United States by River City Publishing LLC, P.O. Box 551, Montgomery, AL 36101.

Library of Congress Cataloging-in-Publication Data:
Greenhaw, Wayne, 1940-
My heart is in the earth : true stories of Alabama and Mexico / by Wayne Greenhaw.
p. cm.
ISBN 0-913515-16-7 (alk. paper)
1. Alabama--Social life and customs--20th century--Anecdotes. 2. Alabama--Social conditions--20th century--Anecdotes. 3. Alabama--Biography--Anecdotes. 4. Greenhaw, Wayne, 1940---Childhood and youth--Anecdotes. 5. Lawrence County (Ala.)--Social life and customs--20th century--Anecdotes. 6. Lawrence County (Ala.)--Biography--Anecdotes. 7. Greenhaw, Wayne, 1940---Journeys--Mexico--Anecdotes. 8. Mexico--Description and travel--Anecdotes. 9. Mexico--Social life and customs--Anecdotes. 10. Mexico--Biography--Anecdotes. I. Title.
F330 .G76 2001
977.3'76--dc21
2001004618

Designed by Lissa Monroe.
Edited by Jim Davis.
Printed by Vaughan Printing in the United States of America.

River City publishes high quality fiction, nonfiction, poetry, and art books by distinguished authors and artists. Our imprints include River City, Starrhill, Sycamore, and Black Belt. Visit our web site at www.rivercitypublishing.com.

For my nieces & nephew,
Donna, Daren, Anna, & Krysten,
with love

CONTENTS

MEXICO

*

My Home, My Heart

*

I stood between my aunt and uncle's graves in the Montgomery cemetery near the community of Wren, south of Moulton, in north Alabama. I looked south at "the mountain," the first hill that rises up out of Lawrence County and begins the William B. Bankhead National Forest.

When I was growing up near here, my family always spoke of "the mountain," when talking about one-thousand-foot-high Penitentiary Mountain on the northern edge of Winston County, where my great-great-grandparents carved farms from the wilderness before the turn of the twentieth century.

Two Greenhaw brothers had made their way down the valleys of the west Carolinas and east Tennessee. One settled north of the Tennessee River in Limestone County. The other found a rich hillside, where he cleared the timber, built a log house with a chimney and fireplace made from the rocks dug out of the rough ground, and raised a family with the young woman he brought with him. Nearby, my Grandma Greenhaw's folks, the Montgomerys, forged a living next to a stream of water that later became known as Montgomery Creek. Both settlements are in what is now the northern region of the 179,000-acre national forest.

As I stand in the graveyard among my ancestors who are planted here, I gaze across the field toward the remains of the old dogtrot house where my father was born, the youngest of ten children. This place is where John Wesley Greenhaw brought his bride, Martha Susan Montgomery, after they were married in 1891, and constructed a two-room log house with an open hall down the middle, and later added room after room as children came along. They moved from here to Town Creek in 1923, and my Aunt Lucy, who was born in 1900 and never married, lived in that house until she died in 1997.

Standing here, I remember those twilights years ago, when we were heading south toward home in Trussville, when Daddy would say, "You boys stay awake now, because we're coming up on the place where Rube Burrow and his boys made their hideout." My brother and I would sit up in the back seat and peer out into the darkness, and I wondered about Rube and his gang of outlaws. Daddy had told us stories about the train robbers, whom he said were meaner and more famous than Jesse and Frank James, which was hard for us to believe, because we'd seen movies about Jesse and Frank at Saturday morning shows in Homewood.

Now, as I wander through these woods of oak and hickory and hemlock, beneath the 150-foot-tall poplar said to be Alabama's oldest tree, a tree that took root and began its growth about the same time Hernando DeSoto and his band of Spanish explorers traveled through the Alabama wilderness in the early 1500s, I think about the generations of my own family that have made their home here.

Alabama is much more than a *place* to me. It's a state of mind. Not only a place where I grew up, it is a history of people who carved a home for themselves and their children. My mother's father, Granddaddy Hiram Dizzy "Bub" Able, whom I write more about in later chapters of this book, once told me, "Son, it doesn't matter where you are, as long as your heart is in the earth. When your heart's in the earth, you know you're home."

Once we hiked through the virgin forest and found a place covered in thick emerald grass and soft moss. A gentle voice told a harrowing story about lovers getting lost in the Sipsey Fork, where the landscape is still breathtaking. I walked down a pathway walled with velvet-like moss and laced with frilly ferns. I heard the rush of water. The sound grew louder and closer, and the forest became cooler.

Deep in the woodlands, I stopped suddenly. I gazed toward a series of waterfalls. Framed in splotches of multicolored wildflowers, the splashing water beckoned me to rest. I put my head against a rock and enjoyed the outrageous beauty of the place where my ancestors once dwelled.

Within minutes, I lost myself in the place. I stripped and put my feet into the cool water and walked until it was waist-deep. When I was finally under the waterfall, I felt the cobwebs of workaday stress wash from my body and soul.

Later I lay once again in the dark green comfort of the forest, and thought about all the yesterdays — that evening when Daddy, proud of his upbringing, told us stories about the outlaw who robbed banks and lived in north Alabama. I sat on the edge of the virgin woodland next to the Sipsey River and looked into the past. I enjoyed my old family haunts — places where outlaws might hide — and I knew exactly why they settled here in the first place.

First published in *Alabama Magazine's* Back Porch Talk column, this remembrance appeared in a slightly different form in *Sojourn* magazine with a circulation of nearly three million. This piece, which I called "In the Forest," became the germ that grew into my remembrance published as the book *Beyond the Night* by Black Belt Press in 1999.

*

My Heart

*

In my eighteenth year I had the opportunity to travel, from my beloved Alabama home, to a region of Mexico previously unknown to me. In this book I go back in time to that wonderful summer of my youth. At that time I fell in love with Mexico, just as I had loved and continue to love my home state of Alabama. Through the years I have found many mysteries in both places. Both are laced with myths true and untrue. Both are filled with delightful people who amaze and confound. As Alabama has been viewed as a backward state, Mexico has often been written off as a third-world country. Neither is true.

In Mexico I have found warm, wonderful, generous, intelligent, interesting, and tragic people, and the same is true in Alabama. As anyone who knows me will tell you: I am Southern through and through. My roots are deep in Alabama soil. My ancestors came south out of Ireland and England, passing through Virginia, South Carolina, and Tennessee as early as the late eighteenth century. In Mexico I found a kinship in the people and in the history. Just as Alabama has been torn apart by the *Grand Causes* of the Civil War and the Civil Rights Movement, Mexico is a blend of contradictions. Once I walked among the thorns and briars of cacti

15

in the desert of the Bajio in central Mexico. I came upon an old Mexican with leather-like brown skin and I told him that I was from another country. He looked at me with wide-open black eyes that seemed to stare into my soul. He said words to me that I did not understand. I took the words back to the hacienda where I was staying. That night I asked my friend from California who had lived in San Miguel de Allende for years what the old man had said to me. He translated, "My heart is in the earth." I smiled and remembered the words that had been spoken by another old man of my youth, my granddaddy, Bub Able, and the words resonated with an eerie meaning.

The next day I went back to the place where I had found the old Mexican in the brown desert sand amid the thicket of cacti. He was not there. I walked over the area for several hours, but I never found him. I wanted to ask him about his words. I wondered how it was that he could have had the same thoughts of my own grandfather. I knew the old man had never been to Alabama. My grandfather certainly had never been to Mexico, although he loved to listen to me tell tales about my own youthful journeys to the fascinating foreign country. The words stayed with me, echoing in my brain, and they stay with me even now. When I think about the two countries that I love dearly, the American South and Mexico, I know that the words of the old men ring true even for me now: My heart is in the earth.

ALABAMA ☞

In Search of the Past

1.

Driving the backroads of Alabama—a singular pleasure that I learned from my father, the traveling salesman—I am transported back in time.

In the summertimes of my youth, my younger brother, Donnie Lee, and I rode with Daddy when he traveled Alabama and east Mississippi, stopping at barber and beauty shops, bringing them the latest stainless steel razors, smelly perfumed wave lotion from Revlon, the fanciest new dryers, and a tonic that would plaster hair to the scalp while turning it dark brown. *Agh!* as Donnie Lee might say.

It was on a highway in south Alabama that we were passed one afternoon by a pink Cadillac with a pair of cowboy boots sticking out the rear window. "That's ol' Hank," Daddy said.

Donnie Lee and I looked at each other, puzzled.

"In a minute or two there'll be another one just like that," Daddy said.

Donnie Lee questioned his statement.

But, sure enough, in a few minutes, the first car's twin, down to the snazzy fins shining brightly in the sunlight, passed us with a beep of its horn. Daddy answered and shot an abbreviated wave.

Lighting a new Kool cigarette from the butt of the one he'd been smoking, Daddy said, "We'll find 'em up ahead," then flipped the butt onto the shoulder of the road.

In the next town we found the two Cadillacs parked side by side facing the curb outside the drugstore. Daddy pulled his Chevrolet parallel to them. We followed him inside, where a skinny man wearing a white cowboy hat rose from the table where he sat with three friends and, grinning from ear to ear, greeted Daddy like a long lost relative. They hugged and carried on, Daddy introducing us as his "number one assistants," and told us, "Boys, this is Hank Williams, the most famous singer and songwriter ever to come out of Georgiana."

The skinny man hooted. "Now, that's about the best introduction I've ever had," he said, and ordered a round of Cokes, which we accepted with thanks. We slunk back on the edge of the shallow breeze from the slow-moving fan centered over the marble-topped table. In the shadows of glass-squared display booths we sipped our drinks while the men talked about "the road," Daddy asking where they'd played, Hank and his boys saying they'd had a big crowd down in Andalusia the night before, a lanky man with slender, almost feminine wrists and delicate, long-fingered hands saying, "There was a sassy little thing put her eyes on ol' Hank and didn't take 'em off for hours," and a heavier man with a stubble beard concluding, "Until somethin' else dropped off," and they all chuckled with an evil edge, and Daddy glanced toward us, smiling with the chatter.

With his bladed face cocked just so, the shadow of his wide-brimmed hat muting his features, Hank caught my eye and grinned and said, "What kind-a music you like, big 'un?" and I tried to hide behind my glass of Coke, pushing back shyly against the glass case. "Cat got yo' tongue?" he asked, and I put my mouth to the edge of the cold glass to keep from saying anything, feeling the heat of all their eyes on me. I wished we'd never seen the Cadillacs or the men, and I wondered when Daddy was going to take us on down the road, where he said he had more shops to call on.

When I finally did glance up, I looked directly into the bluest eyes I'd ever seen on a man. His thin mouth stretched into a generous smile. "How's about you boys coming out here to the car with me?" He pushed his chair back. "I got some things for y'all."

From the trunk of one of the pink Cadillacs he took two black-and-white eight-by-ten glossy photographs of himself, scratched out, "For Wayne, a fine young man," and signed it, then did the same for Donnie Lee. As we moved to the Chevrolet, he called, "You got a Victrola?" I nodded. Then he handed me a half-dozen 78 rpm records. "Y'all share 'em, okay?" I nodded.

When we returned home to Trussville on Friday, Mama questioned us about our week with Daddy. We showed her the photographs. We took the records to our room. As the first started to play, Donnie Lee made a face. I frowned and shook my head. I'd heard hillbilly sounds when we lived with my mother's parents, Granddaddy and Nanny, in rural Shelby County. They loved the country sounds of the Grand Ole Opry from Nashville every Saturday night. I listened but never enjoyed the guttural sounds, the guitar twangs and nasal drawls.

In memory, that trip with Daddy unwinds in shades of black-and-white colored with a streak of pink. Today, as I listen to the powerful poetic slur of his music, hitting notes that even he could not find on a scale between five parallel lines, sounding words that ring against the heart like coins dropped into a deep clear pool at the bottom of a deep dark cave, I am so moved that I am stunned

21

almost senseless with its beauty. Somewhere between then and now I learned to fathom the depths of his genius.

"Did you hear that lonesome whippoorwill? He sounds too blue to fly. The midnight train is whining low. I'm so lonesome I could cry."

How could any eleven-year-old ever know the naked strength of such words prayed to such sounds? The plaintive voice cuts to the heart that knows the secrets of being twisted and torn, battered and bruised, where the scar-tissue grates against old feelings that cannot — will not — remain hidden.

"I tried so hard, my dear, to show that you're my every dream. Yet you're afraid each thing I do is just some evil scheme. A mem'ry from your lonesome past keeps us so far apart. Why can't I free your doubtful mind and melt your cold, cold heart?"

When a man wakes alone in an old-time tourist court on a lost highway in the middle of nowhere with a hangover and a memory, last night's cigarettes sour in the roof of his mouth, the sound of a sweet thing's laughter echoing sadly in his ears, and a faded picture of Jesus staring down from the rain-stained wall, he knows the resonance of a Hank Williams blues song.

"I went down to the river to watch the fish swim by. But I got to the river so lonesome I wanted to die. Oh, Lawd, and then I jumped in the river but the doggone river was dry. I had me a woman, she couldn't be true. She made me for my money and she made me blue. A man needs a woman that he can lean on. But my leanin' post is done left and gone. She's long gone and now I'm lonesome blues."

Wandering through the old frame house that was the man's childhood home in Georgiana, listening to the song's words moaning out in the pained voice of the stranger I met in the drugstore so many years ago, I think back to that black-and-white day when Daddy was with us.

When Hank gets to the words, *"I'm goin' down in it three times, but I'm only comin' up twice,"* I feel his hurt, the deep-down hard

22

tones, the knowledge of my own hurt, my own pain in a technicolored world. I remember my father's hurt eyes in his last years, before he died at age fifty-three, long-suffering and lonesome.

As I stare into the face in a photograph on the wall, a photograph exactly like the ones Hank gave me and Donnie Lee so long ago, I see the playful glitter in his eyes, knowing more now than he could ever communicate to an eleven-year-old. I feel a hard spot form in my sternum, knotted in a knowledge that I had known him, if only for an instant out of time.

2.

Outside, I drift down the black-top highway westward, then south on County Road Five, bordered by thick pines draped with blankets of rich green kudzu, a world scented by rosin seeping from the stumps of clear-cut trees, where modern machines unearth roots and leave gaping wounds of red clay, to be washed by fall rains to form gullies that the kudzu was brought here to cover and protect in the first place.

Down County Road Five, moving slowly around lazy curves where I hear ghosts whispering amid scrub oak and lilac bushes and dogwoods crowded in clumps of wilderness, I remember a time before my time, when this was the Federal Road, used by pilgrims moving southwest out of the Atlantic coastal colonies of Virginia, North and South Carolina, and Georgia, following the natural pathways southwest, venturing into the frontier where they would seek a new life. It was down this road in the late 1700s that James T. Bates brought his wife, Elizabeth, and their children to a trickling stream called Burnt Corn Creek where spring water burst from the flat land. He took it as a sign from God that here was a place that was meant to be his home and he started clearing the thicket, plowing the land, and building a house.

As I ride down that same path through the same woodlands that James T. Bates and his family traveled more than two hundred years ago, I spot a fire-watch tower high above the two-hundred-foot-high pines. And I can't help but wonder what it would have been like to stand up there nearly two hundred years ago, watching as a hundred or so white soldiers attacked a trading party of fifty or so Red Stick Indians on their way back from Pensacola, where they'd bought and traded for flour and salt and sugar and other necessities, and where they had been given guns and ammunition by agents of Spain in their feeble attempt to stop the westward movement of new American pioneers into the territory. If you could have been high up, looking down from a distance through the sweltering humidity of that July afternoon in 1813, you would have seen the beginning of the Indian war, when the James T. Bates family, including six children, the oldest of whom was then a child of fourteen, heard gunfire in the distance.

Somewhere along the trail to the south and east, the fighting commenced.

3.

After Captain Samuel Dale was hit breast-high with a lead ball from an Indian rifle, he was carried into the darkness of a nearby swamp by one of his volunteer soldiers. Rebecca Bates, the oldest daughter of James and Elizabeth Bates, who had been sent to the spring to draw a pail of water, heard the men struggling in the dark foreboding wilderness. She ran to the house, where her father had built lean-to rooms for her and her siblings. She rushed in and told her parents about the men. James, who'd already taken down his long-barrel gun from its hooks over the mantel, ran to the edge of the thicket where his timber-clearing had stopped. He stood silent, listening, hearing the distant sounds of shots and then the rustling of the men in the swamp that was thick and dark with underbrush. Standing straight next to a large oak, he heard their excited talk in his own language. He then stepped out, raising his arms, signaling his peaceful intent.

Together, Bates and a young soldier named Thomas Guin assisted Captain Dale through the knee-deep mosquito-infested water to the high land, through the field where corn and beans had been planted in neat rows, and to the safety of Bates's house. Elizabeth Bates tore Dale's shirt from his body and extracted a lead ball from his chest and bathed the wound. "The Indians are armed and angry," Thomas Guin stated, and that message echoed from settlement to settlement. Frightened families fled south into what later became Baldwin County and took refuge in the home of Sam Mims, where barricades had been constructed and where settlers talked about keeping a full-time watch.

That watch was not active at noon on August 30, 1813. In fact, the security had become so lax, the inhabitants had allowed sand to heap up in a pile that blocked the main gate from closing. Red Stick Creeks, led by William Weatherford, known as Red Eagle, attacked the fort. An eyewitness account by Dr. Thomas G. Holmes, interviewed thirty-four years afterward by A. J. Pickett for his *History of Alabama,* described hours of slaughter, beginning when:

> . . . five of the principal prophets rushed with all their infuriated fanaticism to the centre of the fort over the body of [Major Jack] Beasly who had been dispatched with a war club—after reaching the centre of the fort, they got to dancing in defiance of the citizen soldiers, for they had assured their deluded followers that they could dance in defiance of American powder or ball for reason

25

if they attempted to shoot them, that their balls would split, but to their great disappointment they met their fate, and that very suddenly, for they were all five shot down, which it was said dampened the feelings of the whole Indian army—for much confidence had been placed in whatever they said, those deluded followers had evidence that they could not split balls, for before five o'clock five hundred had been pierced by American lead.

4.

On the day I listened to those words being read by Mr. Sam Lowrey, the proprietor and operator of the Burnt Corn General Store and Post Office, as well as the Lowrey Family Trust, which consisted of thousands of acres of southwest Alabama timberland, I wondered about the authenticity of such an account. "It is not whether every word, every detail, every figure, is exactly correct," Mr. Sam told me. "Listen to the cadence of the old man's talk, his remembrance of such an awful happening, probably the most important event to take place in the history of our great state." I listened, and I knew that he was right: Dr. Holmes's words are poetry in retrospect. They are powerful, especially when you consider their importance to our history. That day, according to Holmes, 453 women and children and another 100 citizen soldiers were killed during the afternoon. "The way that many of the unfortunate women were mangled and cut to pieces is shocking to humanity, for many of the women who were pregnant had their unborn infants cut from the womb and laid by their bleeding mothers," Holmes remembered, detailing the scalpings.

"It was this horrendous act—whether Dr. Holmes was exact in his emotional reminiscences or not—that was described to Old

Hickory as he sat on his porch at the Hermitage outside Nashville. After hearing the account of the massacre, General Jackson sent out the message that he needed his men to reunite for a new war. Then ol' Andy and his volunteer army marched south into Alabama with a mission: to drive the Indians to hell and beyond. And that's what they did at Horseshoe Bend."

Mr. Sam Lowrey sat at his desk in his newly paneled office in the rear of his old store. He was a man whose ancestors went back to those first Europeans who settled this wilderness, and he was very proud of his rich heritage. "The Indian war was what started it all," he said, resonating with feeling. "The first battle of the Indian war took place right down the road a piece." And later that day he showed me the trickling stream that is the beginning of Burnt Corn Creek and told me about Big Sam Dale and about the skirmish, and about James T. Bates and his family.

In a quietly dramatic fashion Mr. Sam built the drama, as the battles between the Indians and the settlers escalated. By the time Mr. Sam got to the description of General Jackson's attack at Horseshoe Bend that drove the Indians into the bloody Tallapoosa River, his voice was almost a whisper. Thinking back on it, he was a one-actor show, building to the climax, when Red Eagle rode onto the grounds near the confluence of the Coosa and Tallapoosa rivers in what later became Elmore County, near the spot where Fort Toulouse had stood as a French outpost to guard its territory. "Weatherford sat high on his horse. He was a proud and brave man, a leader of the Red Sticks, and his surrender did not come without a great deal of thought and heavy weight on his conscience. I think that he must have seen the inevitable: that without proper surrender, Jackson would slaughter and starve as many Indians as he could."

I shivered when Mr. Sam told me that story. Whether every exact detail is true or not doesn't matter. The essence of the tale is true. It is haunting. And I knew, when he told me I was sitting at the same place where two young writers before me stood, when they visited Burnt Corn and sat in the shadows of the store and listened to Mr. Sam tell his stories, that I was indeed in privileged company. "I remember Truman Capote came home one time driving a Jaguar. It was a fancy car, all spiffed up and shining. He was very proud of his possession and he wanted to show it off to his aunts and uncle and his friends in Monroeville. He and Harper Lee came down like they'd done many times before. And they sat right where you're sitting, and they asked me all about the history of this country." His eyes brightened with a quiet excitement. "It's a fascinating history, don't you think?"

I was enthralled with the history as he told it, as I read it in A. J. Pickett's book and Virginia Van Der Veer Hamilton's book, and others.

Without the excitement of discovery, what is history? For Mr. Sam, every dark corner of his tens of thousands of acres of history was exciting. As far as he was concerned, Captain Samuel Dale, Big Warrior, Red Eagle, the Bates family, all of them and their existence made Alabama what it was and what it is. As long as history lives for us, our state is vibrant.

I continue to ride the backroads, often slowly, always on the look, stopping at every historical marker, meeting the people in the little houses in the hollows, listening for the sound of a whippoorwill echoing just after twilight.

*

The Sunday of
"Seven Bridges Road"

*

When I heard the full mellow sounds of country singer Alan
Jackson's voice singing "Seven Bridges Road" on national television, I remembered a spring Sunday more than thirty years earlier
when the song was written.

It was a Sunday morning coming down, a slow breeze whispering through the trees next to the antebellum mansion in
Montgomery, Alabama, where I lived in an apartment carved from
many haunted rooms. It was a house that resonated with mysterious happenings in past and present. As I cradled a cup of hot coffee, new leaves fluttering outside, there was a feeling of expecta-
tion in the air.

When my friends showed up, beeping their horn for me, I was
fully awake, revived from a night of reveling, and ready to find
new adventure. My old college friend Jimmy Evans was driving.
Tall, thick, fast-talking when he talked at all, he was a young
lawyer home from graduate school in New York, a labor-law
expert now but still able to quote collegiate poetry through the
strings of a guitar. I sat shotgun. I listened as Jimmy talked about
the man we were going to see.

"C. P. Austin's a great guy. He's been around. He can play the box, man. I'm telling you, he can play." He laughed. "He knows the blues. He's been with all the greats, including Robert Johnson. Learned 'Key to the Highway' from the man himself. And 'Crossroads.' Plays 'Crossroads' as close to the man himself as anybody I've ever heard. He *feels* that song, like he feels life. You'll see."

In the backseat, Steve Young sat sideways, fumbling with the old guitar he'd picked up in a pawnshop after he'd gotten his second paycheck as a three-o'clock-in-the-morning milkman delivering for Hall Brothers dairy, south of Montgomery. Brown-haired with sensitive eyes, the native of Newnan, Georgia, who grew up in Gadsden, Alabama, strummed the box that lay like a baby in his lap. His fingers worked the strings easily, getting to know it, feeling it, twisting the tuning knobs between runs. He too knew guitars. He had been to California, written songs, played in famous rock 'n' roll bands, and now he was down here in Montgomery — stopping over to earn a little money, relax, refill his creative jug with the right juices, and smell the magnolia. He was a man whose talent ran thick and deep.

Heading southeast out of Montgomery on Woodley Road under a thick canopy of wistful Spanish moss, we traveled over several concrete bridges. The backroad pavement turned to dirt. We bounced over several more wooden bridges. In the backseat, Steve mumbled, "Y'all know this road's got seven bridges?" in his guttural Bob Dylan-esque growl. We paid no attention.

At the small community of Orion in rural Pike County, Jimmy pulled into the grassless yard of an unpainted frame house with a wide, inviting front porch. Children poured from the door. Chickens scattered from beneath the house. Sounds came from the rear, where an outhouse sat next to a red clay ravine.

After each child, the rickety screen door slammed shut. By the time we were out of the car, a slight-built, dark-skinned man with big bloodshot rheumy eyes stepped onto the porch. He rubbed the balls of his eyes with the back of his hands, blinked, and said, "How y'all?" in a voice that sounded like gravel in a grinder.

Everybody situated themselves on the front porch. C. P. Austin, master of the house, took his customary perch in a straight-backed cane-bottom chair. No doubt, that was his chair. Jimmy sat nearby. Steve took a seat. They held guitars. I leaned back against a post. I fumbled with a camera that I aimed at a child now and then, bringing hands to mouths and giggles of delight, punctuating the music that began momentarily.

After Mrs. Austin brought coffee, they tinkered with their instruments that came alive slowly and awkwardly in their hands.

"C. P. played Mississippi blues way back," Jimmy said.

"Did," C. P. said, and leaned into the guitar and ran long, knotted, loving fingers over the strings. The slightest frown touched his African lips. He adjusted. Ran again. *Do, do, do, do!* Down, then up the scale. Adjusted. Ran again: *Do, do, do, do!*

Then, with lively fingers, he made the box a walking, talking, singing, animated, living thing that took shape and character under those old knotted hands. The callus-layered tips of his fingers worked. Even his wrists contorted at an odd angle, adjusting with his thin shoulders bent forward, every movement calculated to get just the right sound, which poured forth and filled that little corner of the world.

The children—and even the chickens—hushed. Jimmy and Steve listened with guitars silent in their laps.

When C. P. finished the old-time tune with a slap of his wide palm against the wood, C. P. said, "I learnt that from a Miss'ippi blues man."

Then he started into another instrumental, narrating as he played, "I played once upon a time with Blind Lemon Jefferson and drunk whiskey over music with Leadbelly and hung out on the cross-corner from Robert Johnson, the bes' in the whole land. In a little ol' Delta town we matched one another stroke-for-stroke." He grinned. "I tried."

They were all old ones, from a slave version of "Barbary Allen" that his great-great-uncle had taught him when he was a boy on a farm in the Alabama Wiregrass, to Leadbelly's "Goodnight Irene," sung that same sad way Leadbelly sang it, leaving the last chord to echo a memory of her poor lost soul.

As soon as the final sound of one song was over, C. P. grinned again. "I knowed 'em all. I seen some good singers down in Atmore at the prison camp, voices full of loneliness and despair, and there were some good 'uns up in the Tenn'ssee River bottoms, cotton pickers who'd learnt 'em from their pappies and their pappy's pappy." He nodded. "Those boys had hurt deep down from way back in history, calling to them, the sound coming out whether they knew it or not." He grinned a knowing, awkward grin.

He took a break and we all drank beer and ate fried chicken, and Jimmy played some new old blues on his portable tape recorder. C. P. oohed and ahhed as his oversized ears pricked at the sounds.

C. P.'s brother-in-law came and talked a little and ate some and set up a chair in the yard where he cut the children's hair, and the boys continued playing on the porch.

Between numbers, C. P.'s hands reached out for the guitar, palming it, looking at it from end to end, examining every inch, like it was a brand new toy and not something he'd known all of his days. Before his second piece of chicken was finished, he had the instrument in his greasy hands again and was playing expertly what he'd just heard for the first time on the recording. Halfway through, he stopped. Started again. His eyes brightened. "I'll get it this time," he said.

"I played here and there. I don't stray too far from Orion no more." He glanced up and caught the stare of his young wife. He grinned, leaned forward, slammed a fan-sized palm against the guitar face and made it ring with an almost angry sound. His fingers danced across the strings, calluses catching the downbeat, and he sang loudly, full of heart, *"I got a gal, she be mine. I got a little gal, sweet as wine."*

When he finished, his eyes glistened, looking toward her again, grinning again, softer this time. "That 'un's mine." His leathery skin shone with the spring sunshine against his sweaty cheek. "Some blues songs is happy."

They played until late afternoon and their fingers were numb. All of the children's hair had been cut; the brother-in-law folded his stuff into a bag and put it into his car. We said goodbye. Looking back, I got one last glimpse of C. P. and his wife and three of the children on the porch. Jimmy drove off and I lowered my head, closing my eyes, with the sounds still running through my brain.

As the car bounced over a wooden bridge on Woodley Road, I awakened. I heard a new sound, a new rhythm, and Steve's voice announced, "This road's got seven bridges."

They didn't go home. They came to my apartment in Winter Place high on a hill above Montgomery. An old mansion where Scott Fitzgerald had courted Zelda Sayre in the elegant parlor in the 1920s, and where Hank Williams had once done a private gig in the basement where slaves had been kept a hundred years earlier. First, Steve jotted words on a piece of scrap paper balanced on Jimmy's rear fender. Inside, upstairs in the living room, Steve kept picking at the song, chording and finding phrases, like, *"I loved you*

*like a baby, like some lonesome child. I have loved you in a tame way —
and I have loved you wild,*" but it didn't all fall together that night.
He said he still had the sounds of C. P. Austin in his memory, and
that memory haunted him all the way north to Montgomery with
the moon shining through the moss as we headed home.

The next week, in Peek's Barbecue on Commerce Street in
downtown Montgomery, where Steve Young started at 10 P.M.,
playing until he took off on his three-in-the-morning milk route, he
told his audience he'd written a new song after traveling Woodley
Road. "It's called 'Seven Bridges Road,'" he said and started, "*Now
there are stars in the Southern sky, southward as you go. There is moonlight and moss in the trees down the Seven Bridges Road.*"

SEVERAL YEARS later Steve Young recorded his song, and in the
late '60s it became a hit by Joan Baez. In the '70s the Eagles flew it
to the top of the charts. Rita Coolidge recorded it, and so did Iain
Matthews. When Steve read somewhere that Alan Jackson was
also born in Newnan, Georgia, he wrote the famous country singer
a letter. He heard back that Jackson would like to meet him, but
they never came face-to-face. In 1998, "Seven Bridges Road" had
the powerful voice of Alan Jackson carrying its tune on the national airwaves during the Music City News Country Awards show.

After he wrote the song, Steve Young left his milk route
behind, started a California country-rock group called Stone
Country, cut an album, then went solo and made several more,
including *Rock Salt & Nails, Renegade Picker, Switchblades of Love,*
and *Honky Tonk Man.* For his 1991 CD recorded live in Houston,
Charlie Hunter wrote, "Steve Young is one of the greats. He's driv-
en, twisted, tortured to find what the truth of a situation is; be it
the truth of a relationship, the truth of his heritage as a Southerner
or as an American; the truth of the world in which he's chosen to

work and in which he and we must live. He's angry, didactic, filled with wonder. He's hard, proud and sometimes fighting mean. He's funny, sad and passionate. And he believes unerringly in what he does." Also on the jacket of that work, Townes Van Zandt wrote, "He is a spiritual hero of mine, and I love him." Some of his top hits include "Montgomery in the Rain," "All Her Lovers Want to Be the Hero," "Ragtime Blue Guitar," "Long Way to Hollywood," "The White Trash Song," "Many Rivers," and many more. Hank Williams Jr. made a hit of "Montgomery," and Waylon Jennings made "Lonesome, On'ry and Mean" his signature tune.

Part Cherokee Indian, Steve grew up in Southern Baptist fundamentalism. Mix that with some New Age Zen and you've got something to behold. "My songs contain blues, folk, rock, Celtic and gospel feels, black and Native American elements, and many other influences," he says. "My music is not just country, it's Southern music."

Within a year of our Sunday in Orion, Jimmy Evans became a municipal judge in Montgomery; then district attorney, then attorney general of the state, until he was defeated for re-election in 1994. Later he was just another laid-back guy who still played a mean Sunday-afternoon guitar.

Little more than a month after our visit, we received word that C. P. Austin fell from his front porch, hit his head on a rock, and died in a Pike County hospital.

This recollection first appeared in *Alabama Magazine* in a shorter version. *Music City News* published this account in the fall of 1999.

REMEMBERING BOBBY SHELTON
AND THE KU KLUX KLAN

*

When Robert Shelton, Imperial Wizard of the United Klans of America, recently claimed the KKK was having a resurgence, painful pictures were brought back into my mind. He declared that, because President Jimmy Carter was elected by "94 percent of the black vote and 84 percent of the Jewish vote," there would be a white people's revolt.

I remember when Bobby Shelton pumped gas at a filling station down the street from my home in Tuscaloosa, Alabama. We used to pass by on our way to and from school and look out the corners of our eyes at him. He was a "tush hog"—a tough guy—or thought he was. He was a friendly enough good old boy, full of himself, talked loudly, and pranced back and forth in his father's store. He always spoke out on issues in an Archie Bunker manner.

We knew he was head of the Ku Klux Klan. I told my friends what that was. I had seen a Klan head when I was a little kid. He had been a big and burly railroad man who lived down the block. When we visited kinfolks in Holt, a coal-mining suburb where my uncle ran a grocery store in a predominantly black neighborhood, my cousins and I would play in the yard until after nightfall. One night, we heard a female screaming and rushed down the gravel drive to see what was going on.

A half-block away we saw the darkness brighten with hand-held torches. Hooded men stomped in a circle in a black man's yard. Within minutes, the figures threw the torches onto a pyre. A yellow-blue blaze leaped upward, parting in the middle of a cross and flaming angrily toward the sky.

Silent and breathless, we crouched behind a honeysuckle-covered fence and watched. The men chanted something we could not understand, marched off, got into their cars, and drove away as slowly as a funeral procession. They left behind a silence as remorseful as a new grave.

The next morning, when I saw the frightened eyes of the black children as they were being pushed past the charred ashes, my father told me the people there did nothing to deserve such treatment. The cross was burned, he said, "because they're colored people." I asked no more questions, but the memory stuck.

After I got to know Bobby Shelton, I always remembered back to that time in my childhood. In my senior year in high school he campaigned in the Alabama gubernatorial race against George Wallace, the moderate candidate. After he was defeated in the runoff, Wallace declared, "I'll never be out-niggered again." Four years later Wallace had the support of Bobby Shelton's Klan group.

In 1962, as a reporter, I watched Bobby Shelton speak to a group in a lot in Warrior, Alabama. Dressed in his special red-satin gown with its fiery dragon stitched across the chest, he lashed out against the "nigger-loving, Jew-embracing Kennedys." He spoke on behalf of Wallace's candidacy for governor. Wallace, he said, "will stand in the schoolhouse door and keep our children from becoming mongrelized by the degenerate races."

A half-dozen years later, after the schoolhouse stand and public schools in Alabama were integrated, Bobby Shelton was impris-
oned for contempt of Congress. And after he was freed, his power
diminished. The membership in his organization dropped.

But not long ago a splinter group in Alabama advertised the
largest cross-burning in history. I traveled to Theodore, Alabama,
near Mobile, and watched three dozen hooded and robed Ku
Kluxers gather in the twilight. After a prayer by the Kludd, their
chaplain, the group, including several pint-sized four-year-old
robed and hooded figures, marched around and around the huge
cross, which looked as though it were made of railroad cross-ties.

When night fell, torches were lighted. When the torches were
thrown, the flame climbed the wood. The dancing flames blinded
the stars. And while the Klanspeople were jubilant, the spectators
where I stood were stunned.

I blinked my eyes, fighting tears. It was a hateful cross. To me,
it was not as large nor as mean as the one that had burned in my
childhood. Hopefully, I thought, it would be the last cross.

This article ran on the Op-Ed Page of *The New York Times* on Saturday,
July 8, 1978. Shortly thereafter I would learn about a man with a dual
identity. I had already known Asa Earl "Ace" Carter as a friend and associate of Bobby Shelton and a speechwriter for Governor George C.
Wallace in the 1960s. Next I would discover his new role.

*

ASA EARL CARTER:
A MAN WITH TWO IDENTITIES

*

In the aftermath of defeat in the Alabama governor's race of 1958, George C. Wallace chomped on his cigar, gritted his teeth, and brooded with his cronies in a smoke-filled room at the Graystone Hotel on Commerce Street in downtown Montgomery.

Race was the issue that had beaten him, he declared. He hadn't pounded hard enough. If anything, people saw him as too easy on the race issue. He was painted as a moderate, if not a liberal. He promised, as reporters would hear later, that it would never happen again.

Not long after, Wallace was introduced to a man who changed his life, reinforced his political ideals, and confirmed his destiny as the white voters' champion of the Southern cause. He shook the hand of Asa Earl Carter, a burly, brooding, dark-eyed, broad-shouldered poet from the northeast Alabama foothills of the Appalachians.

Asa, also known as Ace, was a bona fide Ku Klux Klan original, espousing a hard-boiled anti-black and anti-Jewish philosophy. He had been fired as a radio announcer by several stations for

41

his sudden racist outbursts. He had even been arrested several times after racist-inspired violence.

One of Wallace's well-heeled cronies hired Carter to write speeches Wallace would deliver on the campaign trail. And after Wallace won the governorship in 1962, his famous declaration, "Segregation today! Segregation tomorrow! Segregation forever!" flowed from Asa's pen before it sprang from George's mouth.

As time passed, Asa Carter broke with Wallace, declaring, even weeping, that the governor had abandoned their sacred cause. Then, mysteriously, Asa broke with Asa—inventing a new identity for himself. He became Forrest Carter, the writer known for novels such as *The Outlaw Josey Wales*, and more famously for cooking up an Indian childhood for himself and spinning the popular yarn *The Education of Little Tree*, lauded by New Age prophets as the gospel for their way of life.

But the Asa Carter story might make the best book of all.

WE BEGIN this Asa story in the middle, back in the 1950s.

Leaving the Navy, after the *Brown v. Board of Education* ruling by the U.S. Supreme Court struck down segregated schools, Asa Earl Carter turned up as a talk-show host on Denver, Colorado, radio, railing against the "nigger-loving Supreme Court."

Not long thereafter he was back in his home state of Alabama, making similar statements on radio, where he was hired by the American States Rights Association, a group of local businessmen opposed to integration of the school system. On station WILD, he ranted against National Brotherhood Week, sponsored by the National Conference of Christians and Jews. After this tirade, even the most conservative station in Birmingham thought he had gone too far and dismissed him.

He surfaced again to form a White Citizens Council that flourished after the Montgomery bus boycott got under way in December of 1955. Soon he counted as many as thirty chapters under its charter. "We will not allow Jews in our organization," Carter told journalists. "We believe that this is basically a battle between Christianity and atheistic communism, of which the Jewish people are a part."

He developed his own brand of political incorrectness. In speeches, he held up copies of *The Birmingham News*, which he called "*The Birmingham Jews*," and pointed toward the *Blondie* comic strip, telling his audience that Dagwood's foolishness "undermines fatherhood, a sacred value in the Christian family."

When Montgomery native Nat King Cole returned to Alabama in April of 1956 to sing at a concert in Birmingham, Carter and four others picketed the hall, and later threw eggs at the entertainer and physically attacked him on stage. They were taken to the Birmingham jail, but within a few hours Asa Carter was out. Unlike his friends, he was never prosecuted. Asa Carter walked free.

Carter recruited several dozen white men from small towns and suburbs north of Birmingham into an organization he called The Original Ku Klux Klan of the Confederacy. He wrote the bylaws, designed its Confederate-gray cloaks, and was paid from membership dues as its "political adviser," a position he later claimed was his only Klan connection.

In 1957, a gunfight broke out at a statewide meeting of The Original KKK of the Confederacy. Two men were shot and left for dead. One later identified Carter as the culprit, according to several accounts of the time. Again, the state arrested Carter, but the case fell apart for lack of evidence after the victim recanted his story.

That same year, six members of Carter's Klan abducted a black man on Labor Day, carried him to woods outside Bessemer, a steel-mill town west of Birmingham, and sliced off the man's scrotum. A Carter friend, Oxford bartender Buddy Barnett, said Carter told him that the Klansmen should not have tortured the black man: They should have simply killed him, rather than pouring turpentine on his wound and making him scream. "It would have been better to have killed him than to do that," Barnett said, quoting Carter, according to an interview given to *Texas Monthly* writer Dana Rubin.

In the late '50s, Carter swore that he would spill his own "blood on the ground" to put an end to integration. As for federal judges, he stated, "If it's violence they want, it's violence they'll get."

WHEN WALLACE met Asa Carter, who with Grand Wizard Bobby Shelton of the Tuscaloosa-based White Knights of the Ku Klux Klan had backed John Patterson for governor in 1958, Carter had run fifth in a five-man race for lieutenant governor in the Democratic primary. At that time in Alabama, the Democratic nomination to a statewide office was tantamount to victory. Wallace's longtime friend Oscar Harper said he had been told that Carter "was a good man, believed the way we did, and was one helluva writer."

With the help of Seymore Trammell, then district attorney of Barbour County, where Wallace was still circuit judge, Carter came on board the Wallace campaign for governor in 1962 as a speechwriter, paid by a printing company owner, a road contractor, and an insurance executive — all Wallace cronies.

In the rear office at the Wallace campaign headquarters in Montgomery, Carter worked virtually unnoticed. He conferred with Wallace or Trammell or another of Wallace's close associates, disappeared into the office, then reappeared with a sheath of paper for the candidate. After Wallace won, Carter arranged for one of the most important policy meetings that the governor-elect would participate in.

In a mezzanine conference room at the Graystone, Wallace gathered with some of the kingpins of segregation, who were looking for someone to represent their Southern way of thinking. Wallace, a cigar clenched in one side of his mouth, told them, "I'm your boy," as witnesses, one to become a state Supreme Court justice, would later recall.

Seated around the table were Governor Ross Barnett of Mississippi, Judge Leander Perez of Plaquemines Parish in the marshlands of southern Louisiana, and James Gray, who would run for governor of Georgia in 1966.

Sitting against the wall were Asa Carter, Trammell, who had been appointed finance director in the new administration, and several other Wallace lieutenants.

Perez, a heavy-set man with a booming voice, broke the ice. "We don't let the niggers have their way down in Plaquemines." His high white pompadour seemed to bob as he spoke.

"We're going to show everybody in this country where we stand," Wallace promised the judge.

"I hope you let 'em know loud and clear, governor," Perez said.

Carter struggled for several days to whittle a sharp, silver-tongued and memorable inaugural speech for the new governor. Early on inauguration day, January 14, 1963, Carter brought Wallace his latest revised version. Editor Grover Cleveland Hall Jr. of the *Montgomery Advertiser* read over the speech, polished a few phrases, chopped away some of the most inflammatory words and returned it to Wallace. But Wallace, disregarding Hall's advice, decided to keep the declaration, "Segregation now! Segregation

45

tomorrow! Segregation forever!" Carter said the words would resound across America. Anything less, he said, would be "weak and phony." Wallace agreed.

Listening that cold afternoon on the steps of the Capitol where Jefferson Davis had taken the oath of office as president of the Confederate States of America 102 years earlier, Judge Leander Perez told his rebel-rousing friends, "That's our man for president."

In June, Wallace stood outside a doorway at the University of Alabama, raising his hands to turn away two young blacks who came to register for summer term. When confronted by Assistant U.S. Attorney General Nicholas Katzenbach, Wallace once again spoke words that Asa Carter had composed for him, calling the federal intervention "unwelcomed, unwanted, unwarranted, and force-induced intrusion."

A year later, when Wallace decided to "take the Alabama message" to Ivy League campuses in an abbreviated bid for the presidency, he used Carter-prepared texts. Speaking about the *Brown v. School Board* decision, he said it did not, "as some seem to think, spring instantly into existence full-grown and ready for action, equipped with injunctive process, preferred appeal, set bayonets, and all its accouterments, like Botticelli would have us believe Venus came to the shores of Greece, full-grown and full-blown, on the breath of Boreas."

Jabbing at the air with his pointed finger in staccato movements, shifting forward with his shoulders like the Golden Gloves boxer he once had been, Wallace declared, "To ask us to equate our children, classroom for classroom, with a race that is two years behind at the sixth grade and three years behind at the twelfth grade is to ask us to deprive our children of the education to which they are entitled."

WALLACE WAS a country boy, like Asa Carter. Like Carter's family, his had felt the brunt of the Great Depression. They were poor. Their fathers had lost what little they had. Wallace knew, when he spoke at the colleges, that he spoke not to Ivy League children, though they comprised his audience. Rather, he spoke to white working men and women, middle-aged and middle-class, the first generation out of the Depression, growing up and building families after World War II, proud of their gains and not wanting to lose ground.

In the South and in the North, these whites were scared of the black man, scared of his impact on their neighborhoods, house prices, and schools, scared of competing with him for their jobs. Wallace and his speechwriter recognized it as a down-deep gut-felt fear. It was very real.

In 1966, when the Alabama Senate refused to pass a law to allow Wallace to succeed himself as governor, he talked his wife, Lurleen, into running. At first, she read whatever her husband and his people put in front of her. Later, she refused to speak the words written by Asa Carter. "That's not the way I talk," she said. "I'm my own person. I'll write my own speeches." Seymore Trammell remembered, "She didn't want hate in her speeches. She refused to ball her fist and spit words of hate." George's brother, Gerald, said, "She let us know straight-out that she was her own woman. She wouldn't have a thing to do with Asa Carter. I think she saw straight through him for what he was."

Carter was gone. By the time Lurleen died in office eighteen months after her inauguration, George Wallace was ready to run for the presidency on a third-party ticket. He knew what to say to the people of America. He could say it, he felt, better than Asa Carter could write it. He was his own pollster. He talked to the taxi drivers and short-order cooks, bellhops and barbers, and he knew that talking in short, direct sentences was his way now, not alliteration or poetic metaphors.

Although he did not use Asa Carter's words, he did use the man and his old buddy, Klan Grand Wizard Bobby Shelton. The two were dispatched to the Midwest where they spoke with numerous Klan factions in favor of Wallace's candidacy. They reported back to the national headquarters in Montgomery that their trip had been a success: the Klan was solid behind Wallace. Wallace won ten percent of the vote in the general election of 1968 against Republican Richard Nixon and Democrat Hubert Humphrey. On the campaign trail, Wallace had said there was "not a dime's worth of difference in the two."

In 1970, when Wallace ran for governor again, his old wordsmith was on the other side. Carter, running on the Segregationist Party ticket, was a candidate himself, and a losing one.

At Wallace's inauguration the following January, Carter and a few of his associates from Oxford picketed the event. They carried placards reading "Wallace Sold Out" and "Free Our White Children." They handed out pamphlets written by Carter called *The Southerner*, stating that "the white people and their state government are being quietly and slyly sold out to the Negroes and their communist bosses."

I was covering the day's activities for *The Alabama Journal* newspaper in Montgomery. After the governor's speech, I sat on the back steps of the Capitol with Carter.

He began telling me that "Wallace is a no-account liar" and "a cheat who has stolen the integrity from the office of governor" and "a phony filled with the hot air of hypocrisy."

Within moments tears were pouring down Asa Carter's cheeks. He shook his head. "I believed in him," he said. "I sat with him. I held his hand. I nurtured him. I believed deeply that he was the great man we had been waiting for. And now . . .

48

"God! The office of governor has a *nothing* filling the chair where greatness is supposed to sit. There is a void. It is pitiful, absolutely pitiful!

"If we keep on the way we're going, with the mixing of the races, destroying God's plan, there won't be an Earth on which to live in five years."

He rose and walked to the car where his friends were waiting. He turned to me with tears still streaming down. "Farewell," he said, got into the car, and they drove away.

PUBLIC RECORDS in Birmingham and Calhoun County show that, in the subsequent months, Asa Earl Carter fell on hard times. He set up a statewide paramilitary group whose members wore gray arm bands emblazoned with Confederate flags. He spoke to the group several times, passed buckets to take up a collection, but netted only a few dollars.

He attempted to organize an all-white private-school system, but Alabama Attorney General Bill Baxley sued to stop tax illegalities. Carter struck back in *The Southerner*, writing that Baxley had hired a "bushy-headed black buck" as an assistant. That assistant, Myron Thompson, a graduate of Yale Law School, later was appointed U.S. District Court judge by President Jimmy Carter, no relation to Asa. By the end of 1971, Asa Carter was arrested three times within a year on alcohol-related charges.

Then Carter left Alabama. It has been explained that he disappeared to seek redemption; that he fell into deep depression after a personal wrestling bout with alcoholism, and fought his way out of the dark chasm by attacking empty pages with a pen as his weapon.

"When I visited with him several times," recalled an old friend, "he asked, 'Have you ever seriously studied the problems that existed for Southerners at the end of the Civil War? It was as bad for them then as it is for us now. We have been faced with two great wars: the Civil War and the battle over so-called civil rights.

"'Following the War Between the States, good law-abiding citizens like Jesse and Frank James up in Missouri had to continue the fight against the phony establishment that moved in and began enforcing illegal laws. They became outlaws because they fought against the tyranny of Union reconstructionists who twisted and turned the so-called laws to benefit themselves.'

"By the time he finished talking," his old friend said, "I was mesmerized."

Carter and his wife, India, sold their house outside Oxford, moved to St. George's Island off the Florida panhandle, and soon they drifted west. By the time they found a home in the Indian nation of Oklahoma and northeast Texas, Asa's identity had changed almost entirely. It was as though the new environment changed his persona and his history. He took the name of Forrest Carter from his hero, Confederate General Nathan Bedford Forrest, the first head of the Ku Klux Klan. This new name posed no problem for Carter. Through the years he had been known as Bud as a boy, Earl in Colorado, and Asa or Ace in Alabama. Some of his distant kinfolk lived on the Cherokee reservation, and to them he claimed to be a half-Indian known to his tribal relatives when he was a boy as Little Tree. Later investigations showed he was probably one-eighth Cherokee. His great-grandmother on his mother's side was apparently full-blooded Cherokee and his great-grandfather was part-Cherokee.

Carter adopted the role of a cowboy, wearing jeans, bolo tie with turquoise stone, and a black wide-brimmed Stetson-style hat. He would while away the hours in honky tonks, listening to cowpokes talk. He had given up hard whiskey and occasionally sipped a beer.

In 1973, he traveled back to Alabama where he self-published his first novel, *The Rebel Outlaw: Josey Wales*, using a small-town printer and a local graphic designer. In Montgomery, he delivered several copies to old friends around the Capitol, including one to Secretary of the House John Pemberton, signed, "From your old buddy, Asa 'Forrest' Carter," and one to Pemberton's assistant, Ray Andrews.

Back in Texas, Carter continued to write. He sent *Josey Wales* to a half-dozen New York agents, telling them a story about having sold thousands of copies across the South and the West out of the trunk of his car. One person to receive a copy was well-known agent and editor Eleanor Friede, who had become famous in the publishing world for having discovered the book *Jonathan Livingston Seagull*, which sold in the millions. Married to a Manhattan Jewish publisher, Mrs. Friede had been close friends with Truman Capote, whose image as a homosexual Southern writer had infuriated Carter, who preached against "New York Jews and queers controlling and destroying the media in this country."

From long distance, Carter told Mrs. Friede that he was "a good old country boy who was awestruck by the great, huge publishing world in New York," remembered a Carter buddy, while in the darkness of his honky tonk world "he railed against his natural enemies: blacks, Jews and homosexuals."

With the help of several men, one a rancher named Don Josey, a Confederate-history buff whose name Carter apparently borrowed for his hero, and Ron Taylor, an Alabama friend, he sent telegrams and letters to Mrs. Friede from around the South and West, making her think that he was constantly on the move. In various messages he told her he was "hidin' out," contemplating ideas and writing. He painted himself as a drifting cowboy, needing "quiet time to meditate and create," as Taylor said. "He kept feeding her these side stories to confuse her," Taylor told *Texas Monthly* reporter Dana Rubin.

In the meantime, Delacorte Press, with which Mrs. Friede published a line of books under her own imprint, contracted to publish *Josey Wales* under the title *Gone to Texas*. When it was published, publicity material stated: "Forrest Carter is a cowboy, an Indian, and the author of an exciting and authentic novel of the Reconstruction period."

The novel sold well in hardcover. Clint Eastwood bought the story and made it into a motion picture. Carter was on his way as a novelist.

With the publication of the sequel in 1976, *The Vengeance Trail of Josey Wales*, Carter flew to New York and appeared on the *Today* show, interviewed by Barbara Walters. Tanned and slimmer than he had been in his Alabama years, he had also grown a thick mustache and kept his black hat pulled down low on his forehead.

Nevertheless, his Alabama acquaintances were quick to recognize him. George Wallace confidant Oscar Harper was shaving when he received a call from Ray Andrews, who said, "Ol' Asa's on TV. He's pulling the wool over Barbara Walters's eyes." Harper turned on NBC and "sure enough, it was Asa putting on some kind of cowboy act." Also seeing him was another man from his past, Montgomery Circuit Judge Richard P. Emmet, who said, "Asa proved that morning that he was a terrific actor. There was no doubt about who he was, but he kept saying he was Forrest Carter, a cowboy and a storyteller to the Cherokee nation. He'd always claimed to be part-Indian, but it was the first time I'd heard about his being raised out West. He'd always said he came from northeast Alabama near Oxford."

None of his old friends were particularly alarmed at Asa's new identity. He had been a mysterious sort throughout the years of his life in, out, and around Alabama. After all, he was writing fiction under a fictitious name and a made-up identity. Other writers through literary history have done the same.

But then, in June of 1976, *Publishers Weekly* carried an advertisement announcing the fall publication of *The Education of Little Tree*, a true story of "Cherokee wisdom imparted by his grandparents to the orphaned Little Tree."

At about this time, Forrest Carter began adding to the end of his signature a circle with a tiny tree inside. It was to become his literary trademark.

BY LATE summer I had become aware of the double identity. As a reporter for *The Alabama Journal*, the capital city's afternoon newspaper, for twelve years, having won numerous awards for journalism, including a year at Harvard as a Nieman Fellow, I recognized this as a good story. It had the irony and notoriety that would give it national import: the author who wrote the enormously popular Clint Eastwood movie was also the author of George Wallace's famous speech resounding with the words "Segregation forever!"

I interviewed numerous people who had known Asa and who knew Forrest, and were sure beyond a shadow of their doubt that Asa and Forrest were one and the same. One was a lawyer who represented Carter in several of his Klan-related incidents in the early '60s. He told me that "Asa's writing stories that are selling in the millions." He also said if I pursued the story "you might get hurt and members of your family might get hurt."

In late July, Carter's editor, Eleanor Friede, who told me that Forrest had assured her he was not Asa, sent me a copy of the galley-proofs to *The Education of Little Tree: A True Story*, scheduled for publication under her imprint by Delacorte in October. She told me I could not speak with the author, who was in England promoting the publication there of *The Vengeance of Josey Wales*.

In August, I telephoned Mrs. Friede and told her I would very much like to talk with Carter. I told her I believed the autobiography to be a hoax. I related several facts of which I was sure: one, Carter was no orphan; two, his grandparents were not full-blooded Cherokees; three, he was not raised in the wilderness.

"How do you know this?" she asked.

At that moment, while talking with her, I was looking at a photograph of "The Carter Family" in a brochure Asa had given me in January of 1971. It had been an information piece distributed during his race for governor on the Segregationist ticket. The headline read "To Save Our Children." Shown in the photo, along with Asa, his wife, three sons, and a daughter, were his father and his mother. Among other information in the brochure was this background: "Asa Carter was born and raised on a small farm near Oxford, Alabama. His date of birth is September 4, 1925. He is 44 years of age." It also stated: "Forebears of Asa Carter settled in what is now Calhoun County in 1826. The Carter family lives on a farm in the small community of White Plains, located between Oxford and Piedmont, Alabama." There was not one word about Cherokee or any other Indian ancestry.

However, the same brochure did praise Asa as "a unique figure of our times. With his abilities and talents, he could have made a personal, comfortable place for himself in the profession of politics. He has refused. This would have meant compromise. This refusal has led the professional politician to uncomfortably regard him as unreasonable. He is a stubborn and knowledgeable foe of the communist and liberal. He has chosen the hard road where all uncompromising men must go. He has cast his lot in the mold of the gut fighter, to die or live as the Cause he loves must die or live. He is inextricably a living part of that Cause."

Mrs. Friede said she could not believe "the loving and gentle giant I know as Forrest Carter could ever have been a segregationist, much less a Klansman and definitely not anti-Semitic."

On his return to the United States, Carter telephoned me from Kennedy Airport in New York. "Hey, old buddy, you don't want to hurt old Forrest, do you?" he asked in a jovial growl. I assured him I did not wish to harm him in any way.

"Awe, come on, Asa, 'fess up," I said, being just as down-home as he. Then Carter denied being Asa or a political figure in Alabama and said he was both a cowboy and an Indian and insisted *Little Tree* was the faithful story of his own childhood. His wife, India, wrote a long letter to Mrs. Friede telling the story of having been married to a mean and cruel man, Asa Earl, back in Alabama, where they were visited by Asa's nephew, Forrest, who was bright and clear-headed, kind and generous. She told of falling in love and running away with the nephew, leaving Asa in rural Alabama.

After my original article appeared in *The New York Times* on August 26, 1976, Carter wrote a four-page letter to Eleanor Friede further perpetuating the hoax of *Little Tree*. Not only stating there would be retractions forthcoming from several of the people whom I quoted — retractions that were never made — he also insisted that "I did not have a family" and that "I am a bastard." Because he lived by a "code," he wrote, he did not wish to go on television again to promote *Little Tree* "because they ask questions, and keep boring in about people."

In an attempt to explain himself and his book, he continued: "I hope you understand, and you are the only person I care about understanding, that I feel [an] obligation toward protecting old folks and not making them a laughing stock in the world they live in. That is why I went West when I was young. Maybe I was wrong in coming back and asking for family records, which were not really records that belonged to me, but all of them were kind, and I substituted pieces of their family, and they said this was all right, because I did not hurt anybody in writing the *Little Tree* book, and they wanted me to succeed."

He continued, after stating "I am a bastard": "People think that children do not listen and understand, but before I was five, I knew that they said my ma was no good. And so this sort of sets you awash, with no anchor; but Granpa and Granma gave me an anchor; and if she wasn't any good, according to whatever the rules was, this you must remember that all Indians are disgusting when they touch the rules and codes of the city, and breeds are even more perplexing."

Years later, his younger brother, Doug, told reporters he doubted that there was any Indian blood in the family's history. He also stated that Granpa in *Little Tree* was based on their great-grandfather, James Weatherly, who died when Asa was only about five years old. In the tale, Little Tree lived with Granpa. In real life, Asa never lived with him, according to Doug Carter.

Forrest Carter's last published work was a novel based on the life of Geronimo, *Watch for Me on the Mountain*. It was such a compelling account that, in a review, Pulitzer Prize–winning author Larry McMurtry said Carter came "closer than anyone to writing the great American novel of the Indian."

Such words of praise from a writer-historian of such stature as McMurtry, it would seem, would validate Carter's standing as a major novelist.

Shortly after the novel was published, Carter was passing through Texas on his way to Hollywood to talk with producers about making *Mountain* into a movie. Having gained back much of the weight he had lost, he was also drinking again, and friends said he looked dissipated.

While visiting the home of his son near Abilene, he died on June 8, 1979. The cause of death was listed as "aspiration of food and clotted blood" due to a "history of fist fight." According to the *Texas Monthly*, "The ambulance driver told one of Carter's friends that Carter had had a drunken fight with his son, fell, and most likely choked on his own vomit."

His funeral was as intriguing as his life. A Calhoun County photographer remembered that Asa's body was returned to White Plains several days after his death. "Late that morning I went to the funeral home, found several of his relatives—his widow, India, and two of the sons—and several people from New York. I followed the hearse to the cemetery, where words were said over 'Forrest Carter,' and an Indian did a chant. I went back to Anniston but was called by a friend at the funeral home several hours later. It seemed that the coffin was not buried. After the New York people left, the coffin was brought back up, the entire family and friends from around here listened to the words of a preacher who spoke about Asa Earl Carter, and he was buried again."

MORE THAN a decade later, after hundreds of thousands of copies of the trade paperback edition of *The Education of Little Tree* were sold by the University of New Mexico Press, once again the mystery surfaced.

Shortly after the *Los Angeles Times* published a tribute in 1991 to "the greatest memoir for New Age followers," a piece appeared in *The New York Times* by historian and Wallace biographer Dan T. Carter of Georgia, who had borrowed my extensive file on Asa-Forrest to assist in the writing of his book, *Politics of Rage: George Wallace, the Origins of the New Conservatism, and the Transformation of American Politics*. Dr. Carter once again wrote about the double identity. Subsequent articles followed in *Texas Monthly*, *People*, and elsewhere.

Later, India Carter finally admitted that Asa and Forrest were one and the same. She stated unequivocally, however, that he was not anti-Semitic and was never in the Klan. Afterward, Elizabeth C. Hadas of the University of New Mexico Press issued a statement that "in all new editions, we will remove the label 'a true story' from the book's jacket and cover."

Though *Little Tree* continued to sell well, Asa's ghost seemed to follow it. In December of 1997, *The New York Times* published an article by reporter Bernard Weinraub telling about the just-released movie of *Little Tree* and asked rhetorically, "Can *The Education of Little Tree* overcome its origins?"

Jake Eberts, the producer who remained interested in *Little Tree* after Steven Spielberg and others dropped interest after the Asa Carter revelations, defended the book, telling the *Times*, "It's a beautiful story."

Director Richard Friedenberg added, "Here was a guy who did bad things, disappeared off the face of the Earth in Alabama, where he was a Ku Kluxer, and reappears in the Oklahoma-Texas area near the Cherokee reservation of the western Cherokee nation, where he proceeded to write several books. It strikes me he spent his literary life, and whoever he was in his second phase, in some kind of grand apology for his first life." He added, "No one knows the absolute truth."

"Absolute" is a difficult word to define when writing about such an elusive person as Carter: Asa, Ace, Forrest, Little Tree. Since I first uncovered his multiple identity in 1976, reporters and columnists from Alabama to Great Britain have been trying to untangle the web that he wove of his life. That life remains much more interesting than any fiction he ever put on paper.

On one level, he was obviously a great deceiver and a racist tyrant. On another, he was a fabulous poet and a weaver of great tales of the spirit. He put words of hate and hatred into the mouth of one of America's greatest demagogues and yet he left behind one of the most gentle stories of all time. I believe that the man known as Asa Carter went through a great personal and intellectual metamorphosis. He tried to shed his evil skin, but a part of him remained tainted even unto the end.

My original article about Asa-Forrest was published in the culture section of *The New York Times*. Some years later the *Times* published a similar story on its Op-Ed Page by Dan T. Carter and *The Los Angeles Times* published my account. The full story as it appears here was published by *The Mobile Register*.

✳

ANOTHER TIME, ANOTHER PLACE

✳

When I was a boy, growing up in rural Alabama, it was a favorite pastime to listen to the world around me. I paid attention to what the grownups were saying and doing. Luckily, my grandfather, Uncle Bub Able, owned a little country store that was the meeting place for the people of the community. It was a narrow, long, plain building with cigarette, cigar, and snuff advertisements nailed to the front, a wooden counter down the left-hand side, shelves filled with canned goods, and a big round hoop of cheese under flimsy cloth back next to the sliding scales. Past the counter was a black potbelly stove that glowed red in the winter. And behind that sat the makeshift table surrounded by straight-backed cane-bottom chairs. Most every afternoon, Granddaddy and his friends circled the table and played dominoes or checkers. And while they played, they told stories.

This was the milieu from which I gained the experience to write. Of course, not every tale that was told has become or will become a story. In the past and in the future, I hope I will expand on what was first gained here to broaden the horizons of my writing life.

Recently, in an Op-Ed Page piece for *The New York Times*, I reconstructed that nostalgia in a scene about Granddaddy, using techniques that could and should be applied to fiction as well.

Granddaddy had bought his first car, a Ford, and he remembered that day:

> "I got it on a Saturday morning. We were living in Tuscaloosa. I drove it to our house, out close to the university, and pulled up and honked the horn. It was loud. Neighbors came out of their porches. Your mama and Nanny came out. Their eyes were big as saucers. Aw, they had a fit over it.
>
> "I sat up there behind the wheel and said, 'Y'all want to go for a ride?'"

With this excited quotation, the character of Bub Able looms three-dimensional-plus. He is proud, boastful, and realistic about himself. Through the style of short, almost repetitive sentences, the scene is set and the character is deepened. With his one line, "Y'all want to go for a ride?" he is a prideful middle-class Southerner. If he had been in Chicago's west side or the Bronx, he certainly would not have used the same words.

After my family moved to town, during my teenage years I frequented Roy's Pool Hall in downtown Tuscaloosa, despite the warnings from my father that the people there were "hoodlums." Many an afternoon I sat fascinated on the edge of a tattered seat and watched the drama take place around the front table where the sharks strutted their stuff.

In my first novel, *The Golfer* (published by J. B. Lippincott), I remembered those lazy hot afternoons when men squared off across the green felt playing field. A pivotal scene between the protagonist Hank Martin, a professional golfer whose life is at a turning point, and his two young friends, a black boy and a white boy, takes place in a smelly, dimly lighted pool parlor in central Alabama. "This is just like golf," Hank Martin explains to the white boy. "You putt the same way you play pool. In both you have to have an accurate eye." Then Billy Boswell misses his shot and Roscoe Robertson takes up the cue stick. Hank comments, "You can't learn it all in one simple lesson" — which might be said of writing as well as pool playing or golf shooting. Then Roscoe:

> . . . looked at the table, his eyes squinted low, his right hand working in quick semicircular motions at the tip of the cue stick with a piece of blue chalk. Roscoe moved close to the table. He bent down to the green felt surface of the table and stretched his left arm forward, toward the white cue ball. His left hand made a quick and accurate bridge on which he placed the cue stick. His right hand and arm came back in pumping, stroking motions. He aimed. He struck.

You know by the style of the writing itself that Roscoe nearly runs the table, and the lesson of endless hours of hard work looks easy when finally applied.

Again, the rhythm and word usage correspond to the world of the characters. To make the world come alive, the writer must make the correct choice.

On another occasion, writing about my granddaddy Bub Able, I described his "finest clock in the whole wide world." On the face were the tin figures of a fife player and two drummers. The hand of one drummer ticktocked loudly with every second's beat. The face was a circle forming the middle of a ship's helm next to which stood President Franklin Delano Roosevelt, shoulders wide, face aloof, and eyes focused on the future. Across the base of the clock was the inscription: *FDR: The Man of the Hour*.

Letting Granddaddy tell the story, I wrote:

"I'll never forget that night when I bought that clock. Me and your Nanny and your mama were living in a tent in Sheffield. It was hard times back then. It was the middle of the Depression. I had worked every job I could get, but nothing came steady. We moved in that tent all over Alabama, Mississippi, part of Tennessee. Your Nanny and your mama never complained. Every time I'd get a new job, they'd pick up and we'd move."

This was his rhythm, his words, again bringing the scene to life with "living in a tent," "middle of the Depression," "worked every job . . . but nothing came steady," and finally the fact that they "never complained."

He continued:

"When I went to work for TVA, I signed on with the union. I had worked as a carpenter off and on for five years or better. I had all the experience I needed. I knew what to do once an engineer told me what the plans were. When I signed with the union and attended the first meeting, and heard those fellows talk about brotherhood and working regular, and putting meat on the table along with the blackeyed peas and turnip greens, I felt kind of funny-good all over."

This was what work was all about: "putting meat on the table." Then he described the union meeting as:

". . . kind of like a church meeting almost. It made me feel real good. I told Emma (my grandmother) that night that it was the best thing I'd ever done. She told me that was fine. I told her everything was looking toward tomorrow instead of worrying about today. They could see something better coming in front of us. She said she could see

64

why I felt the way I did. She hugged me and kissed me.
She wanted to believe just as much as I did."

Whether in fiction or non-fiction, the language draws from the character the feeling surrounding the described action.

Bub Able's feeling of goodness led naturally to his conclusion:

"That Friday when I got paid the biggest amount of money I had ever got for a week's work, I stopped off with some of the other labor union people I worked with, toasted the president of the United States with a drink of straight whiskey, and started home.

"When I got to the drugstore I saw that clock in the window. Franklin Delano Roosevelt was standing there." (His voice almost cracked.) "I don't think I even looked to see how much the price was. I went inside and bought it. I carried it home and put it next to my chair. Emma looked at it and shook her head. Your Mama touched it very softly. I told 'em we'd have to keep that clock forever. It was a sign that everything would be all right."

Of course, I still have the clock. And every time I look at it I'm reminded of the story, which, once again, pushes forward with emotion to the last syllable because of *his* rhythms and word usage. I emphasize *his*, because it is the *character* who is speaking, it is the person's place in the world about which you are writing, that dictates rhythm and usage.

In another story, about a woman named Lottie Lett who did not know how old she was, I allowed her to speak:

"I was born way back yonder. I was born right on this place. It belonged to the Simpsons then, the great-granddaddy of the people who live down in the big house now. My Mammy, she was a slave. I don't remember much about back then. It was a long time ago."

Her words could have been whittled down to phrases, misspellings, and monologue in dialect, like the tales of Uncle Remus, which I loved to hear my mother read to me. However, when I reached adolescence and began reading everything I could put my hands on, I discovered the stories were nearly impossible to decipher because they were written in dialect. I tried and tried, but I was never able to pick the words apart and make them flow. At the time, I made a promise to myself that when I started writing I would not confuse my audience with the foreign language of dialect. If I had reduced Lottie Lett's speech to Uncle Remus language, I believe it would not only make the story incomprehensible but also reduce her portrait to caricature.

We sat in front of the fireplace in the simply furnished living room. She had poured homemade wine into peanut-butter glasses. We drank the sweet liquid and she talked.

"When I was a little girl, times were rougher than they are now. My mammy was a slave, she worked in the house, tended to the children, cooked food for the Simpsons, and I did the same thing. When I was little, I'd go there with Mammy and I'd play with the white children. When we got up seven or eight years old they went off to school. I went to school for two years. Nobody cared whether colored children went to school or not in Wilcox County back then. I just didn't go to school anymore. I stayed home and took care of my brothers and sisters while Mammy worked at the big house.

"I don't remember my daddy. Mammy said he was a slave too. He left when I was a little girl. He went up North, best I recollect. Seemed like everybody went up North if they got a chance."

The tale is more alive with *her* words and *her* rhythms, straight-forward, and without fanciful apostrophic dialect.

It should be emphasized that although this sounds easy, it is, like the pool shooting, the result of many hours at the typewriter. The writer must listen to the sounds in his or her reverberating memory. What was the cadence of the talk? What made it jubilant? What made it sad? Why did I feel the way I felt?

The writer carries the saddest and happiest memories locked away in the unconscious mind, ready to be mined when he or she sits down to work in the solitude that produces a finished piece. For years I listened to my friend, novelist Borden Deal, talk about the collective unconscious before I realized one humid Alabama afternoon exactly what he meant. For days I had been sweating over a particular scene. I labored with it, twisting it and turning it, trying to mold it into my idea of perfection without giving my characters their due. Finally, I pulled myself to the foreboding black typewriter and pushed my fingers to the keys. I looked out the window at a cardinal sitting on a tree limb. Suddenly I did not see the bird, the trees, the sky, I saw that time long ago about which I was writing. My characters came alive in my head. They played out the scene. And afterward, I wrote as quickly as my fingers could move, while my mind did an instant replay. And after that, I rewrote slowly and carefully. Out of that collective unconscious came the remembering. From the hours of tedious work came the final version.

During the 1970s I wrote many pieces for the Op-Ed Page of *The New York Times*. As a result, in 1980, the editor of *The Writer*, Sylvia K. Burack, asked me to compose a piece about writing nostalgia. The result was "Another Time, Another Place," from which I received considerable correspondence thanking me for sharing my ideas.

＊

NANNY WAS WRONG ABOUT MISTER ROOSEVELT

＊

Nighttime was scary when I was a boy. We didn't have the energy worries like the ones President Carter has been telling us about. It seems nowadays that we conserved more energy then.

We lived on a farm in Shelby County, Alabama, near the highway going toward Florida from Birmingham. When I lay in my bed at night, after the three hours of radio listening was finished, I stared at the gray ceiling. When an occasional car or truck passed on the curve outside, beams from the headlights cast shadows inside the room. The shadows crept across the walls and ceiling and finally disappeared into the night, and sometimes I imagined people standing outside the large windows looking in on me.

Granddaddy ran a roadside grocery-and-gas store. It had one bare bulb in the front and one in the rear. The only heat came from a potbellied stove in the back of the store. Summertime cooling was furnished by a breeze created in the draft between the back and front doors.

I helped Granddaddy sometimes, putting up cans of Vienna sausage, potted meat, and ten-cent sardines on the shelves he and my daddy built against the concrete-block walls before Daddy went off to the Army. We did things like that for ourselves in those days.

I liked mornings best. We got up at daybreak to the sounds of roosters crowing. I dressed and half-ran outside to the henhouse and took the eggs from beneath the warm bellies of the Rhode Island Reds and Domineckers. I scampered back out and dumped corn into the feeders for the chickens. It was a part of growing our own food and making enough to sell in the store as well.

While I was pumping water to reload the chickens' drinking buckets, I heard Nanny in the barn preparing grain for Bossy the cow. After my jar was filled, the heavy sound of liquid squirting against metal was heard from Bossy's stall. When I finished my chores, I walked down the hallway between the stalls for the cow and two mules. I stood behind Bossy, whose tail flicked back and forth, and I watched Nanny's vein-ridged hands working quickly and smoothly from one teat to the next.

It wasn't long before the pail was half filled and Nanny handed it to me with a warm smile. She was a big woman with a gracious lap in which I loved to sit, and her arms were large from the work around the place. I took the bucket of bubbly white milk and felt hungry with the bittersweet smell of it in the crisp morning air. Nanny slid her stool against the wall, patted Bossy's golden hip, and told her to finish eating in peace. She walked by my side, her wide apron stained from the first splatter of milk, and her high-topped shoes clattered against the wood as we crossed the always-damp low place beneath the pump. Granddaddy kept planks there so we wouldn't bog down in the mud.

I ate hurriedly, afraid I'd miss the bus. Mama cut my eggs into bite-sized pieces, and did the same with a piece of bacon and patty of sausage Granddaddy had made when the hog was killed at first frost last fall. It was flavorful with an ample sifting of sage and red

70

pepper grown in Nanny's garden. I mixed it all up with my buttered grits and scooped it up and shoveled it down. "You're going to ruin your stomach, eating so fast," Nanny commented.

I caught the crowded dusty bus every morning, standing in front of the Bruton Snuff sign. The three women who swapped around the chores drove up in the red Studebaker and picked up Mama, who was still combing her hair as she waved 'bye. They headed up the highway toward Birmingham where they all worked in an aircraft factory. It was their way of contributing to the war effort while their husbands toted arms in a foreign country.

Never do I remember a day passing when we weren't told, "You have to sacrifice for the well-being of the country." We all stood at attention in front of the two-room frame schoolhouse and put our right hands over our hearts and said the Pledge of Allegiance to the flag while Mr. Morrison, the teacher of the third through sixth grades, hoisted the flag up the wooden flagpole.

One time, my best friend and I got to scuffling around the desks and pushed against a blackboard. Somehow the blackboard fell onto a box of light bulbs. When three bulbs cracked, as staccato as a bone snapping, we were taken before the upper-class students. Mr. Morrison made a speech about destroying the public's property, paid for by all of our parents. My friend and I hung our heads while the words lay heavy in the air. Then Mr. Morrison folded us one at a time over his lap and stung our bottoms with his paddle.

That evening when I ran from the bus into the store, I said, "Can I have a soda, please, sir?" Granddaddy was sitting in the back playing dominoes with a neighbor. Without looking up, Granddaddy said, "I heard you were bad today." I shuffled my feet, looked down at the linoleum covering the concrete floor, and clasped my hands behind me. "Were you?" Granddaddy asked.

"Yes, sir, I guess I was," I stammered, and I told him what we had done. He nodded. "You better go on and do your chores and don't take long about it. Better not have a soda pop today."

The thought and taste of a cold Grapico easing down my throat stayed with me while I fed the coon dog, helped slop the hogs, and saw to the chickens again. When I finished, Granddaddy coldly told me to go inside and do my homework. And I can honestly say that I have never broken another light bulb since that day. They are too precious.

That night I brought coal for the kitchen stove from the bin behind the smokehouse. We had green beans and black-eyed peas and chicken stew and cornbread, everything that had been grown on the place.

Granddaddy settled into his rocking chair and whittled a chaw of tobacco from the plug he kept in the breast pocket of his overalls. Nanny sat across from him and worked a match-stick toothbrush into a tin of snuff and dipped it between front lips and teeth.

After the news and *Sky King*, I took a bath in the rain water Nanny had heated over the stove. She poured it up in a large pan on the kitchen floor, and I scrubbed myself, and Mama made sure I rinsed all the soap from my body.

Mama tucked me between outdoor-dried sheets and listened to my prayers. I listened to the sounds of automobiles, and I heard Granddaddy comment, "There are just too many motor cars on the highways. I don't know what's coming of this world." And Nanny said, "Don't you worry, Mister Roosevelt will save us from that kind of evil."

This article about living with my grandparents in rural Shelby County south of Birmingham was published on the Op-Ed Page of *The New York Times* on Monday, May 9, 1977.

*

BUB ABLE

*

My granddaddy, Bub Able, was quite a fellow in his day. I remember him well as a storekeeper on the highway south of Birmingham, sitting in the back beyond the great hoop of rat cheese and the Garrett Snuff advertisements. He and his friends sat next to the old potbellied stove in the wintertime when it glowed red from the heat of the burning coal fire. They sat back in the cool darkness in the summertime, slowly playing checkers or dominoes, and now and then selling something. Mostly, they talked.

Granddaddy was always weaving a story. I'll never forget the time when a tax man from Montgomery came by and huddled with Granddaddy out beside the high red iron gasoline pump that had a glass tank up on top with a yellow and a green ball inside. I used to love to stand next to the wooden bench under the front shed and watch the yellow and green balls bounce when Granddaddy filled up somebody's tank.

That day was hot as seasoned pepper sauce, the sun lying straight overhead, and Granddaddy, a short, square-built man who leaned slightly to one side and used a walking cane, even took off his felt hat and fanned his face with it. The band inside the hat was soaked with sweat, and I knew it had to be an important conversation for him to stand out in the heat that long.

When he came inside, he was shaking his head. He was still fanning with the hat.

"What's wrong, Uncle Bub?" one of his younger friends asked.

Granddaddy chomped on his false teeth for a moment, clicking them in his jaw. "I've got to raise the gas," he said.

"What in the world to?" the friend asked.

"Fifteen cents," Granddaddy said. He didn't just say the words, he thought on them, which was his way when things got serious. I had seen him do the same when he talked to Mama or Nanny about some scripture in the Bible that had been troubling him.

"I just don't understand it," Granddaddy finally said. "These roads we've got, they're pretty good. They've just been laid down by Governor [James E. 'Big Jim'] Folsom. And that man said they've been paid for. He said we've now got to pay for upkeep.

"It sure is something, going up on gas two cents a gallon, just for keeping up a road," he added.

Granddaddy stepped to the door and looked out toward the highway that wound down into the valley and disappeared around a curve.

Back inside, he said that he remembered when gasoline was less than a dime. Settling into his cane-bottom chair and leaning back against a feed sack, he said, "Why, I can remember my first car. It was a Ford. A-Model. It wasn't much. Cost just under three hundred dollars."

He looked down at me and wiped the sweat from his brow. "I got it on a Saturday morning. We were living in Tuscaloosa. I drove it to our house, out close to the university, and pulled up and honked the horn. It was loud. Neighbors came out on their porches. Your mama and Nanny came out. Their eyes were big as saucers. Aw, they had a fit over it.

"I sat up there behind the wheel and said, 'Y'all want to go for a ride?' Neither of them could believe that it was really ours. They kept asking me. And they sort of acted like they were afraid of it.

"I cut it off, turned the switch, and I stepped down and offered them a hand. I said that it was indeed ours, and I was also offering them a ride. When it stopped puttering, they allowed as how they would ride—after they had walked around it and looked it over real good.

"They got inside and I went around to the front and cranked it up. Off we went with everybody staring at us. I guess I was kind of awestruck, like a young 'un with a new toy. And I was mighty proud.

"We rode up and down the streets, through town, and you know we were one of only one or two dozen in the whole downtown. It wasn't like today, when there're ten or twenty cars on every street.

"Finally, I turned us onto a residential street, wanted to show them some pretty homes, and I ran smack into a dead-end street. When we got to the end, I stopped the car and looked around. I pushed one thing and then the other around the steering wheel, but I didn't know how to put the car in reverse. I cut the engine off, walked around, looked it over good, then told the ladies to step down. After they were off, I put my back up against the front end. I lifted. I was strong as an ox back then. I picked that car up, turned it around, helped your mama and Nanny up into the car, and then I drove off. I never said a word about that to your mama or Nanny. I just acted like it was the thing to do. The next day I learned how to put that car in reverse." He slapped his knee and laughed at himself.

This article was published in the August 6, 1976, issue of *The New York Times* Op-Ed Page. It was included in my book, *Alabama on My Mind*, and it has been reprinted in a half-dozen different anthologies in several different languages.

*

Regular Work,
Meat on the Table

*

My granddaddy, called Uncle Bub Able by his friends, was a union man. He had cut his teeth in the labor unions building Wilson Dam for the Tennessee Valley Authority. He was a carpenter then, hammering and sawing to build the cofferdams.

When I was a little boy growing up in his household, because my daddy was overseas in the Army and my mama was working in a military aircraft plant, the most prominently displayed items were a Franklin Delano Roosevelt clock and a picture of a birthday-cake-decorated float. Sometimes I'd stare for a long while at the two prizes.

Once on a sweltering north Alabama night in mid-August, he said, "Son, that's the finest clock in the whole wide world." On the face were the tin figures of a fife player, a drummer, and a man carrying the flag of the United States. The hand of the drummer tick-tocked up and down loudly with every second's beat. The face was a circle forming the middle of a ship's helm next to which stood President Roosevelt, shoulders wide, head aloof, and eyes focused on the future. Across the base of the clock was the inscription *FDR: The Man of the Hour.*

My granddaddy was crippled when I knew him. He hobbled about on a walking cane, injured when he fell more than two hundred feet down an embankment while constructing Wheeler Dam for the TVA.

He was long-since retired from the carpenter trade, but he always liked to remember, "I'll never forget that night when I bought that clock. Me and your Nanny and your mama were living in a tent in Sheffield. It was hard times back then. It was the middle of the Depression. I had worked every job I could get, but nothing came steady. We moved all over Alabama, Mississippi, and parts of Tennessee in that tent that I had fixed on a wagon bed, where I could fold it up and let out bunks where we could sleep. Your Nanny and your mama never complained. Every time I'd get a new job, they'd pick up and we'd move.

"When I went to work for TVA I signed on with the union. I had worked as a carpenter off and on for five years or better. I had all the experience I needed. I knew what to do once an engineer told me what the plans were. When I signed with the union and attended the first meeting, and heard those fellows talk about brotherhood and working regular and putting meat on the table along with blackeyed peas and turnip greens, I felt kind of funny-good all over.

"I had heard a lot about unions. I never did want to join, though. I'd gone to a Ku Klux Klan meeting back in Tuscaloosa in the twenties. I was talked into it by some of my friends. People compared the union with the Ku Klux Klan back then. I went to just one meeting. When I got there I saw why they wore hoods over their faces.

"They were some of the sorriest, no-account people in the community. Several I knew owed on their bills and never intended to pay, and they were sitting there cursing poor colored people. It made me sick. I left and never went back.

"But the union meeting was something else. It was kind of like a church meeting almost. It made me feel real good. I told Emma [my grandmother] that night that it was the best thing I'd ever done. She told me that was fine. I told her everybody was looking toward tomorrow instead of worrying about today. They could see something better coming in front of us. She said she could see why I felt the way I did. She hugged me and kissed me. She wanted to believe just as much as I did.

"That Friday when I got paid the biggest amount of money I had ever got for a week's work, I stopped off with some of the other labor union people I worked with, toasted the president of the United States with a drink of straight whiskey, and started home.

"When I got to a drugstore I saw that clock in the window. Franklin Delano Roosevelt was standing there." His voice almost cracked. "I don't think I even looked to see how much the price was. I went inside and bought it. I carried it home and put it next to my chair. Emma looked at it and shook her head. Your mama touched it very softly. I told 'em we'd have to keep that clock forever. It was a sign that everything would be all right."

When he saw me looking at the photograph on the wall, he explained that it had been made on a downtown street in Sheffield, Alabama, and that the small figure standing on the back of the float was he himself. It was his first Labor Day celebration as an officer in the carpenters' local. He was very proud of that day.

"We worked hard. We built dams. We were paid good wages, for that day. We hoped that our hours would go to develop something good for you and your children," he said, and patted me on the shoulder.

Today, when I look at the clock on my mantel over my fireplace, I remember his words. When I feel sorry for myself because I don't have a Cadillac or a speedboat or some other luxury I don't need anyway, I stare at the motionless clock and think of the suffering and good times that went into it.

Every Labor Day I feel a special happiness when I view the parade of proud union people on their day of rest. Seeing the floats decorated in their many colors, I remember that white float with its red and yellow trim.

It made my granddaddy happy to look at it and remember when he was an officer in his local. And it makes me happy to picture the glow of his eyes in my mind's eye.

"Regular Work, Meat on the Table" was published on the Op-Ed Page of *The New York Times* on Labor Day of 1973.

The Electric Bill

Everybody from President Carter to Willie Randolph is talking about how we can cure the problem of inflation.

Sitting in the tiny electrically controlled kitchen of his unpainted four-room house, Willie Randolph of Selma, Alabama, can tell you in a minute that, as a truck driver out of work, there's not much he can do about inflation.

Bent forward over a steaming cup of coffee on the table with its red-and-white oilcloth covering, Willie Randolph doesn't need much pushing to develop an angry glare in his eyes.

"I can't help it; big people in this world confuse me," Mr. Randolph said.

In this room, he points out the conveniences of living. The one waterline into the house runs to the kitchen sink. In one corner is a secondhand refrigerator he was given for helping a friend move two years ago. In another stands the four-burner stove, which has a short in the oven. When the oven is turned on, it makes popping sounds that frighten his wife, Alma Lee, the granddaughter of a slave from nearby Lowndes County.

81

The family's only toilet facility is an unpainted outdoor lean-to affair with two carved holes in a wooden seat. The waste falls into a ditch dug by Willie's father more than twenty years ago. In the wintertime, cold air sweeps through the cracks in the walls of the outhouse.

"The children usually wait until they get to school to go to the bathroom," Mr. Randolph said. "They go around all winter with sniffles and head colds."

Guiding a visitor through his house, which has two beds in the living room, beyond the nineteen-inch color television set and the portraits of Dr. Martin Luther King Jr. and President John F. Kennedy, Mr. Randolph commented, "I guess we ought to be happy that we have a place as good as this to live."

Willie Randolph, a slight black man whose forty-three years look like sixty on his weathered leathery face, went on, "We got a little collard patch in the winter and grow turnip greens, tomatoes, and okra in the summer. We always got something to eat."

He never demonstrated for his civil rights, he said, because he was always too busy. But since early December he has not been employed at his regular job driving a truck for a local sawmill. He has done some "shade-tree pulpwooding" with other family members. "But it's a tough way to make a living," he said. "You get your nickels and dimes, but that's about all. One agent for a paper company might pay one thing, another will pay something else for a cord. They still don't have the prices down right. It never is enough, and you're always busting a tire or breaking a chain."

Until recently, Mr. Randolph, by working hard and watching every nickel, held his financial head above the flooding water of inflation. "I don't do no complaining. I don't raise no hell. I do my work, I come home, and I work into the night. I want to see my babies and my woman with food in their stomachs and smiles on their faces."

Living with the Randolphs now are six children and a bedridden elderly aunt. Two older children have already moved out on their own. Several months ago, when the first winter cold hit Alabama, Mr. Randolph arrived home one night to find his wife sitting in the kitchen with her head in her hands. "That woman was crying like I ain't ever seen her cry before. Even when her mama died she didn't weep so hard," he said.

Mr. Randolph took the paper that his wife clinched. He read the figures showing that their power bill had jumped from twenty-two dollars the previous month to twenty-nine dollars.

"I didn't have no idea they were going to raise me like that. Here we were with Christmas coming on and no money for anything. That seven-dollar raise might not mean much to somebody making a hundred thousand dollars, but it meant toys for my children and some extra oranges and apples in their stockings," he continued.

Mr. Randolph took the bill down to the street corner where his friends meet to sit and talk and play dominoes.

He discovered he was not the only person in the community who had been raised drastically without warning.

"What happened was, we got hit hard," he said in a low, even, analytical voice. "None of us have anything. I've got four light bulbs, a hot-water heater, a refrigerator, and a stove in my house. Even the outhouse don't have a light. I burn a fire in the fireplace every night of the winter. We didn't know what was going to happen to us next."

Mr. Randolph joined his friends in seeking help from Legal Services Corporation of Alabama, a federally funded nonprofit program to assist poor people in civil matters.

Legal Services intervened in a suit, initiated by Alabama's Attorney General Bill Baxley, to stop the power company from charging its customers the greatest rate hike in the state's history.

Alabama Power Company said it had to have the extra money because inflation had taken its toll on the company's expenditures. Under state law and rules of the Alabama Public Service Commission, Alabama Power is guaranteed a profit.

It wasn't long after the suit was filed before a circuit judge ruled that Willie Randolph and others like him would get his seven dollars back. In the meantime, Alabama Power has asked for another rate increase.

But Mr. Randolph is at least temporarily satisfied. "What it is is inflation, the way they tell it," the trucker said. "I listened to President Carter talk the other night to Congress. And I heard him say he was going to add money to the Legal Services people. All of my friends and me, we're going to write to him and tell him that's a good thing. Maybe it will be fighting this inflation."

"The Electric Bill" was published on the Op-Ed Page of *The New York Times* on my thirty-ninth birthday, February 17, 1979. It was one result of a grant I had received from the Southern Investigative Journalism Project to study the plight of pulpwooders in the South.

*

I'LL TELL YOU ABOUT NUB

*

Nub was the ultimate football fan.

When I was growing up in Tuscaloosa, Alabama, there was only one *real* football team. That was the Crimson Tide of the University of Alabama.

Even before the leaves started turning, when the air began to have that coolish tinge of autumn, people's minds turned to the gridiron. It was all you could hear at the Stafford Hotel breakfast nook or Johnny's all-night hash house.

Nub was the most excited of the citizens who wore the big red A in their lapels. He was a big man with sandy-colored short hair. His left arm had been severed just below the elbow in a childhood accident. He used the abbreviated arm to great advantage in nine-ball games at Roy's Pool Hall, where he hung out.

Between phrases, when he began to talk nervously about the up-and-coming team, Nub sniffed with a habit that added emphasis to his emotions. "We're coming on strong this year . . ." Sniff! ". . . like you ain't ever seen in a hundred years . . ." Sniff! "I'd take the Tide and three touchdowns against Ole Miss . . ." Sniff! "But it ain't time for that yet." Sniff!

He liked the college boys to gather around him and listen to his words of wisdom. He had never finished high school, but he had a certain charm that lasted from one class to the next at the University. The youth never seemed to tire of Nub's enthusiasm.

He remembered teams back when. Harry Gilmer was one of his favorites. "He'd take a drink . . ." Sniff! ". . . of straight old Early Times." Sniff! "He'd be all the better for it." Sniff!

Until Paul "Bear" Bryant became head coach of the Tide, Frank Thomas had been the finest not only at Alabama but anywhere in the nation, according to Nub. He knew, he said, because he had been there.

It has never been unusual for Alabama fans to hire an entire train on which to travel to games. They did it back in 1926 when Alabama went to Pasadena to the Rose Bowl. They took off from a strip of land separating the University from the state insane asylum. It was always a festive occasion, and many professors quipped about which residents from which institution actually boarded the train.

"One time we had this train going to Nashville to the Vanderbilt game," recalled an alumnus. "Students and chaperones rode on all but one car. It was sold to town people. It was Nub and his crew from the pool hall. When the dean of men saw Nub pouring a drink of Early Times into a coed's paper cup, he started raising hell. Finally Nub stood up. He was about six inches taller than the dean. He grabbed the dean by the collar and hoisted him to his tiptoes. Nub said he didn't want to hear anymore of that kind of talk. The dean went back to the front of the train and didn't utter another complaint."

Then there was the time Nub hired a student to drive him to the Sugar Bowl in New Orleans. At the first liquor store they came to, Nub got out, emptied his clothes from his suitcase into the trunk, walked into the store, and told the clerk, "Fill it with Early Times." Somewhere in Mississippi, Nub passed out. When he awakened, he looked around and saw snow falling. "Where are we?" he inquired. "You did say St. Louis, didn't you?" the student joked. Nub almost had a heart attack, fearing he'd miss the game. That was the year Alabama won the Sugar Bowl in a snowstorm.

"Nub was one of the most interesting people I ever met at the University," said an Alabama politician who, as a student, hung out with Nub at the Burchfield Hotel lounge. Nub told all the students who would sit and sip and listen that this year's team "is the best the world has ever seen . . ." Sniff! ". . . bar none."

"If a football player came in during the middle of the week, the joint was his," said a former defensive guard now in the used-car business. "Nub would buy all the beer you could drink, if he'd won that week. He always bet. I remember Joe Namath coming in once; Nub had two drinks in front of him before he could sit down."

Late at night and on weekends Nub wandered eastward from downtown Tuscaloosa to the Jungle Club, now an overgrown gully fast filling with empty beer cans. "Football Saturday nights were the busiest time of the year," recalled the owner of the place, which was razed in 1973. "Nub was one of our best customers. The football boys liked to come out and see if they could pick up the local girls. If they were stars, the girls would fall all over them. It used to embarrass Joe Namath. He'd blush and look at the floor, then they'd go after him even worse."

When Alabama played Auburn in Birmingham year after year, when it was touted as the Iron Bowl, Nub and all the other fans began whooping it up on Friday or even Thursday night. They did not let up until Sunday. If Alabama won, the shouts of "Roll Tide!" echoed over the city through the night. If Auburn won, "War Eagle!" could be heard on every street corner.

The fans, including Nub, were not always screaming cheers. They have been a fickle lot. Once when Nub, who always put his money on the Tide, lost a bet after he'd given up considerable points, he approached Coach Bryant after the game and called him "a wrinkle-faced old s.o.b." Bryant ducked quickly out of sight. And after the 1967 season, when Alabama lost its second game of the year to Texas A&M in the Cotton Bowl, an irate fan sent Bryant, the winningest coach in college football, a telegram reading "RESIGN."

Several former students and former football players have suggested that a plaque be placed in the athletic dorm to honor Nub. They said that he was the personification of the Crimson Tide spirit. Once a player asked that a game be played for him. Somehow that request became lost in the noise of the crowd. Most of them still remember him, although the Burchfield Hotel is now only a concrete foundation. They point to the place where Nub fired a pistol shot through the jukebox when he became overcome by Early Times and football joy one night. And when he died several years ago there were more students and ex-students at the funeral than most folks around these parts can remember.

"I just loved Nub," said a cheerleader of the late '60s. "He was so gross and obscene, but he was really cute because he loved anyone who loved Alabama. With that kind of loyalty to football and the school, you can overlook his faults."

A friend from Tennessee said, "We had a character like your Nub. His name was Casey. He was short and fat and always wore an orange suit to games. When people rode up the Tennessee River to the game on their party boats they'd be met by Casey, waving his pennant and singing the fight song. Everybody loved Casey."

Perhaps every Southern college has a Nub or a Casey. They are nurtured with care by the students and alumni, who revel in their enthusiasm. And their legends live on in the stories told over brew in the campus honky-tonks.

"I'll Tell You About Nub" was published on the Op-Ed Page of *The New York Times* on October 13, 1977.

*

OF THE MULE AND
THE THOROUGHBRED

*

At the round table at the Diplomat Restaurant in Montgomery, Alabama, where regulars hunched over their coffee like vultures in a treetop, the topic of discussion was The Big Game.

Damn the polls! They knew the South had the best football. There was no question about it.

Even a diehard Auburn fan, perennial enemy of University of Alabama football, proclaimed a hardy "Roll Tide!" Wearing orange and blue socks with "War Eagle" woven into the ankles, he doubled his fist and angrily declared, "A whipping is exactly what Woody Hayes and the Buckeyes deserve, coming down here and acting like they know something about football."

Another nodded. "Ara Parseghian couldn't say enough nice words about Ohio State before the Sugar Bowl. Afterward, he was quiet as a mouse. You could tell he didn't like Alabama winning."

The feeling spread like the plague. The passion showed on the faces of insurance salesmen, politicians, brokers, and housewives. They didn't care what the polls said. Alabama was Number One.

They had gone down to New Orleans and had won. Sure, Notre Dame had beaten Texas, which was no small feat. But Alabama had been Number Three. The Irish had been Number Five.

Not one fan worth his Joe Namath T-shirt would give a dime for the entire talented Irish backfield. Everybody knew the Big Ten, which invented the high and mighty football attitude, was about as no-account as Uncle Baxter's three-legged coon dog. Hadn't the Big Ten sent three teams to bowl games? Hadn't all of them been humiliated? Minnesota, Ohio State, and Michigan. Everybody knew Notre Dame was in reality just another Big Ten team that had been whipped by Ole Miss.

Down in the Orange Bowl, Arkansas was hot as August sunshine. Razorback Coach Lou Holtz, looking more like a cheerleader in his red Izod sweater, was absolutely beautiful. He and his whiz kids made the Oklahoma Sooners look like the sack-holders in a snipe hunt. The Sooners didn't know where they were.

We knew we were Number One. We had known it ever since 1926 when the Alabama team rode out of Tuscaloosa on a train heading west toward its first Rose Bowl. Every time the train passed through a town, people lined the tracks and screamed happy cheers. When the team returned victorious, having beaten Washington 20-19, the fans started cheering in Texas. All across the South the team was glorified.

That tradition continued to grow. Southerners weren't refighting the Civil War. They honestly believed in their gridiron superiority.

Comparing Woody Hayes to Bear Bryant was like trying to match a mule with a thoroughbred. Woody was a sycophant next to Bryant's genius. When a coffee-sipper suggested, "It was big of Woody to admit Bama was the best team he played all year," another good old boy stated, "That's what we like—a good loser."

"They can say all they want about the Bear getting old," one man offered. "He's the best. It won't be long before he'll hold the winningest record of all time." Paul W. Bryant, who announced in 1977 that he would coach at Alabama until he broke Amos Alonzo Stagg's record, won his 273rd game Monday. He is within 41 wins of the mark.

Like his players, Bear displayed country style. He was still the lanky boy with the slow drawl who climbed out of an Arkansas hollow and got a taste of winning. He was still hungry. And the fans started telling the story again about the time he walked on water.

This article was published on *The New York Times* Op-Ed Page on January 7, 1978. Three years later, Coach Bryant became the winningest football coach in history after his Alabama Crimson Tide beat Auburn 28 to 17 for his 315th win.

＊

Two Alabamians

＊

During a recent driving trip through southern Alabama, I found two farming men who looked at the national political picture from entirely different points of view. They were not the only two with varying opinions, but they lived in the same community, where they were born and reared.

The peanut farmer was a slow-moving man. He was tall and lanky, dressed in faded overalls, and wearing a scowl across his putty-complexioned face. "I guess I should have sold the forty-seven acres," he said as he moved toward the rusted barbed-wire fence that surrounded his gully-washed rolling red clay hills. "This is about the worst crop I've seen since Pap put the place in sweet potatoes back in 1933," he allowed.

J. D. Simmons's family has lived in southeastern Alabama since before the turn of the century, and now he is not too happy with the looks of things to come for the little farmer.

"Jimmy Carter wasn't no savior. He did a few things for the peanut farmer. But he didn't give us a lot of things people around these parts predicted he would," Mr. Simmons said. "We got some subsidy, according to acreage and family need, but the people at the U.S. Department of Agriculture tell us now there's going to be no subsidies. They're going to open up trading. Get what you can get. It'll be the greediest and the biggest first."

With the most serious of expressions on his naturally long face, J. D. Simmons said, "You know what that'll do to the little farmer? I'm not talking about just us peanut people in south Alabama, Georgia, Mississippi, and northwest Florida, I'm talking about the little man all over the country. It's going to put us at the lowest rung of the lowest ladder, and the big businessman is going to stomp on us like we're boll weevils."

His flat twang told about his great-granddaddy who came out of the foothills of South Carolina. His great-great-granddaddy moved to this country from Ireland after the potato famine of the mid-nineteenth century. "I'm used to droughts, but the drought of 1980 was the worst I've ever seen. Peanuts don't take much water, neither does corn, but you've got to have *some*. Even pine trees are drying up and shriveling up to nothing. It's a shame. I stuck in there with Jimmy Carter because I thought he had this nation in his heart. I believe he was doing everything he possibly could. I know other farmers who blamed the dry hot weather on the man. But I didn't do that. I could see what I believed would happen down the road if he wasn't re-elected."

J. D. Simmons's wife, Eleanor, was also born and reared in the rolling hills of Pike County, and she is accustomed to making do for her family. This winter, she hopes, will not be as bad as predicted. "I thank the good Lord that most of our children are up and grown and out of the house. They've got their own children to tend to. The two that are left will be taken care of, all right. I canned some green beans. We can always have turnip greens. We made some corn that's been ground into meal. We've got some chickens. We'll kill a hog when it gets cold. That'll last us through the winter. But I tell you, I don't know when I've seen such poor times."

J. D. helps her remember, "What about the winter of '32? When I was a child during the Depression, we had it rough. I don't think it was any rougher than right now. But we do have more conveniences now than we had back then. Things cost so much more now. I'm hoping that Mr. Ronald Reagan will put somebody in as Secretary of Agriculture who will listen to the little man. But I've always wished that. I don't imagine there's too much hope."

A FEW MILES down the state highway is the country store, farm-implement-supply company, and commercial hog parlor of Donald Everett.

Mr. Everett, whose grandfather settled the land where he lives and whose father built up the business, stated emphatically, "Ronald Reagan is going to be the president of the farmer. I worked for him because I could see what Jimmy Carter did during his four years in office. I voted for Carter four years ago because I thought he would help us. But Carter sat on his behind and did a halfway job. He never followed through on anything. I believe Reagan will give us somebody who knows our problems and who knows how to solve the problems [as Secretary of Agriculture].

"I lived through the Great Depression. My Daddy had a store right where this one sits. It was a small one-horse operation. He carried folks all over these hills on credit. He carried them for month after month when none of them had a cent to buy a thing. Without his generosity half the people would have had to sell their places and move somewhere else, or give up their places to banks or mortgage companies. I can see a similarity in then and now. People have been borrowing too much money, paying too much interest, and now it's squeezing them. Now they are going to have to slow down. But I believe that the economy is going to go up. It's got no other place to go.

"When Mr. Reagan goes into office, the farmer is going to have a better day. I see a wonderful future ahead. The fields are already looking greener. People are singing louder in church on Sunday morning. It's a looking-up kind of day. Prices are going to stabilize. Peanuts are going to make a good crop. And there'll be a jingle in people's pockets."

Donald Everett rocked back in his chair and held his chin high, and the afternoon sun shone brightly onto his smiling face.

"Two Alabamians" was published on the Op-Ed Page of *The New York Times* on Tuesday, December 9, 1980.

Echoes of Triumph and Defeat

*

In the mid-1960s, when I was walking with my notebook and camera next to protest marchers on the steamy streets of Montgomery, I never dreamed that someday I would be describing the birthplace of the Civil Rights Movement as a tourist attraction.

But today blacks and whites alike have made a mecca of Alabama's capital, Tuskegee, and Selma, where once there were cries of anguish beneath the swinging billy clubs from armed sheriff's deputies, and in the clouds from state troopers' tear-gas. Today, Montgomery, Tuskegee, and Selma draw thousands of visitors to the area.

The simple brick structure of the Dexter Avenue King Memorial Baptist Church, where young Dr. Martin Luther King Jr.'s voice rang out the first sounds of the movement, is today as much a shrine as a place of worship. Its tiny steeple sits only a block west of the Capitol building, where Governor George Wallace's state troopers, again armed with billy clubs, lined the columns on that March day in 1965 as the multitude marched from Selma to push for passage of the Voting Rights Act.

Dr. King stopped his marchers short of the bronze star designating the spot where Jefferson Davis made his inauguration speech as president of the Confederacy. While rain fell on the tens of thousands of marchers packing Dexter Avenue from sidewalk to sidewalk, Dr. King said, "I stand before you this noon with the conviction that segregation in Alabama is on its deathbed. Let us march on to the realization of the American dream."

Walking over the asphalt where they stood that afternoon, a white Southerner like me experiences a strange collision of his own history. I remember those sincere, dedicated faces—people nurturing sore feet and tired backs, but never giving up the dream. And inside the hallways of the Capitol, the creaking and cracking symbol of weary decadence, I think of my ancestors who were defeated wearing Confederate gray in a struggle over an earlier dream.

A life-size bust of the late Governor Lurleen Burns Wallace confronts me as I enter the rotunda of the Capitol. I remember her in 1967 when she was much softer than this cold stone—a kind, gentle countrywoman. Behind her, among the portraits of other governors, is the roguish face of Governor James E. "Big Jim" Folsom, looking as if he is about to repeat his brave 1949 Christmas message to the people of his state, "As long as the Negroes are held down by deprivation and lack of opportunity, all other people will be held down alongside them."

Standing next to me is a round-faced fourteen-year-old black. Next to him, his parents. They're from Birmingham, and they've driven down I-65 the ninety miles to Montgomery and plan to spend the day surveying the city, visiting sites.

We walk out the south wing of the Capitol, down a pathway lined by the flags of the fifty states and stones native to each. Across Washington Street facing us is the newly renovated two-story White House of the Confederacy, with its wide plain front porch. Inside, in the hallway, two young hostesses greet the guests, handing out printed guides to the rooms. To the right is the bedroom with twelve-foot ceilings where Jeff Davis slept for the first few months of his term. On the floor, his old black valise, a leather suitcase, a hatbox. The parlor with its sparkling teardrop-shaped crystal chandelier is too perfect; the study is dark, almost foreboding. Upstairs, the bedroom furniture is polished immaculately; the high bed, the cherry chest of drawers, the fancy stool—no longer do they have the feeling of oldness. Even the wooden floors do not creak as they once did. I liked it better when I was a boy, when I could imagine bearded soldiers tromping back and forth on the porch, and I could still think of them as courageous men.

From Montgomery, it is less than an hour's drive to Tuskegee via the Martin Luther King Jr. Expressway, which is I-85 East outside the city limits. After leaving the Interstate at the Tuskegee-Notasulga exit, the visitor passes Moton Field, the city airport. During World War II black pilots in the Army Air Corps were trained to fly here, separate from the white cadets.

State Route 81 South winds in and out of a maze of small houses, then between antebellum mansions with gabled turrets high above ancient magnolias. On the Old Montgomery Road, about a hundred feet before the entrance to Tuskegee Institute, the visitor sees a magnificent columned mansion, the largest and most majestic of the houses. Built of some 300,000 bricks, handmade by slave labor in 1856, Grey Columns, or the Varner-Alexander Home, is today the headquarters for the National Park Service, which conducts visitor orientation tours on fifty-three of the original one hundred acres of Tuskegee Institute, recently named a National Historic Site. To help carry out its restoration work at Tuskegee, the Park Service recently received a $2.7 million grant from Congress.

On the campus, clusters of the three thousand year-round students linger beneath the trees outside old brick buildings. Two-

and three-story classroom buildings stand on tree-covered knolls, lining quiet sidewalks, not unlike the way Ralph Ellison described them in his classic novel, *Invisible Man*.

At the end of a cul-de-sac at the bottom of a hollow sits Rockefeller Hall, paint crumbling, tin roof rusted. Several one-story frame buildings need fresh paint. The school has been plagued with financial problems since the day in 1881 when the Alabama Legislature created it with a grant of $2,000 for a Normal Industrial School for Coloreds.

Beside the winding drive that runs through campus, the founder, Booker T. Washington, is recognized in a life-size stone sculpture; he is shown lifting the veil of ignorance from the head of a wide-eyed, innocent young black. Sitting on the concrete bench that makes a semicircle beneath the statue, the white man who was raised in a middle-class community in Alabama realizes again that his black neighbors never had the opportunities he has always taken for granted. At the turn of the century, Dr. Washington was granted lifetime voting privileges; only after the Selma-to-Montgomery march were other blacks given that right.

Because of Dr. Washington's influence with the powerful white community, he was able to make Tuskegee Institute grow into the most important educational institution in the South. Presidents Theodore Roosevelt, Woodrow Wilson, and Franklin D. Roosevelt visited the campus. Andrew Carnegie, John D. Rockefeller, and other wealthy industrialists served on its board and made large contributions to Tuskegee's survival.

Today, Dr. Washington is not lauded by all blacks. By some he is seen as an Uncle Tom who sold out to the highest bidders. "He wanted more and more for himself, bowing and scraping to the whites, never making the blacks proud of themselves because of what and who they were," says Mumba Kata, a graduate student in philosophy. Milton Davis, a Tuskegee native who graduated from the Institute, attended law school at Iowa State and returned to his home to practice law, sees it differently. "From the first days when Booker T. Washington and his students made their own bricks with their hands and built the first classroom, Tuskegee Institute has been rich in a tradition of doing much with little."

Beyond the statue of Dr. Washington, across an expanse of emerald grass, where the summertime freshness of pecan and sweetgum trees perfume the air, a sweeping brick arch soars skyward, topped by a concrete cross. The Tuskegee Chapel is dramatic but simple. The interior gives a feeling of exaltation: exposed brick and polished wood come to focus beyond the pulpit and choir loft, in the three massive "singing" stained-glass windows depicting the history of blacks in America through scenes from spirituals.

No more than a hundred yards from the entrance to the chapel is a simple stone beneath a cedar tree marking a grave. The words proclaim simply the name, Booker T. Washington, and the dates, 1856–1915.

As part of a program being completed this summer, the Park Service is restoring The Oaks, Dr. Washington's three-story brick home that was constructed by his students. The inlaid oak floors, set in crisscross patterns, are immaculate, and the murals, covering the two feet between the cornice and ceiling of four downstairs rooms, show a simple pastoral view of the countryside. The study is not unlike that of Jefferson Davis in the Confederate White House. Dr. Washington also had a box for a top hat. The desk is ornate and without clutter. In one corner is a square wooden sofa with thick pillows. And a chair of the same design, with its own ottoman, looks as though he had many comfortable moments of thought while resting there. On the walls are photographs of Frederick Douglass, the nineteenth-century black leader; and autographed portraits of Andrew Carnegie and Theodore Roosevelt.

Down a quiet, shaded lane, the George Washington Carver Museum waits for the visitor with its own version of *Roots*. Twenty scenes from black history are shown in display windows, beginning with the First Great Builders of the pyramids of Egypt, through black slaves being captured in Africa, Benjamin Bannecker planning the streets of Washington, D.C., the beginning of black businesses, to the symbol of the Four Independent Negro Nations in 1940: Haiti, the Dominican Republic, Liberia, and Ethiopia.

In another section of the museum's first floor, the dreams of the black scientist George Washington Carver fill one glass case after another. The first shows his most famous discoveries: products from the peanut. But I had never known that he developed Hi-Brown Vanishing (facial) Cream with peanut oil and other ingredients, or Carvoline Rubbing Oil, which according to the label was good "for sore arms, back or legs, also soothing and healing to bruised, burned, chapped or callused skin." Hundreds of other items, including bricks from peanut hulls, building materials from sweet potato skins, and a park bench from wood shavings and cement, are on display.

Dr. Carver was also a skilled artist. He mixed his own paints from plants grown in central Alabama soil. On the walls hang his still-lifes of peanuts, sweet potatoes, green beans, berries — and Macon County pastoral countryside scenes.

Hanging on the walls are his intricate and delicate needlework, crocheting, and weaving, all artistically accomplished by a man who came here to teach for one year and remained until his death in 1943. He made his mark from a small laboratory overlooking a rolling pasture, where today Tuskegee Institute agricultural students develop new breeds of cattle for South American and African nations.

Climbing down into the basement of the museum on a circular stairway, I find myself facing the remains of his old laboratory. On a scratched wood bench sits a Bunsen burner, a rack of glass tubes, complex instruments. Standing before the small black press on which he worked with the peanut and other products, I can almost smell the fragrance in the humid summer air.

Next to me are three small children and their parents, Mr. and Mrs. Roy Lawson, and they are "amazed at everything we've seen." From Atlanta, about a hundred miles northeast, this is their first trip to Tuskegee. They are five of more than sixteen thousand who visit the museum every year.

As I leave the Institute, heading south toward the town square, I am pointed directly toward the monument to the Confederate dead. The stone soldier in the campaign hat, a symbol of the defiant dream of what used to be, has long been the centerpiece of the lazy, slow-moving downtown area. But today the men who sit in the shade of the statue are black. The governing bodies of county and city are controlled by black leadership. The county is eighty-five percent black, and that percentage is growing every year. "None of the whites stay unless they're making a living off the blacks," explains a businessman. But the Confederate monument remains.

PUBLISHED IN the travel section of *The New York Times* on Sunday, September 4, 1977, this article caught the attention of many leaders of the time. Today, black heritage tourism has expanded throughout the South and Alabama. Tuskegee Institute is now Tuskegee University. Instead of having only a few rooms to offer tourists, the multimillion-dollar world-class Kellogg Conference Center hosts educational and business conferences on the campus. And a new museum is being developed at Moton Field to pay tribute to the black airmen of World War II.

In Montgomery, the Southern Poverty Law Center commissioned Maya Lin, the famed designer of the Vietnam Memorial in

Washington, D.C., to build the Civil Rights Memorial at the corner of Washington and Hull streets. Troy State University built the Rosa Parks Museum and Library downtown near the spot where Mrs. Parks refused to give up her seat on a city bus in December 1955, sparking the yearlong bus boycott that became the foundation on which Dr. King built the Civil Rights Movement. And after the new federal building named for U.S. Judge Frank M. Johnson Jr. was completed in 2001, the old Greyhound Bus Station (where the Freedom Riders were attacked and beaten by a mob of white thugs) was restored as a visitors' center for the Civil Rights Trail.

Continuing to Selma along the path the marchers took to petition their government for voting rights, high on a hill overlooking U.S. 80, is a stone memorial to Mrs. Viola Liuzzo, the Detroit housewife who had come south to help the marchers. She was transporting marchers back to Selma the night after the march ended when she was run down and shot to death by Ku Klux Klansmen who were later found guilty of violating her civil rights.

Over the Edmund Pettus Bridge (where marchers were teargassed and beaten by Dallas County deputy sheriffs and Alabama state troopers on Bloody Sunday, March 7, 1965, several weeks before Judge Johnson ruled the demonstrators had the right to protest peacefully on the federal highway) turn left on Water Street. On the first block, in a building backing up to the Alabama River, overlooking the bridge, is the National Voting Rights Museum. Deceptively simple, it is one of the most touching museums I have ever visited. Each room is dedicated to a different aspect of the fight for voting rights. In one room are photographs of women who gave leadership through the years. In another is a simple but moving shrine to the members of a family who preached equal rights. In a small glass display case is a pair of shoes worn by Marie Foster, an elderly activist, that Sunday when she stepped alongside her brothers and sisters to cross the

Edmund Pettus Bridge toward a quest for freedom. Photos in the case show Mrs. Foster with Dr. King, the Reverend Jesse Jackson, and numerous other black leaders.

One of Selma's most distinctive antebellum homes is Sturdivant Hall, an example of Greek Revival neoclassic architecture. Edward T. Watts purchased the lot at Mabry and Union streets for $1,830 in 1852 and began building the home, at the cost of $69,000, the following year. Donated to the city in 1957, it is now a fully restored museum with period-piece furniture and elegant pastel walls. The free-standing kitchen is equipped with antique biscuit-makers and pie pans.

Next door to Sturdivant Hall is the White-Force Cottage, an Italianate-style structure built in 1859 by C. B. and Martha Todd White. She was the half-sister of Mary Todd Lincoln, the wife of Abraham Lincoln, and was a lifelong outspoken Confederate patriot.

On Lauderdale Street is Grace Hall, built by Henry Ware in 1857. It is another example of neoclassic architecture.

In the same Heritage Village area is Fairoaks, also known as the Henderson house. After the Battle of Selma in 1865, when Union raiders commanded by Major General James H. Wilson destroyed the Confederate arsenal, munitions works, naval foundry, and the stockade prison at nearby Cahaba, Fairoaks was occupied as a hospital by Union troops.

Live Oak Cemetery is one of the most beautifully serene places, especially early in the morning when the fog shrouds the unique gravestones and dew still drips from the Spanish moss hanging from the broad drooping limbs of the gigantic trees. Move slowly through the boulevards of the dead, feel their history seep up through the hallowed ground. Here, buried among the citizens of the past are also the famous: U.S. Vice President William Rufus King, Senators Edmund Pettus and John Tyler Morgan. We found the 1905 marker of a man named Indiana Jones, and had to wonder.

On the opposite side of town, on Martin Luther King Jr. Street, is the Brown Chapel AME Church, where many of the early meetings of the Civil Rights Movement were held. A life-sized bust of Dr. King stands outside on a monument to the struggle for the right to vote.

At the east end of Water Street is the Old Depot Museum with its own Civil Rights display, also with numerous other exhibits highlighting Selma's rich history. A half-block toward the river is an old building that once housed the Confederate arsenal.

Nearby, also on Water Street, is the renovated St. James Hotel, originally built in 1837, with forty-two rooms, including four suites, each with a balcony overlooking the Alabama River. Furnished in period 1870–85 antiques, the wall coverings and fabrics were chosen carefully to follow that period's design. With a brick courtyard surrounding a spewing fountain, the St. James was known in 1860 as The Troupe House and was used by Union troops after they ransacked the arsenal just a few hundred feet to the east. The hotel is surrounded with its own mystery, with stories floating through the air about the time Jesse James stayed here. It is a true fact, you are told, that Jesse did place a few wagers in the gambling room now occupied by the lounge called aptly enough The Drinking Room.

Out Broad Street to the north, visit Jerry Siegel's Art Gallery in a Greek revival cottage where you will find the finest collection of local and regional art in Alabama. It is a virtual museum of excellent paintings by Alabamians and Southerners.

Drive west on State Highway 22, turn south on Cahaba Road, and visit the site of the state's first capital, where the Cahaba River flows into the Alabama. As you wander down the old streets, you will uncover a saga of antebellum history in the columns that still stand at the Cochran house, high on a bluff overlooking the rivers. Following the battle here, General Wilson and Confederate General Nathan Bedford Forrest met in the Cochran house to discuss the exchange of prisoners. At the place where Union prisoners were held, called Castle Morgan, pace the walls and step on the old bricks that formed the walls to keep the men in these cramped quarters. After the war, the men were loaded onto the steamship *Sultana*. They sailed down the Alabama River to Mobile, over to Louisiana and up the Mississippi River. At a place near Memphis an engine exploded. The *Sultana* sank and most of the former prisoners were killed. As you feel the tragedy of Cahaba's history — how it finally became a ghost town after nineteenth-century floods — you are also surrounded by the natural beauty of the landscape. While you witness the destruction of tombstones in the old cemetery, you feel the cooling breeze after a quick summer's shower.

IN THE summer of 2000, a couple of young friends from Montgomery rode with me to Selma to pick up my old friend Kathryn Tucker Windham, the celebrated author of *13 Alabama Ghosts and Jeffrey, The Bridal Wreath Bush, Alabama: One Big Front Porch,* and numerous other books.

Ms. Windham, whom I call Kathryn, is a beautiful lady. Like a fine Kentucky bourbon, she mellows gracefully with age. I could sit and look at her and listen to her for hours on end. But she's not a person to sit still long, as much as she loves telling a good story.

She knows history, our state's, her own — the days of growing up in the slow-moving world of Thomasville, back when she was a student at Huntingdon College, the hectic deadlines as a young reporter for *The Alabama Journal*, when an editor snatched paper from her typewriter and shouted, "Write, girl! Write!" — and afternoons and evenings of turmoil during the struggle for civil rights in Selma, where she has lived during the last decades of her life.

Kathryn, at 82, is a lively person. There's excitement in her eyes. It glitters there. And her voice lilts when she talks, like good music. The cadence of her talk generates joy in her description of the wildflowers growing in her beloved Black Belt, the way the young people of her community respond to the issues in current affairs, or her relationship with various people.

Kathryn is forever a student. She inquires. She seeks information about what is going on in the world just beyond the bounds of her own geography. Last summer, she traveled to France as a part of a celebration orchestrated by the artist Nall, whose extraordinary book *Alabama Art* includes a portrait of Kathryn, showing her with drooping bunny's ears. It is Nall's own inimitable way of describing one of his artistic heroes.

On our day with Kathryn, she guided us to Jerry Siegel's gallery where we perused his eclectic collection of paintings. She and Jerry are not only friends, they were born on the same day in the same year. When they're together, their voices overlap, like music played in sync.

We pick up thick barbecue sandwiches from Hancock's, her favorite eating place, which has been making good smoked pork forever and a day. She takes us on a whirlwind tour of the fragrant kitchen, introduces us to the folks who apply tender hands to the tender meat, and they all smile welcome smiles. And then we're off to Cahaba, Alabama's first capital, where William Lowndes Yancey edited the Cahaba *Reporter*.

On the bank of the Alabama River we spread our picnic near the site of the old prison. Kathryn tells tales, and we dig into her homemade potato salad and a jar of pickles unlike any we'd ever experienced.

We remember Anna Gayle Fry's *Memories of Old Cahaba*, in which the author quoted John W. Duboise, "In all America, in town or country, no people sat down to more bounteous dinners, served by better servants, on rich mahogany; no people wore more fashionable clothes, rode better-groomed horses, wrote a purer vernacular, or spoke it with gentler tones" than Cahaba in 1836.

We visit the artesian well with its crystal-clear cold water, and the old graveyard where visitors have overturned stones and destroyed crypts. We speak out angrily against such stupid destruction of our history.

On the hillside above the spot where the Cahaba River flows into the Alabama, we stand and gaze up at the four great columns. Kathryn reminds us that it was the old Cochran house where General Forrest and General Wilson met.

We stop at the visitors' center on the way out and find two couples from the Midwest. They are introduced to "The Ghost Lady," and Kathryn has an impromptu signing party for the people who have bought her books.

In the fall of 2000, I had the privilege to be in the audience when Kathryn was presented the Humanities Award by the Alabama Humanitarian Foundation at its eleventh annual luncheon at the Wynfrey Hotel in Birmingham. My friend accepted the award with dignity, intelligence, grace, and charm, saying, "My family always warned me when I was called on to appear before a crowd: wipe your nose, pull up your hose—and don't sing."

Parts of these stories were originally published in *The Montgomery Independent*.

Half Pints and Rain Barrels

＊

A dark-skinned woman with a sharp straight nose, aged twisted lips, and legs slightly bigger around than a half-dollar, Annie Bell Brown looked surprised when more than forty people walked into her scrub-brush front yard.

She sat on a ragged old sofa somebody had discarded years ago. She leaned forward and dipped Garrett Snuff, and she cradled gnarled arthritic fingers gingerly around a swollen elbow that hung limply in a sling. Pain creased her forehead and entered her rheumy eyes. A week before a local teenager had found her lying in a dirt street of Black Jack. Her arm was broken in several places. Small dogs played around her frail body. The young man lifted her up and carried her to an emergency room nearly twenty miles away.

Annie Bell Brown is one of about two hundred residents of Black Jack, a no-man's-land tucked between Saraland and Satsuma in Mobile County in south Alabama. Neither the county nor the towns will claim the territory. It's looked on as a useless strip of dirt.

A native of nearby Plateau, where she was born with a twin sister seventy-four years ago, she now whiles away her time on the porch of the one-room unpainted shanty for which she pays twelve dollars a month. The dwelling is furnished with a wood heater-stove, a rundown mattress on rusted springs, a refrigerator, and a rickety chest of drawers she picked up on the side of a Mobile street.

When the forty-some-odd people from Alabama, Mississippi, Georgia, and Washington, D.C., visited her on a Coalition Against Hunger tour in the spring of 1980, Mrs. Brown, a widow, showed surprise in her big brown watery eyes. "I don't get no food stamps," she said. "I don't have the strength to stand in line all day," she added. Asked if she could use food stamps if somebody brought them to her, her face lighted. "I sure could," she said.

"I don't know nothing about no Medicaid, Medicare, or anything like that," she said. She receives a monthly check for about $150 from Social Security. "That's from my husband, who passed," she explained.

In a narrow cupboard near the stove sat a one-pound plastic container of black-eyed peas and a partial can of Luzianne coffee. In the refrigerator was a half-pint of milk and a jar of peach preserves.

Asked about plumbing, she pointed toward the rear of the shack where an outhouse teetered at the edge of a ditch. And she said the pump where she got her water was some fifty paces down the dirt road.

Sipping the strawberry Kool-Aid offered by Bill Edwards, a young man who has been fighting Alabama hunger most of his adult life, she half-whispered, "The Lord sent y'all. I know He did." And local black State Senator Michael Figures took down her name and address. He said he would have someone with a food stamp form on her front porch by nightfall.

112

ON THE way north into the Choctaw Indian country of northern Mobile County and southern Washington County, Bill Edwards said that this is what his Coalition Against Hunger is all about. "We want to make the public aware that problems like this exist in our communities." And a man from the U.S. Department of Housing and Urban Development agreed. "It's not just in the big cities of Washington, New York, Newark, Atlanta; it's everywhere," he said.

Within an hour the group bumped down a clay road in the Piney Woods near the Alabama-Mississippi border. Tall, handsome, Roman-nosed John Rivers, a fourth generation Choctaw, told about the problems of being the third race in a rural south Alabama county "where nobody ever wanted anything to do with you. We were told by the white people that we were not theirs. And the black people didn't want us. When I was a boy we had three separate schools for the three races of Washington County."

He guided the way to a small frame house where a sickly olive-complected child clung to the skirt of his undernourished mother. The woman said her husband had died six months earlier. She was on food stamps, but they barely provided enough food for her and her four children. The other two boys and a girl were in school. As the group tromped through the crowded cabin, a representative from the county pensions and security office almost fell through the floor when her foot weighed down upon a loose board.

Less than a half-mile away the group pulled into the grassless yard of a tiny house. It looked like something a middle-class child would build as a play hideout in the backyard of a suburban home. Out of the front door of the plywood and cardboard dwelling ran a three-foot-high little boy with a beaming round face and twinkling brown eyes. "Hi," he greeted, "my name's Bubba." And the first woman of our group reached down and swooped him up into her arms and uttered, "Give me a hug, Bubba," and he hugged with a huge grip.

Inside the ten-by-fifteen-foot two-room house stood a barefoot woman in a red print dress. Two girls slightly smaller than Bubba held to her sides. She had sharp Indian cheeks, raven hair, soft brown eyes, and skin the color of the deep red clay. She invited the group into her neat well-scrubbed home.

Standing on the back stoop, she pointed out where she, her husband, and their three children had lived in an old house that had burned to the ground. There had been no insurance. There was no way to rebuild. They lived from hand to mouth week by week when her husband found work with a pulpwooding outfit. If it rained hard, as it tended to do in the spring and fall, there was no work.

"We tote water from up there on the hill. And up yonder—" she pointed, "—we go to the bathroom. We catch water off the roof. We bathe in washtubs. And I wash the clothes in that there pan.

"There ain't no electricity. It got cut off. The power company got my bill mixed up with a fellow up the road. By the time we got it straightened out they said we owed $124 and I'd have to pay it to have the electricity turned back on. But we don't have that kind of money.

"It gets kind of cool in the winter. We have that canned gas. Have to have it filled every week, and I cook with that."

Holding her head high and defiant, she said, "When you are poor, you do what you have to do."

ON THE way to yet another place, Bill Edwards reiterated his old fight against an apathetic public. An angry young man, Edwards has been shaking his finger in the face of the rich and the fat for at least a decade.

A Californian, Edwards grew up in Orange County, "which I guarantee you is just as backward in its way as much of Alabama,"

114

he said. Studying history and political science at California State College in Fullerton, he came to the University of Alabama's graduate school in 1969 and took a master's degree in social work.

Working with the National Democratic Party of Alabama, a predominantly black splinter group in the early 1970s, Edwards developed a quick and deep insight into the state's political world. He also worked with VISTA through Miles College in Birmingham. Again with Miles College, he moved to Greene County where for four and one-half years he had "quite an experience, saw poverty at its worst, watching the splitting-up factions of the black people's political life." Then for two years he directed the Alabama Migrant and Seasonal Farm Workers association. He and his wife, a teacher from Birmingham, moved to Loachapoka between Auburn and Opelika in east central Alabama and he began work with the Coalition Against Hunger.

Showing his commitment, Edwards slipped into a passionate speech punctuated with cold hard facts. He looks back on President Lyndon Johnson's War on Poverty as the beginning of the dream to rid the country of hunger. "At that time the nation began its dream about actually doing something about poverty, actually getting the people out of poverty.

"All you have to do is look and see, and the myths about poverty die hard and fast. Some people believe all poor people are lazy, drive Cadillacs, eat gourmet meals from food stamps. These poor people actually work hard, keep their houses clean, and barely have enough to eat," he stated.

With Edwards that day was Hollis Geer, staff attorney of Legal Services Corporation of Alabama, the co-sponsor of the hunger tour. Geer, who represented many of the Mo-Wa Indians (short for Mobile-Washington counties), rode the country circuit at least once a week to check with her rural outlying clients.

A native of Boston, Geer moved with her family to Huntsville, Alabama, when she was twelve, and after graduating from Duke in anthropology spent two years in Liberia and Ghana. Back in Boston, she worked with prison reform groups and attended Boston University Law School.

While still in school, she worked with Legal Services Corporation offices in Knoxville one summer, "and I knew I wanted to come back South and do this kind of work."

In the push-and-shove world, she made room in local churches for intake sites to meet with her clients. And soon she hoped to share an office in Chatom, the seat of Washington County, with the Coalition Against Hunger workers.

As the dust-coated school bus rocked back toward the tour's starting point, Bill Edwards creased his forehead and spoke again about the people. Leaning forward, he hit his fist into his palm with emphasis. "There is so much that we have to do," he declared. "It's an uphill battle, but we think we can do it." And at his side, Hollis Geer nodded her head in agreement.

"Half Pints and Rain Barrels" was published in the June 1980 issue of *Southern Changes*, a magazine published by the Southern Regional Council in Atlanta.

*

GOLDVILLE, ALA., DIDN'T PAN OUT

*

I've loved gold ever since I was a little boy in rural Alabama and looked down into a rugged hand and stared into a glowing nugget.

The men around my Granddaddy Bub Able's country store used to tell tall tales about finding the mother lode right in the hills of Shelby County.

I remember John Everett, who lived about two miles down the Florida Short Route from us. He was a great big man with huge horny hands. His fingers could encircle a pickax handle twice, and his shoulders were as thick and strong as a young bull's. "If they keep finding coal around here, I guarantee you they'll hit gold sooner or later," he declared, and my eyes bulged at the listening.

Another time, a stranger to those parts came in and told about seeing a man south of us, down in Chilton County, who claimed that a group of settlers had found a room filled with gold. He said it had been part of a ransom paid by the early Indians to the explorer DeSoto when his Spanish outlaws tromped through Alabama way back in the sixteenth century.

When I asked my schoolteacher, she chuckled and said, "That's just some old man's story." But I never could get the sound of it out

117

of my craw, and I must have dreamed about a whole room filled with gold for weeks on end. It was the kind of story that made a boy's imagination run wild.

I thought back on a lot of those stories the other day after visiting a more-or-less ghost town in central Alabama named Goldville, population fifty-three, not counting coon dogs and scattered livestock.

Behind the Last Chance Grocery in the bend of State Highway 49 sits a pale green mobile home where Miss Mary Powell and her little terrier live.

Her gray hair tied up under a sunbonnet, Miss Mary made her way through the tiny fenced yard with its big-lettered sign warning "Beware of Dog." She sat back on the metal spring chair, dipped her snuff, and pointed out across the hollow to the half-tumbled-down two-storied log house in the middle of a pasture.

"That's the only thing left standing from the old days," she said. She grinned widely, showing smokeless-tobacco-stained teeth. "They say it was a sporting house," she added.

"Goldville was a boom town. That was before my time. Back in the early nineteenth century. In the early 1840s, after gold was struck back to the west of here and to the north, people come in from the North, from Carolina and Georgia, and by 1845, they say, more than three thousand people lived here. Goldville was the trading center for the Tallapoosa territory and was one of the biggest towns in Alabama. That was after the Indians had been defeated at Horseshoe Bend and shipped west on the Trail of Tears.

"There was buildings all in here," she said, pointing with her walking cane from the last standing buildings to the unpainted store sitting on piles of flatrock. "There were twelve or thirteen stores, a hotel, a schoolhouse, three or four saloons, a racetrack down in the lowlands, and two or three churches.

"The good churchgoing Christian people in Goldville got fed up with all the carrying-on that come with prosperity. They didn't like it that there were fewer churches than drinking places and other kinds of funning places. So they moved down to Newsite with their preachers. But Goldville kept going.

"They had gold mines all around in here. There was a tent town west of here. More than a thousand people lived there. They worked the mines owned by New York companies. They got paid wages, and they figured the companies made all the money. The big mines were up yonder on Hog Mountain, where there was a water-powered crushing mill and where they say the ore ran better than a hundred dollars a ton. That was a big price back then.

"When they got the news in 1849 that gold had been struck in California, everybody just up and left. Just like that. It happened overnight. One morning folks woke up and the tents were gone, the miners had moved out, other folks followed, and the town was near empty.

"A few folks stayed, but sure not many. They dwindled along on the land, farming what little bit they could plow, making corn whiskey, and doing some pulp-wooding."

Several years ago, former Alabama Governor John Patterson, who was born in and still maintains a farm in Goldville, researched state law and found that if a town had ever been incorporated it could become a city again. Prophesying a booming future, Patterson filed all the papers, formed a town council, levied a tax on beer sold at the Last Chance, and even received several federal grants.

"Folks keep coming around, 'cause they know there's gold in this sorry old beat-up land," Miss Mary Powell said with a grin.

"It used not be worth a plugged nickel. Some folks are now paying two thousand dollars an acre for it. It won't grow nothing, but maybe that's why the Lord saw fit to let it churn gold down in its innards. The big city folks from Atlanta are coming in and giving big money for the mineral rights, but not all that many are selling. A lot of 'em remember the stories their fathers and mothers, grandfathers and grandmothers used to tell about the days way back when, when people packed in here and mined the gold. Back then, they had dreams about Goldville giving 'em treasures."

She cackled her crisp laughter against the cool air and leaned back and looked out over the countryside.

While she talked on about the price of land and the price of gold, I remembered that Granddaddy once told me that the price of an ounce of gold should always be the same as the price of a good suit of clothes.

Back in the 1930s the price of gold was down to about thirty dollars an ounce, the price of a good suit, and I wondered what kind of suit I could buy for seven hundred dollars plus.

"Goldville, Ala., Didn't Pan Out" was published on the Op-Ed Page of *The New York Times* on Saturday, March 8, 1980. Governor Patterson became a judge on the Alabama Court of Criminal Appeals. After he retired he moved back to his old home place in Goldville.

＊

LOTTIE LETT. 90 YEARS. ALABAMA. NEVER "BED SICK." GONE NOW.

＊

She died. That's what they told me at the country store down the road from the empty house. Four years ago I was driving north on the strip of highway in rural Wilcox County in south Alabama when I saw smoke billowing up into the gray sky. As I passed I saw a black woman dipping clothes into a black pot under which a fire was smoldering. Within a hundred yards I stopped, turned around, and returned to her.

Her name was Lottie Lett. She was a great broad woman with a magnificent African face, stood about five feet six inches, and had a bandana tied about her hair. Her clothes were tattered but clean. She wore old men's shoes without strings. She worked diligently with a pile of clothes on the scrubbed shelf near her smut-black wash pot. The smell of the burning hickory and scorched lye soap permeated the cool winter air.

"I was born way back yonder," she said, not remembering the exact day or year. "I was born right on this place. It belonged to the Simpsons then, the great-granddaddy of the people who live down in the big house now. My mammy, she was a slave. I don't remember much about back then. It was a long time ago."

The best she could recall she was ninety years old, give or take two or three years. "Thank the Lord, I've always been in pretty good health. My old bones ache a little now and then, but I ain't ever been bed sick."

While she talked she wielded an old broomstick, stirring the clothes around and around in the smoke-capped pot. Now and then she raised the stick and a white shirt or sheet clung to it, dropping slowly back into the liquid.

"This place is the same as it always was, far as I can see," she said. The frame house behind her had never been painted, lacked underpinning, and was without screens on the windows or doors. A makeshift stone chimney had been fashioned in a helter-skelter manner up the northern wall. Chickens danced about the yard that had no grass, but was evenly lined where she had meticulously swept with a brush broom.

She had buried three men in her lifetime, she said, and had seven children scattered from Detroit to Newark to Birmingham. "They used to go off way up North. My first child went to Detroit when he was eighteen. He never did finish high school. Only thing for him around here was farming.

"These ol' cotton rows get long out there. That's the kind of work that'll kill a fellow before he gets all his growing in. He went up to Detroit and went to work in a plant and came back down here driving a two-tone Buick. My oldest daughter went off to Atlanta, then went to Newark. She married a fellow that drives a truck up there. They've got a good bit of money, they come down here to see me, they've got seven young 'uns themselves. I've got twenty-two grandchildren altogether."

Her face nearly glowed as she spoke the joyful words. She talked on and on about her various children, and finally said, "They used to go way off up North, but now the young 'uns go to the big cities of Birmingham and Mobile, and they can come home more than the other ones."

A daughter died young and left her with a grandson to raise. He was fourteen, and he accounted for the large amount of white T-shirts and blue jeans that had to be washed. "I just keep on working," she said with determined resignation. "If I didn't have something to do every day when I get up, I'd shrivel up and get blown away by the wind." She smiled as she said the words.

"When I was a little girl, times were tougher than they are now," she said later in front of the fireplace in the simply furnished living room. She had poured homemade scuppernong wine into peanut butter glasses. We drank the sweet liquid and she talked.

"My mammy was a slave, she worked in the house, tended to the children, cooked food for the Simpsons, and I did the same thing.

"When I was little, I'd go there with Mammy and I'd play with the white children. When we got up seven or eight years old they went off to their school. I went to school for two years. Nobody cared whether colored children went to school or not in Wilcox County back then. I just didn't go to school anymore. I stayed home and took care of my brothers and sisters while Mammy worked in the big house.

"I don't remember my daddy. Mammy said he was a slave too. He left when I was a little girl. He went up North, best I recollect. Seemed like everybody went up North if they got a chance.

"I've been to Montgomery. I never went to Birmingham. I never went to Mobile. I go into Camden ever so often.

"I never did want to leave down here. This is my home. I've lived here all my years. I churn my butter out on that porch. I wash those clothes out in the yard. I like to hear the whippoorwills calling and the mockingbirds answering. I milk that ol' cow over yonder, and she gives a fair amount of milk. When they kill a hog down at the big house they send me some fatback and part of a ham. I usually ask if I can clean up some chitlins. I like good, clean, fried chitlins. In the winter I make some collards in the patch, and they sure are good with chitlins."

She was proud of the picture of Dr. Martin Luther King Jr. her daughter had given to her. She displayed it over the mantel, and she said he was the greatest black man who ever lived.

When I drove to the house this winter it was empty. I walked across the yard where sprigs of grass pushed their way up between the knotted roots of the old oak. I sat on the steps and looked across the road to the pasture beyond. I remembered her words.

"Lottie Lett" was published on the Op-Ed Page of *The New York Times* on January 19, 1976.

*

A Girl's Story

*

She's sixteen.

Not a Madonna lookalike. But close.

Five-foot-two, eyes of blue.

She's slight-built with drooping shoulders. Over one shoulder hangs an imitation-leather, fashionably ragged western-style vest. Her jeans are worn thin and tight and torn at the knees.

At first, she gives a don't-give-a-damn look and a pert, puppy-dog twist of the head. She's tough, she wants to signal. She's thick-skinned. She's been around.

The mouth is painted just right. Kewpie-doll sexy. Probably took ten minutes to make those corners perfectly pointed. It's not quite don't-give-a-damn. It's not quite grownup. But it tries.

After quick introductions, after social workers assure her I won't divulge any identity, she lowers her eyes. For a moment she had wanted to speak out, be tough, then she's faced with the reality of what has happened.

"I went with 'em on my own," she says. The eyes do not look anywhere but at the table dividing us. "I wanta be liked. I want 'em to like me, to make me one of 'em, to put me up. You know?"

She went with twelve boys, she says, to a place west of town.

125

"It was a place they go to. It's a shack, a clubhouse, where they meet. They got Rambo stuff on the wall. They got Michael." It's covered with posters, she says.

That's where it happened. It was an initiation. Gang stuff. They all had sex with her over a period of about two hours. Then they started over.

She did not describe every detail. I didn't pry that hard. My reporter's instincts, by now, were not quite as sharp as they once were. They were deadened. My eyes didn't look at hers anymore. I, too, was looking at a spot on the table.

"It's what you got to do, if . . ." Her words shrugged into a slow slur, like drifting into another language.

If what?

". . . if you're gonna make it big with 'em. They like me, they said. They made me one of them."

The boys are members of a gang, she said. The members are from high schools and junior high schools.

They like the girls who go with them, she said. That's what makes you popular. The more you please the boys, the more popular you are.

The afternoon after her ordeal, she went home and cried. She cried and cried. Couldn't stop. She was hemorrhaging, she said. When she could not force it to stop, she panicked. Finally she called her mother.

At first, she did not tell her mother what had happened. Later, when a doctor explained in cold hard medical terms, she broke down again. This time the story flowed from her.

Now, the story remains an enigma to her parents. They can't believe their little daughter could have done these things of her own free will. She *had* to be forced.

The girl shakes her head. It is no longer cocked in defiance. It hangs in defeat.

126

She does not deny what happened. She tried that and she discovered it did not work. She wanted to push it away, she said; as soon as it happened.

Then she became afraid. She knew she had done something to herself. Something physical. Something more than physical. Now, the doctors say, she is okay physically. Her body is healthy.

When you see her watery, downcast eyes and the not-so-perfect lips, you know that she remembers. Something is happening in there, somewhere.

While one element of society is worried and questioning about how young people get into gangs, she has been the victim of one. She knows that there are people worried about her too, but probably not half as worried as she is about herself. Yet she cannot say it. Not now.

But I see it in her, I think. She knows what she has done, and she knows there's a whole life in front of her. And she's afraid.

This article was one of my About Town columns published twice-weekly in *The Alabama Journal* in the early 1990s.

*

TIME RUNS OUT
FOR GEORGE WALLACE

*

The first time I met George Wallace, in 1954, I was sitting in a barber's chair in a shop in south Alabama. He was campaign manager for Governor James E. "Kissin' Jim" Folsom, who was running for a second term in office. Wallace was a tough little guy even then. He stood easily in the middle of the floor, bouncing up and down on the balls of his feet. I was fourteen, traveling with my father, who sold barber and beauty supplies. We listened to Wallace talk for a while, then proceeded toward the next town. My father said, "That man's not going to stop until he's governor of Alabama."

Ten years later, after I became a reporter for a Montgomery newspaper and George Wallace was elected governor, the feisty politician never forgot Daddy or any other constituent. Every time I saw him he asked about Daddy. He was like an enthusiastic machine, shaking hands and greeting people and calling them each by name. But in the past few years even Wallace could joke that his memory was failing. He told about campaigning in a small town and meeting a small boy. "Hello, son, how's your daddy?"

Wallace asked. "He's dead, sir," the boy said. "Oh, I'm sorry," Wallace replied, and kept shaking hands. After he had gone through the crowd he met the same little boy again, shook his hand, and inquired, "How's your daddy?" The boy replied, "He's still dead."

In the not-too-distant past, George Wallace was that kind of never-stop campaigner. Alabama Attorney General Bill Baxley, an heir apparent to the governorship Wallace had held almost constantly for sixteen years, has commented that while he and Wallace are philosophically opposed, they have had the same kind of vigorous approach to campaigning. "There never was a Wallace machine. People rallied around his strong personality. He was the one thing so many varied people in the state had in common. They came together at election time for him," Baxley said.

During those first months I was a reporter for the *Alabama Journal*, I was in awe of Wallace's power. His stranglehold on the state was felt in every hallway down which I walked. My first exposé of the Wallace administration was an article about a giant color printing press bought from a Wallace crony. A wall in the basement of the Highway Department had to be torn out for the press to be installed. After a year, the press was still sitting in its crate. Not only had it never been used, but no state employee was qualified to operate it. When I talked to bureaucrats about the machine, they literally cringed. Occasionally an administrator would cast a wary eye toward the wall, where the ever-present portrait of George Wallace stared solemnly down.

Shortly after the printing press article appeared, I covered a news conference. Twisting his head cockily to one side, Wallace snapped, "I suppose the newspapers will start looking into my toilet paper supply before long." Reporters snickered. "I suppose they'll be looking for the printing on my toilet paper." Again, they snickered. Within three days, I discovered that the state's office paper was all bought from one company owned by a Wallace supporter and relative.

When he wasn't lording over state affairs or making friends and family wealthy, Wallace was gaining nationwide headlines by standing in the schoolhouse door. He became known as the leader of the white racists. He walked and talked with Leander Perez of Louisiana's Plaquemines Parish. He met with Governor Ross Barnett of Mississippi. And his speeches were written by a former employee of the Ku Klux Klan, Asa Carter, who later picketed Wallace's 1971 inauguration speech for being too liberal.

Wallace country changed during the years, and the adept politician changed with it. By 1970, because of the governor's stubbornness as an administrator, preferring to keep blacks out of schools, state jobs, or public facilities, Alabama had been put into the hands of U.S. District Judge Frank M. Johnson Jr. Unlike Wallace, an old schoolmate, Johnson did not sit idly by and allow traditional powerholders to exercise their strength without restraint. When Johnson ordered schools desegregated, Wallace called him an "integrating, carpet-bagging, scalawagging, race-mixing, bald-face liar." After Johnson ordered the state's mental institutions upgraded to meet minimum national standards, Wallace said, "Some federal judges need a barbed-wire enema."

In the mid-1970s, serving his third term as governor, Wallace began courting the growing black electorate in the state. From his wheelchair, his means of mobility since he was shot while campaigning for the presidency in 1972, Wallace told the Conference of Alabama Black Mayors the future "looks bright for all races in Alabama." Later, after meeting in his office with Rosa Parks, the black seamstress whose refusal to give up her seat on a Montgomery city bus sparked the boycott of the early 1950s, and ultimately became the first symbolic action of the Civil Rights Movement, Wallace said, "Blacks and whites have moved together in a spirit of progress throughout the South."

131

During much of this time, however, Wallace showed little interest in the day-to-day affairs of state. He was more interested in running for office than he was in holding office.

When he ran for president in 1976, he felt sincerely that he had a good chance at the Democratic nomination. He and the South had looked away from the old "segregation forever" days. For months he had been walking a few steps at a time on aluminum crutches. He dragged himself slowly along, picturing himself a Southern FDR before the Democratic convention only a few months away. If he could only make a dramatic and tear-jerking entrance, rising to his feet, pulling himself to the podium, and facing the American public as a standing up, finger-pointing, strong-voiced leader, they would open their arms to him. But in the first week of the Florida primary, while being lifted from an airplane, his paralyzed leg was fractured. His campaigning was drastically hindered. With the plastic cast making his leg stick straight out from the wheelchair, he looked more than ever like a helpless cripple.

He lost Florida to a vibrant, well organized, clean-cut, smiling Jimmy Carter, who had come along in the aftermath of the Civil Rights Movement, portraying a scrubbed image of the New South. Carter defeated Wallace by two percentage points in Florida. Then, after Wallace lost his old North Carolina stronghold, he was doomed. He could only sit back and watch while Carter's snowball grew. As he said later, "I paved the way for Carter," but his time as a viable national candidate had passed.

Back home in Alabama, Wallace finally decided to govern with authority. After years of inaction, he took on a rowdy legislature. He pushed for a package of bills designed to stop the utilities from what he considered gross overcharging. He came on strong, reminiscent of the New Deal–era populist Huey P. Long, but the legislature held its own against him. His utility package was defeated. And as a result, the greatest hindrance he leaves his successor is a totally fouled-up legislature that recessed this year without even passing a state education budget.

Wallace said that he would run for the U.S. Senate to fill the seat to be vacated by the retirement of Senator John Sparkman. But he did not solidify his supporters behind him, although they were waiting for his call. Meanwhile, his opponents gained strength. The heavy, humid days of campaigning through July and August did not look inviting to a man in a wheelchair. All in all, he was tired.

It has been twenty years since he made his first big speech for governor. He had met people in barber shops. He had talked to tiny groups in civic clubs in one-horse towns throughout Alabama. But his first major speech of 1958 was to the Alabama League of Municipalities. His longtime friend, Ed E. Reid, executive secretary of the League, had been talking the Wallace line to his people, and it showed when the candidate stood. Wallace received his first roof-raising applause, and from that moment his popularity increased across the state. He didn't win the election. He lost to State Attorney General John Patterson, who had the support of the Ku Klux Klan. Wallace was perceived as the moderate on the race issue. After the election, Wallace declared to close friends, "I'll never be out-niggered again." Four years later he became governor.

Twenty years later, he was wheeled into the convention of the Alabama League of Municipalities in the same town, Mobile, where he had made that first major speech. As a postscript to a mild talk, Wallace announced that he would not run for the U.S. Senate.

The following morning in his office in Montgomery, a tanned, smiling, but almost totally deaf Wallace told reporters, "I won't have you to kick around any more." But his joke fell flat. When reporters pushed, he said, "I simply don't want to run for the Senate."

His voice was an empty shell of what it had been sixteen years earlier when he stood defiantly in Montgomery on the spot where Jefferson Davis had been inaugurated president of the Confederacy. At his own inauguration Wallace predicted, "Segregation forever!" He had been a cocky little white supremacist back then. Now he insisted to everyone, "I'm not a racist."

In retrospect, I do not believe he is a racist. But he used racism as a political tool without regard for the consequences. In using it, he created an atmosphere in which racism flourished.

As I sat in his new conference, I couldn't help but feel a little sorry for him. There had been a time when I had feared, even hated, him. Now he appeared twisted and torn. Question after question had to be repeated because he couldn't hear. And his answers were uncertain. When someone asked if he thought he could have been president if he had not been shot, he answered, "I feel like I could have been president." But his words didn't have the old vigor. They contained an edge of bitterness. He knew he would never have another chance. And we knew it too.

In my book, *Watch Out for George Wallace*, published in early 1976, I called him "the most dangerous politician in America today." Now, he was the bantamweight prizefighter hanging up his gloves after one fight too many.

"Time Runs Out for George Wallace" was published in the summer of 1978 on the Viewpoints page of *Newsday* on Long Island in New York. It was not the last time I wrote George Wallace off as a politician out of politics. However, four years later he did what he loved doing: he turned the tables on everybody who had written him off and ran for his fourth term as governor. He won, this time with the solid majority of black voters voting for him.

※

GOODBYE, GEORGE

※

As I stood in the chambers of the Alabama House of Representatives in the Capitol on Goat Hill and listened to the resounding voice of George C. Wallace, I cried.

I could not help myself, watching his eyes tearing up and his lips quivering.

I remembered politics past. I remembered a day thirty years earlier when he came bouncing into a barber shop somewhere in south Alabama and extended his hand to my father and introduced himself.

Wallace was a feisty, greasy-haired, quick-talking fellow.

Dad was a traveling salesman of barber and beauty supplies, and he judged George Wallace as a comer in politics. Daddy had seen many of them come and go in his years on the road.

I remembered a day in the early '60s, after Wallace stood in the schoolhouse door at the University of Alabama in Tuscaloosa and tried to keep two young black people from registering as students, when I was covering state government for the *Alabama Journal* in Montgomery.

I remembered the day that he stood on the steps outside the state capitol and declared to the nation that he would lead his beloved South against the tyranny of a central, federal government

135

for "Segregation now! Segregation tomorrow! Segregation forever!"

He smiled for the cameras, sneered at Washington, D.C., and was congratulated by his segregationist buddies, Judge Leander Perez of Louisiana, Governor Ross Barnett of Mississippi, and Ku Klux Klan wizard Bobby Shelton of Tuscaloosa, all of whom had come for his first inauguration as governor in 1963.

I remembered the time when he summoned all the reporters in the capitol to his office and swore he would stop "this foolishness," as he called the planned march by Dr. Martin Luther King Jr. from Selma to Montgomery.

Several days later, he allowed his public safety director to lead state troopers with tear gas and billy clubs against a defenseless group of marchers as they crossed Selma's Edmund Pettus bridge on an otherwise quiet Sunday afternoon.

Wallace was a flag-waving rebel with a cause. He was the leader who went out into the nation carrying the banner of defiance.

His kind of cocky leadership led many white people in Alabama to proclaim the state Wallace Country. They proudly displayed the Confederate Stars and Bars. A few even rode openly wearing the white hoods and gowns of the KKK.

Wallace was their public image. Because he spoke defiantly, mocking the U.S. Constitution, the U.S. courts, and the Congress, he gave them a false respectability.

On the very night after he stood in the schoolhouse door, a white man shot and killed civil rights leader Medgar Evers less than a hundred miles away in Mississippi.

In the midst of the turmoil — which Wallace stirred with angry words, such as snapping back staccato sentences at U.S. Attorney General Robert Kennedy when he visited the governor in Montgomery — a church in downtown Birmingham was bombed and four little black girls were killed.

The investigation into the bombing was foiled when Public Safety Director Al Lingo, a Wallace appointee, called detectives off after they began questioning Klansmen about their involvement.

Wallace never pulled a trigger. He never lit a fuse. He was the bully on the block who incited action from others by his tough words, and these words created an atmosphere of fear for the man, woman, or child who just happened to be black.

After he was defeated for governor the first time he ran in 1958, he had allowed racism to haunt his political career. He believed he had been beaten because he had been the most liberal candidate and his opponent had the support of racist groups such as the Ku Klux Klan.

He told close friends then, "I'll never be out-niggered again."

Because of his staunch stands against the encroachment of federal powers, articulated in racist terms in dozens of speeches, he traveled through the Northeast in 1964 speaking on Ivy League campuses. He had little sympathy for the long-haired jeering mobs and expressed his feelings privately and publicly.

In 1968, he ran for president on a third-party ticket and amassed more votes than any other candidate running outside the two major parties.

When he returned to Alabama, he was eager to show off to reporters his collection of photographs from '64 and '68.

And although many of us had accompanied him on the trips, he called us into his office on many occasions and reached down and pulled out his collection of pictures. He showed photo after photo of crowds in civic centers throughout the Midwest.

It became humorous to us, but his voice was never without enthusiasm.

"They listened to every word I said," he would say. "They gave me a standing ovation that was longer than ten minutes! I swear it was."

Wallace had natural charisma and was a gifted politician, but rather than labor as an innovator to find a way to mold public opinion, he moved with the flow of social history. He allowed the current of popular sentiment to wash his political beliefs from a shore of hatred to a shore of moderation.

He used racism as a tool to win elections in Alabama in the 1960s, and in the 1970s he looked back and said, "I was never a racist."

During the past few years, Wallace attempted to soften his stance on civil rights. "I was wrong about the law," he said. "I admit it. Now I want to do what is right."

In 1965 at Selma, he had tried to keep an entire race of people from demonstrating on a U.S. highway for their voting rights. Once blacks got those rights, he went to them hat in hand and asked for their votes. And he finally got their votes in 1982 when he won his unprecedented fourth term as governor.

Wallace was a child of the Depression who could not stand seeing people go hungry, and worked hard to make sure that they were fed and clothed. That same sense provided him with the political antenna to know that the common man was more than simply disenchanted with the liberal inclinations of the federal government and the candidates of the national parties. He spoke with the populist's passionate cry of the little man.

In later years when he courted the black vote, perhaps it was this compassionate plea for the desires and hopes and dreams of the little man that appealed to the many black voters who pulled the lever for him.

It was certainly amazing to see a politician prevail through a time when few blacks voted to a time when 5 of 35 Alabama state senators and 19 of 105 state representatives are black, and black officeholders sit on city councils and county commissions throughout the state.

Wallace moved from a time of standing in the schoolhouse door to his own appointment of a black press secretary, a black director of pensions and security, and a black commissioner of pardons and paroles. In 1982, he received the great majority of the black vote when he was elected to his fourth term as governor. Before finishing that term, he was awarded an honorary doctorate by predominantly black Tuskegee University.

Wallace changed in other ways, too. Once he had referred to Chinese as "*commonists.*" But in 1985 he traveled to China and asked leaders there to consider Alabama as a location for new industry. As a result, a group of Chinese officials visited Huntsville to look at possible locations for expansion of their industries.

While business leaders continued to criticize his inaction, Wallace maintained that his administration brought more jobs into the state than any other, and the statistics bore him out.

Listening to his voice as he told about sharing the good times and the hard times and about paying "a pretty high price in 1972," I remembered seeing his body fall to the asphalt in the parking lot in Laurel, Maryland, and feeling a sudden emptiness in my entire being.

For the first time, he spoke publicly of the five bullets that struck him down while campaigning in the primary for the Democratic nomination in 1972.

Since that day he has said numerous times that if he had not been shot and paralyzed, Hubert Humphrey would have won the nomination instead of George McGovern, and that Humphrey would have asked Wallace to be his running mate.

"We would have won and I would have been vice president of the United States," he has said, noting that Humphrey visited him many times in Montgomery after the shooting.

He remembered days gone by and the tears came to his eyes. No longer did his voice strut like it was something separate and apart from the man, as it did when he defied federal law in the 1960s.

He held his head high and declared, "I have climbed my last political mountain. For now, I must pass the rope and pick to another climber and say, 'Climb on. Climb on to higher heights. Climb on until you reach the very peak. Then look back and wave at me. For I too will still be climbing.'"

His voice broke, tears clouded his eyes.

"I conclude by telling you that my heart will always belong to Alabama. I expect to be around, the Lord willing, a few more years. But as for the governmental and political arena, my fellow Alabamians, I bid you a fond, affectionate farewell."

The people who packed the room stood and applauded. They stood and stood. They clapped louder and louder. It was his best audience in years. And I hoped someone was making a good photograph of it for him.

WALLACE LASTED more than a handful of years. I visited him occasionally at his home. We'd talk about the old days. He continued to insist he was never a racist, told me he'd never called Dr. King or Judge Johnson by name. "No, but everybody knew who you meant, Governor," I said. His teeth chomped on his smelly cigar. He couldn't hear my words. I wrote them on a yellow pad and handed them to him. At some point a friend brought him a videotape of some of his old audiences from 1968. His man, Eddie, who tended to him, patted pillows and sat him up in bed. With his handy clicker, Wallace played the scenes over and over again. He could not get enough of the applause.

"Goodbye, George" was published in *The Miami Herald*.

✳ Mexico ✳

The Same Earth

In 1954 I spent months in a hospital in Birmingham being treated for an acute case of scoliosis resulting from childhood polio. I was encased in a body cast from the top of my head to one of my knees. When my body was twisted to an appropriate position, I underwent two operations to strengthen my backbone.

In the children's section of the hospital I made friends with several wheelchair-ridden patients. One brought me a magazine that contained an article called "How to Live in Paradise on $100 a Month." I clipped that piece and kept it for the next four years. I also wrote to the director of the Instituto Allende at San Miguel de Allende in the state of Guanajuato in Mexico. He sent me catalogs showing photographs and describing the creative writing center.

In the summer following my senior year in high school I rode trains to the foreign country. I knew only several words of Spanish, but I was eager and anxious. It was my first trip into a country I found muy simpático, although it was filled with mystery and wonder and tragedy, and I have been returning frequently ever since.

*

Secrets Behind Walls

*

1.

I knew her only a few weeks, but it was long enough to make an impression that would last a lifetime.

I was eighteen. Filled with ambition to become a writer, I traveled south from my home in Alabama to a place very strange to me.

I caught a passenger train, the *Southerner*, from Tuscaloosa to New Orleans; then the *Southern Pacific* to San Antonio, where I paid a taxi driver $5 extra to rush me to a station across town, where a steam engine and two cars were ready to pull out and head across the south Texas desert to Laredo, where I climbed onto the *Aztec Eagle* and upgraded to a first-class Pullman berth for $14 American.

Less than a half-hour later we were rambling through Boy's Town, where long brown faces with big sad eyes gazed up at me with pure disdain and envy as I settled into a soft seat beneath the plastic bubble in the observation car. A Mexican general bought my first *cerveza*, a Golden Corona in a long-neck bottle, served

145

with a cold glass. The general in his khaki uniform grinned, show-ing gold-capped teeth, and asked, "*Cuantos años tienes?*" to which I replied with a smile and a shrug. "How old?" he translated. I told him, and added that I graduated from high school last week in Alabama, and he said I was old enough to buy and drink Mexican beer, and taught me *cerveza, tequila, pollo con rehejo,* and *puta,* the word for prostitute, which he said was *muy importante*. He waved *adiós* at Monterrey, and left me alone with my beer and new vocabulary.

In the Pullman berth, I peeped from beneath the shade and saw my reflection in the glass. Outside was only darkness as we rumbled through the night. I slept fitfully, awakening several times, looking out, seeing nothing. I lay awake, wondering if per-haps we had passed my destination in the middle of the night. As my imagination worked, I shivered and pulled the covers up to my chin and closed my eyes.

I awakened in a stupor of surprise, a bright yellow sun glim-mering around the edges of the brown shade. I rolled toward the light and lifted the shade and stared out at the sun-bathed rocky hillsides of the Sierra Madres. Above was the clearest, bluest sky I'd ever seen. I looked at that outside world that I had dreamed about: an open universe that was completely new to me, even its language something akin to the next page of a strange and fasci-nating foreign classic, something frightful but eagerly anticipated. Here was reality from the celluloid images I had followed thor-oughly from John Huston's movie and B. Traven's novel, the men seeking treasure in the Sierra Madre mountains and losing all con-tact with their consciences when the desire for gold became so overwhelming they could think of nothing else.

When the *Aztec Eagle* stopped at the remote depot at 11 A.M., I stepped down with my two bags and portable typewriter. I was suddenly surrounded by children chirping like hungry, excited birds, all reaching toward me, grabbing eagerly at my bags.

"No!" I said. "Get away!"

When they persisted, I slapped at their dirty little hands.

"No!" I said.

They continued, grabbing and pulling.

As the train disappeared down the tracks, the tattered children carried my bags away. I ran after them, thinking my bags would disappear and I would be left without clothes, books, or typewriter.

When I caught up with them, they were placing my bags into the trunk of the only car in the dusty yard. Next to the car stood a driver who asked in broken English if I needed a taxi. I looked around, saw no building other than the dusty depot and no other car. I nodded.

The children surrounded me. They poked their open palms toward me. Their large dark eyes stared hungrily, like baby birds at feeding time. I looked toward the driver, who ignored me.

While the driver slid under the wheel of his old car, I reached into my pocket, pulled out a handful of change, and tossed it toward the children.

I scrambled to get into the backseat while the children dropped to their knees and grappled for the coins.

"*Casa Jorado, por favor,*" I said.

The driver started out across the desert. No town in sight. Nothing but flat brown desert and hills in the distance.

Then came a shout behind us.

The driver slammed on brakes. The car slid to a stop.

I wanted to shout, "Go!" but I had already exhausted what little Spanish I knew. I felt helpless. I twisted and saw a man running toward us. He was saying something frantically. I had no idea what his words meant. He opened the door and slid inside. He turned and grinned and said something. I nodded.

The driver released the clutch and off we went across the desert in a cloud of dust.

147

Instantly, I wondered if I was being kidnapped. These two Mexicans were in cahoots. They would take me out into the desert—a strange, desolate place to a boy who had known open pastures, thick forests, cottonfields, and friendly villages of the South. I had never been away from home alone. Once, when I was a child, I traveled with Mama and my little brother by train to New York, where we lived near the Army post where Daddy was stationed on Staten Island. In the summertime of my youth we would travel as a family to Florida or the hills of east Tennessee. I had gone with friends to Panama City Beach, where we'd gotten drunk and acted fools, staying for five or six days. But I'd never been away for an extended time, and certainly never into a foreign country where I couldn't speak the language.

I was scared.

Then the car turned eastward. In the distance, spread over a hillside, was a town. White buildings glistened in the midday sun. In the middle of a labyrinth of pastel plaster walls shaped in various-sized rectangles was a giant pink steeple reaching high into the bright blue sky. It was the centerpiece of the photographs of the town of San Miguel de Allende I had previously seen in brochures advertising the Instituto Allende, where I would attend classes this summer.

At the entrance to *Casa Jorado*, I passed through a large wooden door into a dark hallway where walls were covered with old photographs. Standing there, staring at the shadowy, faded faces of Mexicans from past generations, I heard the brusque sounds of "Malagueña" being played allegro on a slightly off-key piano.

At the end of the hallway the hacienda opened to a sunny garden with colorful jacaranda blooms, lemon trees, bougainvillea, and other flowering plants. To the left, through a high doorway, a young woman sat at a baby grand piano. She played the notes of "Malagueña" with verve, turning her dark head from side to side as though she were entertaining thousands in a huge concert hall. She was lost in the sound. When she stopped, halfway through, I applauded. She glanced toward me. Her face flushed pink. She ducked her head, turned, and fled to the far side of the large room.

"*Señorita?*" I called. But she was gone.

Behind me, from a dining room emitting the delicious fragrance of a Mexican *comida* with garlic and coriander and onion, stepped a gray-haired woman. Short, with prominent nose and high forehead, she introduced herself as Dona Jorado, the mistress of the house.

She led me onto the patio, pointed out the honor-system bar, took me to my small room, and gave me serving times for breakfast and comida.

2.

In my spartan room was a single bed without springs. In an old-fashioned chifforobe I hung my clothes. I situated my portable typewriter on a small wooden desk beneath double windows. Here too I placed three books: a tattered paperback of *From Here to Eternity*, a well-worn hardcover Viking *Portable Faulkner* and a paperback Webster's. Then I ventured out to explore the territory.

After I passed several peacocks loitering lazily in the garden, I walked down the cobblestone street toward the Instituto. As I strolled by high walls hiding a very large building with a dome I noticed wooden doors even larger than those of *Casa Jorado*. Near the corner of Dr. Hernandez Macias and San Francisco streets, a gigantic padlock held the very large door shut. The significant lock intrigued me and made me wonder what was hidden behind those walls. It looked like a church. But most churches in Mexico were open to parishioners twenty-four hours a day seven days a week.

I learned soon that throughout San Miguel, like many Mexican towns, the streets were lined with walls. Wooden doors opened to houses or stores. Some were magnificent, some were mere hovels.

Some blocks away, I walked through the large open wooden doors in a high concrete wall studded with iron buttons. Inside the walls of the Instituto was a lovely small courtyard. In the middle, beyond a wall of bright red bougainvillea, was a trickling fountain that looked peaceful and welcoming. In the corner offices I signed papers, then was introduced to a tall man with thinning gray hair and piercing eyes. Stirling Dickinson had come from Ohio to Mexico twenty years earlier and had started an art school. After World War II he joined with a former governor of Guanajuato, Enrique Fernandez Martinez, to establish the Instituto, on the estate of the Canal family that owned the first building of the compound, first constructed in 1735. In 1809 the Spanish family sold the property to an order of Descalced Camelite Sisters, barefoot nuns headquartered in nearby Queretaro. The shoeless sisters planned to build a religious complex, and a chapel was completed by Spanish architect-sculptor Manuel Tolsá of the Royal Academy of San Carlos in Mexico City before the revolution of 1810 interrupted the project.

In his soft Midwestern voice, Stirling Dickinson told the story of Fray Juan de San Miguel walking barefoot from the valley of Mexico, where Mexico City is now located, to this hill 150 miles north. He built a shrine near the train station where I had arrived that morning.

By 1810, after Spanish-born political bosses ruled the country for two hundred years, the Mexican-born Creoles, led by a handsome young landowner from San Miguel, began to talk of rebellion. Ignacio Allende started a club called the Society for the Study of Fine Arts in which the idea of freedom was discussed with enthusiasm. With him was Father Miguel Hidalgo, a priest from nearby Dolores. Together, they organized the rebels. Father

Hidalgo issued his famous *Grito*, "Long live Our Lady of Guadalupe! Long live independence!" that can still be heard on the streets of San Miguel every September 16th. For Allende, Hidalgo, and several other leaders, the revolution was short-lived. They were captured and beheaded. Their heads, on public display in iron cages, withered away for nearly ten years in Guanajuato, until another great Mexican leader, General Anastasio Bustamante, who later moved to San Miguel, took them down and buried them with honors.

Stirling Dickinson told the story as we sat on a patio behind the school looking over the vista of the town. The view up the hill was breathtaking: the spires of the central church, *La Parroquia*, pointing high into the sky, several domes with multicolored mosaic-style roofs, layer upon layer of earthen-shaded rectangles, all fit together like a gigantic cubist canvas.

Back at Casa Jorado, after comida of boiled chicken, potatoes, a stewed cactus-type vegetable, and well-buttered *pan*, I lay on my cotton-filled mattress and listened to songbirds and fell asleep. Waking, I reread a scene from *From Here to Eternity*, my favorite novel. In the quietness of late afternoon I listened once again to the first twenty or so bars of "Malagueña," wondering if she would ever learn more of the tune.

As I started out that evening, first gazing at the ancient faces of the people of yesteryear in the photographs lining the entrance hallway, I heard once again the sound of the piano playing the song I was beginning to hate with a warm passion. I looked through the antique-filled parlor and saw her smooth high-cheeked olive-shaded face lighted by a brass lamp. My first thought: *She's gorgeous.*

She glanced up, her eyes catching my stare, and she cast her vision downward quickly.

As the song started again, I moved out the door toward the center of town, the *jardín*, where I knew I would find the *La Cucaracha* bar where I knew *gringos* hung out.

Four years earlier, hospitalized in a Birmingham children's clinic for surgery and treatment of scoliosis, the result of infant polio, I had read an article in a magazine: "How to Live in Paradise for $100 a Month." It described San Miguel as a writer's haven and told about the people and the happenings at the *Cucaracha*. It was written by an ex-GI named Richard Magruder, whom I would meet thirty years later in the Mexico City airport. I told him how his article in the magazine had changed my life. We became friends, spending time together in Atlanta, Acapulco, and San Miguel, before his death a few years ago. Until the end, when he was suffering mightily from cancer, Richard Magruder displayed a lively enthusiasm for his adopted country.

I wandered up the hillside to the *jardín*, or square garden, across the street from the steeples of the *Parroquia* church, with its pink spires that I had viewed from the patio behind the Instituto. Built by a Spanish mason who had only a tattered postcard of a church in his homeland from which to work on his elaborate design, the church is one of the most unusual in a country filled with interesting and elaborate churches.

The square was decorated with Mexican laurel trees manicured flat across the top and round underneath. Originally planted by devotees of Porfirio Diaz, who governed Mexico with dictator-like power from 1876 to 1911, the trees formed a pattern of triangles divided by walkways lit by black iron lamps that many years earlier burned oil. Beneath the trees, the walks were lined by wrought iron benches. An elevated iron-roofed bandstand stood in the center. In the days to come I learned that on Sunday nights boys and girls walked in a promenade, each in the opposite direction, while mothers and aunts sat on the benches and watched closely.

At the *Cucaracha*, I met a number of so-called writers. Most drank more than they wrote. And they liked to talk. I sat in the corner and listened, seldom joining in the conversation, aware that I had little experience and few years. I had never been to war and had never had a love affair, two favorite topics of most of the men and some of the women. Before the end of my first night, one of these writers said he was friends with Jack Kerouac, and he knew that Jack and his Beat buddies would visit San Miguel during the summer. I went home to *Casa Jorado* with still more mystery floating in my mind.

3.

I went to class at the Instituto. I wrote. I read my stories in class. My teachers did not like my Southern way of writing. They chided me for having my characters "yell" or "holler" and their faces soured at some of my descriptions. I was too clumsy, too Alabama, too country. They instructed me to read F. Scott Fitzgerald's stories about growing up. All of these teachers were from the Midwest or West or New York.

By the time the Beats showed up, I was totally frustrated with trying to write clear unobstructed prose without a trace of Southernness. I tried, but it was very difficult for a boy who had grown up listening to the voice of a different land.

Allen Ginsberg, an overweight bearded poet, spouted philosophy at the top of his shrill voice until he disappeared the first night with a friend and didn't show up again until the others were ready to leave several days later.

Neal Cassady was a square-shouldered athletic sharp-faced railroad brakeman with sunken brooding eyes and a soft western tongue.

On that first afternoon, Ginsberg announced, motioning toward the pale high-boned face of Jack Kerouac, "We all worship at the feet of this great Beat god." As he unfolded from the forest-green five-year-old Mercedes Benz, Kerouac's fine-boned face was haloed in the bright Mexican afternoon sunlight. With downcast eyes, either shy or trying to hide from the sudden brightness, our mutual friend introduced us. I offered my hand, and he gave me a shake as limp as an earthworm. I was surprised. I had expected a good strong manly handshake from the Dharma bum whose writing I admired, especially for its powerful drive that seemed never to cease as it grabbed the reader and carried him along at breakneck speed, riding the rails or the highways, as strong and vast as America. There was no power in his touch.

As he chewed his cud like a benevolent cow from a Buddhist pasture, his light bright blue eyes seemed to focus beyond me on something halfway between here and there. I suspected that he had been gnawing on something that settled his mind on a never-never land far, far away. "Hey, man, I want to meet Montezuma and climb into that soul where something fitful is happening *now!*" he exploded with a sweet gentle loudness.

From somewhere in the depths of the Mercedes appeared a skinny naked girl with breasts the size of small pancakes and stringy dark hair and ribs that showed pitifully. Her name was Callie, but they called her Sunshine, and she'd been traveling with them from the border, where she'd been hitchhiking from some small town in the upper Midwest. Somewhere between Nogales and San Miguel she had lost her clothes. She found a pair of shorts and a halter and sandals. But when she stepped out onto the street our friend Bill Evans, an adventure writer who had lived in San Miguel for several years, warned, "You better find some more cloth to cover yourself. The police will have you behind bars in a minute, dressed like that. Or undressed like that."

"What's wrong?" she asked incredulously, looking down at her scrawny body.

"This isn't Acapulco or some beach resort," Evans said. "They frown on women wearing pants here. If you walk downtown like you are, you'll be arrested. They have very strict laws."

She shrugged, crawled back inside, shucked off her shorts, snapped a knee-length skirt around her waist and pulled a peasant's blouse over her head.

Minutes later we were all sitting in the outer room of the *Cucaracha,* drinking. Kerouac sat in the largest chair and leaned back and gazed up at the ceiling, where Bill Evans was pointing out the three chipped places where movie star Robert Mitchum had shot his bodyguard's revolver, leaving his "autograph" in the early 1950s while shooting *The Big Country.* Gazing upward, Kerouac said, "I wish I had a gun," and someone volunteered, "Chucho's got one."

Chucho was a rotund Mexican descended from the early *Chichimeca* Indians who first inhabited the area more than a hundred years before San Miguel became a town. He was especially friendly to his *gringo* clientele, and before the summer was out invited me and several others to his ranch, where we rode horseback into the hills and viewed his latest fighting bulls from a distance.

Neither Chucho nor the gun appeared. Ginsberg began talking about Jack Kerouac as Saint Jacque, navigator through the wilderness of stars. Kerouac smiled. It was all so much fun: the cosmic joke and jokester, the forerunners of Ken Kesey and his Merry Pranksters, who would come later to San Miguel in their psychomobile fashioned from an old Bluebird schoolbus. These ancient mariners were paving the way, like the literary Columbus or Magellan, watching the horizon for new territory to explore, knowing they were the Huckleberry Finns of the twentieth century.

"Saint Jacque led us to this nirvana, man," Neal Cassady said. "It's the place where I've been wanting to be all my life. I mean, like I was in Denver doing boring shit, man. Major boring! But now, here we are in paradise with the Minerva of Madness, this doll-chick Sunshine, who is light, all light."

Sitting in a corner, sipping my *Cuba Libre*, I listened to Sunshine ramble on in a long monologue about how she spent last summer with a bunch of guys in the mountains of northern California. "We were seeking God in the wind," she said. Kerouac said that was a good place to find Him. "If you're quiet enough and have patience, you will find the jazz brain that you need to carry out the essence of being," he said, and Sunshine tilted her head to one side, her eyes lighting, saying, "I'm aware."

Listening on and on, I wondered if they really knew what the hell they were talking about, and later Kerouac, without being prompted, spoke loudly, "Ride your bicycle upside-down into space and hear the howling of the prophet Allen who sits on yonder throne, sharing the universe of Ignorance that can only be a Kharma dream."

After listening late to the talk, I awakened early next to Sunshine on the floor of Bill Evans's fourteen-dollar-a-month apartment high on the hill above town. Just before dawn we all rode out to Taboada hot springs on a rocky knoll. We undressed and stepped into the steamy fog of the waters while a silvery sun sparkled over the edge of distant hills to the east.

After the soothing baths, we lazed in the early morning sun, bright now and warm, and we went to the nearby village of Atotonilco, the Nahuatl Indian word meaning "the place of hot springs." A dark, foreboding cluster of buildings, the Sanctuary of Atotonilco, with six chapels separated by patios and walkways behind high walls, was built in 1740 by a priest who had inherited great wealth. He spent his entire fortune building the primary chapel, Our Lady of Health, and its surrounding counterparts to celebrate penitence. The priest worshiped by whipping himself with thorny branches of cactus plants, a practice which he passed on to generation after generation of parishioners.

That morning we entered in silence. I stood next to Kerouac as we stared up at the wall covered by the shadowy figure of Christ carrying a cross on bloody shoulders. Inside the sanctuary was another portrait of Jesus bleeding profusely. Thorns punctured his skin at numerous places, even the cheek, forehead, side, and thigh, from which the blood flowed.

We moved silently, our eyes scanning the scenes: Seven Deadly Sins and Seven Cardinal Virtues. Kerouac, whose eyes seemed dilated as he gazed upon the paintings, gasped at the brutal grace of the bright, clear violence.

After Allende and Father Hidalgo were beheaded, the rebels who continued to fight against the Spanish control used Atotonilco as their hideout. Under the shield of night, from 1810 to 1820, they rode out to attack and rob the trains carrying silver from the mines at Zacatecas and Guanajuato.

When Spanish troops captured the village, the priest was arrested and sentenced to be hanged in the morning. They marched him down the dusty street and locked him in the shrine. That night, according to local legend, the priest escaped through a tunnel that led him to the basement crypt of *La Parroquia*, miles away in the center of San Miguel. When the Spaniards returned, they thought the arrested priest had actually vanished or had been rescued by angels.

Outside the sanctuary, Kerouac said, "It is joy we are witnessing. It is the love of hurt—suffering until you are at peace with yourself. It is what life is all about."

I looked back toward the strange place. I had not seen the same thing. But I shivered with a weird feeling.

In the next several days I learned that *On the Road* had been written in "the long night of life" without stopping, on a single roll of paper, "banging on the typewriter like it was a brain-drum," the

157

author said, "beating it out to the tune of the night and the morning and the noonday sun, man, like letting my brain find its own rhythm, because that is the Dharma and the Kharma, and it makes all the difference in the world to have Buddha sitting on your shoulder, conducting the orchestra of your writing, letting it flow. Every day is like today, and it is Saturday."

I, the realist, said, "No, it isn't; it's Thursday."

But he said, "Every day is Saturday, and there is nothing to do."

I went to my little room and wrote his words in my journal, another habit insisted on by my new Midwestern teachers: Fitzgerald kept a journal, therefore all young writers should. At the downtown corner bookstore I bought a paperback of John Steinbeck's *The Grapes of Wrath*, which was not recommended by the professors but which I wanted to reread anyway.

4.

During the next few days I heard Maria Elena Jorado play her first twenty bars of "Malagueña" at least a dozen times. Standing in the shadows of the hall I watched her intense dark eyes concentrating on the keyboard, making her music, and I wondered what was wrong in her world that caused her deafening, maddening repetition.

The next morning, after spending hours the night before with Kerouac and Cassady, I awakened abruptly to the screeching sound of a peacock's cry.

Moments later I heard Maria Elena's voice, frightened and angry. "No!" she screamed. Then came the staccato sound of a slap.

I rushed to the windows. Looking out across the green lawn glistening with dew in the morning light I saw the girl caressing

158

her high-boned cheek. Tears watered her oversized dark eyes. Before her stood a tall, distinguished-looking, gray-haired man who turned quickly and stiffly, like a soldier, and strode away.

The girl's eyes lifted and roamed. When she saw me, she lowered her eyes instantly. She too turned and walked quickly toward the house.

5.

That evening at the Cucaracha, Kerouac talked: "There are empty shapes and empty dreams wandering through the heads of youth. Don't accept reality, don't take it at face value. Forget what any creative writing professor ever tells you. Regurgitate life."

Later I asked him about John Steinbeck, and Kerouac shook his head almost violently. "Don't believe that ragged stupid nonsense, a Dust Bowl mentality that reeks of dishonesty, written with the heart of a historian. You can't believe history! Never! History filters down through the academic world of the intellectual fools who sit in red-brick ivy-covered towers and breathe the tainted air flavored with the tangy taste of money, believing only in their own superior intellects. History can only be told by those who lived it, not by wretched professors who study it. Believe the love letters of saints and whores, not the texts of pampered professors. Believe the weeping, moaning, tear-stained outbursts of mothers whose children have died in front of their eyes, not the dry-heaves of historians. Did John Steinbeck suffer? Did he die a dozen deaths on a flight from Oklahoma to California? No!" Kerouac ranted as I watched, amazed and slightly alarmed. I was eighteen, a child of the Alabama backwoods, and I had seen religious men fling their arms and had heard them shout emotional cries of the spirit; I thought I would hear better from a man whose writing I admired.

159

Saint Jacque of the Beatniks said,"Steinbeck listened to the words secondhand, read about the troubling times, but he never felt the hunger eat at his belly. He was never Tom Joad."

Later, Neal Cassady walked with me out of the Cucaracha. We sat on the high curb, drinking and talking. "Don't worry about what Jack says," he said. "He gets all cramped inside. The joy of the road turns sour sometimes, especially when he gets all wound up inside. After a trip like this, Jack locks himself in a room away from the world and does as he preaches: regurgitates life. And then he becomes whole again. The creativity is part of the whole, but to find the source of creativity, he attacks the world like a soldier attacking the enemy."

I went to my room at *Casa Jorado*. I lay awake and thought about Kerouac and Cassady, about Sunshine and Maria Elena, and I felt deep-down lonesome, empty inside.

The next morning I read Steinbeck's words in *The Grapes of Wrath* and loved them once again. I felt the emotions of the scenes. I started writing a short story about a cousin back home in Alabama, a Southern boy who had Southern ways and loved his coon dog more than moonshine or money. When I read the words to the class at the Instituto I felt pangs of embarrassment as my shaky Southern voice spoke the language of my home. Some of the other, older students chuckled beneath their breaths, but the professor, Ashmead Scott, about whom I will write in more detail later, was kind and gentle and found a way toward some constructive criticism that left me with hope rather than total despair.

Several days later the Beats went on their way. Through the years I read more of Kerouac and liked his work in spite of my memories. I even cried when I read that he had died in a little ordinary house in Florida. He deserved better than that, I thought. And I also cried when I read that Neal Cassady had gone back to San Miguel to find a girl not unlike Sunshine. He started walking the railroad tracks from the depot toward Celaya and joined an

Indian wedding party and drank *pulque* with them, on top of Seconal and other drugs. He sang with them and danced off into the night, counting each rail. The next morning his comatose body was discovered near the tracks, and he died in the hospital at San Miguel.

6.

Early on a July morning after I finished reading *The Grapes of Wrath* I was awakened to the loud pop of a gun firing.

In the garden, Maria Elena Jorado stood in the brilliant early morning sunlight with a long-barrel revolver hanging from her limp hand. Her face was tilted forward, her dark eyes streaming with tears.

On the perfectly manicured green slope lay her father, Don Alejandro Jorado, the scion of a Creole family that had dwelled in San Miguel since the days before the first revolution.

I heard a near-silent gasp and saw Dona Jorado float in her sheath of loose garments toward her daughter, enveloping the girl into her arms and leading her away from the body, upon which she cast a quick and disdainful glance.

By the time a team of medical people arrived, Maria Elena had been whisked away into the bowels of the residence.

Over coffee, another guest who had lived at the hacienda for years said, "She finally did it."

"How long . . ." I started.

"Over a year," he said. "She tried breaking it off three or four months ago. He wouldn't. When she cried out to him, he beat her. Sometimes unmercifully. I would hear it, but . . ." His voice trailed off.

Don Alejandro lived. Maria Elena was taken to Mexico City to live with her aunt, her mother's sister, who had married an industrialist there. I later heard that the girl had entered a convent to disappear from the world that she had known.

7.

The happenings described here took place during several summers of the late 1950s and early 1960s.

As I returned to San Miguel in the years to come, I purposefully did not visit Casa Jorado. I never again stepped through the wide doorway into the hall that held the fading photographs of a once-grand family. I was told that Maria Elena came home after her father died. She took care of her mother in her waning years. A teacher at the Instituto said that Maria's younger sister married a North American who came south to study the language and the culture. A brother became a successful businessman in the community.

In the late 1990s I visited the town for several days, contacted Sterling Dickinson, and we had a pleasant comida at his lovely home on the banks of a wooded steep *barranca* where he grew a variety of orchids. He spoke quietly but eagerly about his beloved Mexico and told me he looked forward, at age ninety, to visiting the Mayan ruins of Bonampak deep in the rain forest of Chiapas. When I told him I had been there several years before, his eyes brightened. He leaned forward. "Tell me about them," he said. I tried to describe the special quality of the murals within the low-ceilinged stone ruins deep in the jungle near the Rio Usamacinta. As he listened Sterling Dickinson half-closed his eyes and nodded his head.

Returning once again to San Miguel in the winter of 2000, I talked with several people from the Instituto. Sterling Dickinson had died earlier that year in a freak automobile accident. Prior to

162

his death, they said, he had made the trip south into Chiapas, had walked the miles into the rain forest, and had spent the night on the damp ground before visiting the murals, where he sat on the floor and gazed into the faded representations of a cruel and unusual Mayan world.

Behind Another Wall

1.

Every time I passed the doorway fastened with a padlock as big as my hand, I wondered who was being kept out and what was being locked inside.

After I asked my friend Roberto Barry, who had lived at Casa Jorado for years after the Korean war, after he'd come to Mexico to attend art school on the G.I. Bill, he said he would open the doors for me. Roberto's thick black brows arched as he said, "It is another of the great mysteries of this town. You will soon learn: there is mystery everywhere here. That is a part of the charm of Mexico — and particularly San Miguel."

As Roberto knocked, a young Mexican rode up on a rickety bicycle with a smile covering his face. "*Mi amigo*," he said to Roberto, who introduced me to Fernando Alvarez, who had been the caretaker of the Instituto de Bellas Artes since it closed eight years earlier. I learned later that he was older than he looked. He had known many students, professors, administrators, and the famous muralist David Alfaro Siqueiros, whose artistic tribute to Captain Ignacio Allende was hidden beyond the locked gate.

As Fernando led us down the solemn corridor beneath the massive masonry arches that looked out onto the overgrown central garden with its multi-tiered broken fountain, he talked about the artist Siqueiros, whom he said was *"el mucho grande artiste"* at the time of his San Miguel tryst with destiny. "He was one of the top three in all of the country," according to Roberto, who looked so much like Siqueiros he could have easily passed as the artist's brother. "First there was Diego Rivera of Guanajuato, who has been judged the greatest. Then there was Jose Clemente Orozco of Guadalajara. Then came Siqueiros. Many experts say that Siqueiros surpassed Orozco in greatness and importance. But Diego is definitely first." In the late 1980s an art student from the Universidad in Mexico City told me that the greatest Mexican artist of all time was without a doubt Rufino Tamayo, whom I had also met in San Miguel. Later I also heard arguments in the Cucaracha bar that Siqueiros himself was *número uno*. It is about such things that Mexicans—and those who live with Mexicans— argue with emotional gusto: to them it is worth the words, the emotion, and the weight of argument. It is like baseball in the U.S. The opinions of aficionados are sacred.

Before we entered the room, the young Mexican with fiery dark eyes and thick unruly hair raised his arms toward the ceiling. "Señor Wayne," he said, "this is an honor. This is your privilege. You are about to enter the dining room of the nuns who lived here at the convent many, many years ago. Once they entered the front gate, they escaped these walls only in a coffin. You will walk into it just as though it was eight years ago, the afternoon *el maestro*, Don David Alfaro Siqueiros, was driven out of it. Do you understand?"

I nodded. I thought that I understood. I really did not. I knew it was a place where an artist had started a piece of work and was interrupted by some political or social upheaval that seemed always on the verge of happening in this country, and he walked away from it to return to his home in Mexico City.

However, when I entered, my breath caught. It was gigantic. The curved ceiling was about thirty feet high. The large arches from the corridor were repeated in triplicate. Between each of two arches, the ceiling came to a point in the center. There was no doubt in my mind that Siqueiros had been struck by the grandiose room of huge proportions and architectural splendor, although it was dark and forlorn without the tables and chairs where the nuns once sat and ate. As I gazed across its expanse, the drawings of Siqueiros' plan erupted from each angle and every arch. Dark orange earthen tones expanded to squares of purple, and an ultramodern underbelly of a bomb or rocket ship stretched from front to rear of the ceiling, and a baptismal font was drawn on a wall directly in front of us. Heavily penciled lines were drawn across the floor from the door to the rear, where twin small openings expanded streams of light through the room.

We stood in the corner and stared through the crisscrossed shadows. We stood in silence, reverently looking out over the landscape, and I couldn't help but wonder what Siqueiros himself must have thought when he first looked at the room. Suddenly, a bird's wings fluttered and flew from the opening at the far end.

"In the late afternoon, as the sun is going down, the colors change," Fernando said. "Sometimes the objects that he has drawn actually move with the extension of the light."

On the floor were dried paint brushes, pencils bigger around than my thumb, squares of paper with drawings and scribbled notes, even an old dirty shirt. When I squinted to read the notes hastily written in Spanish, Fernando touched my shoulder. "Everything remains as the maestro left it," he repeated. I did not touch, although I wanted to feel the trowel that the great artist had held in his palms. I wanted to know the words that he wrote or were interpreted by a student and to explore that powerful personality if only by some spiritual osmosis. When I breathed, it was the same heavy dank air that he had breathed. The smell of old concrete and generations of religious women and excited artists permeated the room.

Standing there, my shoes not daring to touch one line that had been drawn by the master before he was chased away amid chaos, I knew that I was in the presence of something truly magnificent. Each of the lines drawn at an exact angle, all of the points coming together in the center of the floor, this exact spot became the center of life. Made holy not simply because it had been the home of women married to God, it was as though the winds of centuries were blowing through this tunnel. Here I was in the middle of the artist's tribute to the martyred hero of the Mexican Revolution, Captain Ignacio Allende, who took up arms alongside Father Miguel Hidalgo in 1811 against the *gachupines*. The solemn power of these moments, standing and studying the first and last markings across the entire interior of the nuns' dining hall, rocked me with a hunger to discover more about Siqueiros.

2.

It was fitting that David Alfaro Siqueiros pay tribute to the most famous revolutionary in Mexico's history, for Siqueiros himself was a revolutionary soldier from the time he was a teenager. In his first act of aggression, he threw up his hands in disgust with his father, who had abandoned him early to the care of his paternal grandparents in Chihuahua. The father had brought David and his sister Luz back to Mexico City to live in his house, where the boy might learn strict discipline. David was sent to San Carlos Academy to study art under Gerardo Murillo, who went by his Nahuatl name, Dr. Atl. It was under Dr. Atl's tutelage that Siqueiros, at the age of fourteen, joined Centro Artistico to petition the Diaz government to allow public walls to be painted with murals. The same year he befriended Jesus S. Soto, a student from Guanajuato, who introduced him to the writing of the Russian Maxim Gorky. Soto, who later became governor of his home state, encouraged his young friend to begin thinking in terms of "real revolution."

When Siqueiros arrived at the dinner table late one night, a wealthy landowning friend of the boy's father chastised young David as "one of those who say, 'What's yours is mine and what's mine is also mine.'" As his father joined in the chiding, David leaped to his feet and shouted, "The only thing I know is that all the *hacendados* [big landowners] are a pack of thieves." His father threw a glass in the boy's direction and demanded that he get out of his house. Standing straight and tall, young David turned and walked out of the room, slamming the door behind him. As he strode through the house, he ripped down curtains, knocked over lamps, overturned chairs, tore down paintings and kicked his foot through the canvases. He walked onto the street, picked up several rocks, turned and heaved them through the front windows. He marched away and never returned.

He was only sixteen in 1913 when he joined other students shouting and throwing stones at the officers of dictator *El Presidente* Porfirio Diaz. Again, he followed Dr. Alt's support of the forces of Venustiano Carranza, a rich landowner who had become the governor of Coahuila and had recently become a constitutionalist opposed to the military dictatorship of Victoriano Huerta. David Alfaro trained with other young men near Veracruz, forming the *Batallon Mama*, which saw its first violent action near Tehuantepec. After Huerta was defeated, two other revolutionary generals, Pancho Villa in the north and Emiliano Zapata in the south, with their peasant armies, took up the fight against the Constitutional Army of Carranza.

The various factions of the revolution were now fighting each other. Under Carranza's leadership, Siqueiros fought in the states of Veracruz, Chiapas, and Oaxaca, later at Guadalajara and across northern Mexico. He received a bullet wound in the leg at Lagos de Moreno. By the time he was twenty he was a seasoned veteran of combat with the rank of *capitán segundo*. After Carranza declared victory, Siqueiros stayed in Guadalajara, where he began to organize artists who had served in the revolution. Still in the army and receiving a captain's salary, Siqueiros soon returned to Mexico City to take up his work once again as an artist.

However, when Carranza failed to implement the provisions of the new constitution, the new *presidente* fell to an assassin's bullets. General Alvaro Obregon, at whose side Siqueiros had fought when Obregon lost an arm while leading Carranza's army, now ascended to the presidency.

It was not long before Siqueiros once again was embracing socialism as the answer to the massive economical and political problems of his country.

3.

Siqueiros was first and foremost an individualistic leader. He stood out in the crowd. Try as he might to be one of the masses, he nevertheless was always the chosen one; whether it was the writer of propaganda for the Communist party's newspaper, *El Machete*, or the splendid artist that he became; always the biggest, the loudest, the most verbose, and always considering himself the very best. In his personality as well as his art, he was bombastic: his head, like his colorfully painted images, larger than life, his eyes big and dark and extending from his head above his dramatic hooked nose, all of his features topped by a headful of Medusa-like curly unruly hair.

Beginning with elongated modernistic revolutionary soldiers, powerful portraits of male figures, it was not long before his work matured and deepened with a social and historical conscience that virtually shouted its message to the world. On his travels to Uruguay and Argentina he was very impressed with the artistic expression he witnessed. He painted in Los Angeles and then opened an experimental workshop in lower Manhattan in New York. At this time he was not advocating a Mexican school of art but indeed railed against Rivera's murals because "he painted only general themes, abstract symbols, scholastic, pseudo-Marxist lectures." Calling Rivera a "friend of the political portrait," Siqueiros nevertheless criticized the older artist for never employing "the figures of the Mexican feudal [landowning] bourgeoisie who were in league with imperialism."

Siqueiros's outdoor workshops not only resulted in murals with themes of socialism, the work itself was shared by as many as forty laborers at a time, each working as a part of the whole process.

Siqueiros traveled to Spain, where he fought on behalf of the anti-Fascist forces. At the same time, his nemesis within the Communist party, Leon Trotsky, was welcomed to Mexico by Rivera and his wife, Frida Kahlo. Diego and Frida sheltered Trotsky in their *Casa de Azul* in Coyoacan, where he continued to formulate his plans for overthrowing the government of the Soviet Union.

4.

Back home in Mexico, Siqueiros threw himself into his work. He had been away from painting long enough for his creative juices to overflow, and he did numerous single canvases as well as a mural for the electricians' union. But the political situation—and particularly Trotsky's presence in the suburb of Mexico City — was never far from his thoughts. By mid-1940, with the mural almost finished, he began to lay groundwork to stop Trotsky's activities in Mexico, no matter how drastic an action it would take to accomplish his goal. Siqueiros felt strongly that Trotsky was supporting Hitler and the German Nazis, Siqueiros's most dreaded enemy. He had been informed that the Nazis were poised along the Russian border, preparing to make a major military strike against the Soviet Union.

On the night of May 23, 1940, Siqueiros led several of his followers to Coyoacan, where Trotsky and his wife Natalya had been moved to a house on Calle Viena. Early the next morning, disguised as an army major, wearing eyeglasses and a false mustache, Siqueiros and his men overpowered five police guards and tied them up on the floor of their guardhouse. Inside, the marauders discovered Trotsky and his wife, destroyed many papers, and took other documents. The house was left in disarray, the couple unharmed but frightened, and for months Siqueiros and his men were hunted down and some jailed. Other dissenters broke into the house several weeks later and brutally murdered Trotsky. Siqueiros, who fled to New York, insisted he had nothing to do with the murder.

Leading the investigation was General Leandro A. Sanchez Salazar, chief of the Secret Service of the Mexican police. He overheard streetcar conductors in a bar stating that a police officer had led the attack. As various accused conspirators were brought in for questioning, Nestor Sanchez Hernandez revealed details and named Siqueiros as the leader. Having by now returned to Mexico, the artist went immediately into hiding.

The Mexican Communist Party denied Siqueiros had ever represented its efforts and isued a statement that Siqueiros's actions were contrary to the party's ideas and ideals.

Three months after Trotsky's murder, the U.S. government's secret files listed Siqueiros erroneously as "a German agent in Mexico." It could not have been further from the truth.

Siqueiros took refuge near Hostotipaquillo in the foothills of the Sierra Madres Occidental, in the state of Jalisco northwest of Guadalajara. He was hidden and protected by union miners he had helped to organize fifteen years earlier.

In the meantime, General Salazar, swearing that he would find and arrest Siqueiros, left the capital for Guadalajara. Salazar followed Siqueiros's brother, Chucho, to the small mountain town.

Salazar, saying he was a politician from Mexico City, visited the mayor, who was aware of Siqueiros's presence. The mayor insisted that the artist was sick and had gone to the mountains for his health.

After almost two weeks in Hosto with no luck, Salazar was on the verge of returning empty-handed when one of his agents brought in an ailing miner, Cristobal Rodriguez Castillo, who was threatened by Salazar. After several hours of intimidation, Castillo told an elaborate story about how he had helped Siqueiros for years in his labor-organizing, helped him to recruit men for the raid on Trotsky, and gave details of all of the artist's movements since he had arrived in the region four months earlier. To discover Siqueiros's present hideout, however, Salazar threatened Castillo with jail in Mexico City, which would take him away from his large poor family and leave them destitute. Finally, Castillo led them to Magueyito, a village about twenty miles across rugged terrain.

As a matter of fact, Siqueiros was sick. While he was staying at a home in Hosto, he had been treated for a fever. But three days prior to Castillo's being brought in, the artist escaped out of a window. He fled into the hills on foot. For three days he made his way through the cacti-infested hills without food, sleeping in caves and barely escaping the attack of a nest of deadly poisonous coral snakes.

At a primitive roadside lean-to, Siqueiros ate frijoles and tortillas and drank water. The merchant told him soldiers were combing the hillsides in search of a dangerous criminal.

Siqueiros climbed back into the hills to his secret cave, where that evening a swarm of mosquitoes forced him out of hiding. Late that night, after a rain storm, he fell asleep in a puddle.

At dawn, soldiers awakened him with shouts of "Surrender, sonofabitch!"

His hands tied behind his back, a rope forming a noose strung around his neck, he was forced to march out of the hills.

When shots were fired, he was knocked to the ground. His face hit against rocks, blood spurting from his nose and cuts on his forehead. Later it was explained that the gunfire came from a group of lost soldiers, and not miners trying to help him escape.

Soldiers marched him for an hour before Salazar rode up, stopped the procession, ordered Siqueiros untied, offered food and water, and talked about their days as soldiers of the Revolution. Around them, the soldiers stood at attention and listened while Salazar told them Siqueiros was a soldier of the Revolution and a great painter who glorified his country. "David Alfaro Siqueiros is not your prisoner but your chief," he stated.

When Siqueiros was brought into Hosto riding in the car with Salazar, he was met with cries of *"Viva Siqueiros!"* Miners and their families gathered and paid homage to this man who had been their leader in the long struggle to improve their lives.

A great banquet was hastily organized by the mayor and his staff. The artist-prisoner sat at the center of the table. To his left was Salazar, to his right an officer of the Eighth Battalion. Toasts were made, the feast was consumed, and by 5 P.M. the entourage was on its way toward the capital.

174

Siqueiros was held in jail for six months before his trial commenced. He defended himself eloquently, stating that he saw Trotsky's presence in Mexico as "a serious disruptive force" and outlined his own experience in Spain fighting against "the evils of Fascism." In his plea, he stated emphatically, "I considered that, as a Mexican revolutionary, there would be no greater honor for me than to contribute to an act that helped expose the treason of a political center of espionage and provocation that was seriously contrary to the national independence of Mexico, the Mexican Revolution—that counted me among its soldiers and militants from the year 1911—and of the international struggle for the cause of Socialism." After his impassioned plea, he was acquitted of the homicide of Trotsky, attempted homicide, criminal conspiracy, and the use of firearms.

He was exiled to Chile, where he was commissioned to paint two murals: one depicting the history of Chile, the other of Mexico, both to be a part of the history of Latin America with a combined title of *Death to the Intruder*.

As a result of his being brought to the attention of the U.S. ambassador to Chile, the artist announced strong support of the U.S. effort to defeat Hitler and Fascism. Industrialist Nelson Rockefeller provided funds for a speaking tour and commissioned a mural for Rockefeller Center in New York. Even though the U.S. State Department turned down Siqueiros's request for a visa, he still spoke out in Santiago for the Support of the Victory of the Democracies. Even though Rockefeller paid him a sizable grant for a large painting, his travels north were stopped in Cuba and he was denied entrance into the U.S.

Finally, in 1943, he was allowed to return to his beloved Mexico. His first mural was entitled *Cuauhtemoc Against the Myth*, showing his interpretation of the last Aztec emperor, with feet on each side of a pyramid, while he fights off the invading centaur of conquest, who carries his cross as a dagger ready to do battle. It is the view of the conquering Spaniards arriving on horseback, something foreign to the innocent Indian, who with a powerful thrust puts a spear through the centaur's heart. As with most Siqueiros paintings, it reeks with passion and emotion, the muscles aquiver, the drama tense, the message clear.

While Siqueiros's new mural caused ripples across the Mexican art scene, he discovered that, in his absence, muralists had become almost extinct in those environs. What had once been a thriving group of Mexican muralists was now a dying breed. No longer were the revolutionary artists holding their banners high, splashing their paint on the walls of public buildings. Most had scattered across the globe, reducing their political importance back home. Forever the organizer, Siqueiros tried to rally his fellow artists, but with no more than lukewarm success.

In October of 1947, his first major exhibition in fifteen years was scheduled to open at the *Palacio de Bellas Artes*. Showing off his new realism, more than a thousand people, including Diego Rivera with popular movie star Maria Felix, poured through the hallway. Siqueiros was declared one of the leading artists in his home country.

At the age of fifty-one, Siqueiros bought his first home and studio on secluded property at the end of a dirt road in the district of Tlacopac. Here he painted some of his most famous work on canvas, including a portrait of Orozco sitting majestically in the hand of his creator, and *Our Present Image* with strong wide hands outstretched.

5.

Having gained new status as a recognized artist, he was invited to lecture at the *Escuela Universitaria de Bellas Artes*, the forerunner of the Instituto Allende in San Miguel de Allende. More than a hundred U.S. veterans of World War II had come to San Miguel to study art under the G.I. Bill. Earlier, Siqueiros had refused the invitation of Rufino Tamayo, who visited the school to teach at regular intervals. In early 1948, however, it was Siqueiros's first wife, Gachita Amador, who lived at the school and was widely known as a folklorist, who delivered the invitation from the school's director, Alfredo Campanella. Gachita urged her former husband to accept the appointment as *maestro extraordinario* (visiting professor) for the pay of 150 pesos or $17 a day for at least fifteen days. The school would pay his travel expenses but "recommended" he and Angelica, his current wife, stay at the Rancho de Bellas Artes, which Campanella also owned. As part of his contract, the bill at the hotel would be deducted from his teaching fee.

In October, Angelica drove them to San Miguel. As they were escorted along the cobblestone streets, the two were a striking pair: he in his ever-present black suit and his favorite dark gray fedora, she also in black with her raven-colored hair pulled back into a bun. Their heads held aloof, they were magnificent under the Bajio sun.

On the following morning, Siqueiros sat at a table at the end of a large room in the dormitory of the nuns deep within the convent. For the next several hours the artist spoke with gusto about the Mexican Mural Movement. The students who crowded into the room were mesmerized. They had heard about the maestro but none were familiar with his work. During the next four mornings he spoke as he painted: enthusiastically with emotional vigor about the subject that he loved as much as his darling Angelica.

Each day more and more students inched into the room. Each day they left the lecture talking among themselves with enthusiasm. They crowded around the teacher to ask questions and to prevail upon him to teach them how to paint the murals about which he spoke so fervently.

Finally the students took him to the great room where Roberto and Fernando and I stood that morning in 1958. It was where fresco painting had been taught. Siqueiros stretched his head back. His big green eyes explored the enormous cavern-like walls where frescoes, efforts by various students, covered small portions of the walls.

In the middle of other faculty members and dozens of students, his outstretched arms reached toward the vaulted ceiling. "These walls cry out for paint, for images that reach out and grasp, holding the human spirit in a vise-like grip and squeezing the juice of their life's blood from the veins, the way art is supposed to deliver a one-two punch. It must be powerful enough to last for a long, long time, to last forever, an eternal emotion. Remember that a small pebble dropped into the middle of a large puddle will cause a wave. But, by the time it reaches shore, it has dissipated." Roberto Barry remembered the words.

"Needless to say, he was taken by what he saw, and there was youthful excitement in the air," Barry recalled. "It was a time when people could still *feel* youthful excitement," Barry said in his characteristic sarcasm. "David Alfaro *felt* it and made the rest of us know what he felt."

Campanella, hearing of the incident from a number of students who had been critical of the way he was running the school, asked the artist to return, work with students and other faculty members, and create a mural in this room. It was obvious that Siqueiros had gained immediate great popularity among most of the students.

In April of 1949, Siqueiros returned to San Miguel. In the next five months he and a team of twenty-four fellow artists would create a mural to the memory of the early revolutionary, Ignacio Allende. Siqueiros would be paid a total of $1,500 for this work.

In the beginning, Siqueiros huddled in the room with his team. On large sheets of paper he outlined his concepts as he marched back and forth across the width and breadth of the room. "He paced like an officer detailing the strategic plans for a field operation," Roberto remembered. "But his words: they were the words of a poet. He had a grip on art like none of the students had ever seen or heard. Not even the great Tamayo had illustrated such wonderful grasp of his art. Siqueiros began to express the overall concept of the gigantic mural: the life and times and importance of Ignacio Allende. Then he outlined the organization of the man's life as it would fit into this room—or so many of the students thought he was saying—as they listened intently. First, he gave the others a chance to show how they saw the room, and how Allende's life would fit here, and how various aspects might be represented here. He turned them loose with their varied ideas, letting them roam like wild mustangs across the walls of the nuns' dining room. While he went home to Mexico City to prepare himself for the major job, each student was given a portion of the old plaster. It was theirs to do with as they wished, allowing their artistic minds to dwell upon that portion of Allende's being that he had doled out to them."

Roberto Barry spread his arms wide. Fernando and I could imagine the artist himself standing there, talking to the eager students. They spread around the walls, each with trowel and fresh plaster, crayons and chalk, paints and brushes, and from the humming sounds of creation came various scenes from the life of Allende: Spanish soldiers conquering the Indians, putting them into slavery, Allende's birth, his baptism, being taught by the nuns within the walls of this convent, meetings of the literary clubs where the talk of revolution caught fire and spread, encounters with Father Hidalgo, the *Grito* from Dolores, bloody battles, then the capture and decapitation of Allende, Hidalgo, and other leaders.

Upon his return, Siqueiros was both dismayed and bemused. One of the art students who had come south to study on the G.I. Bill after a brief stint in New York, Leslie Hampton, remembered the afternoon Siqueiros walked into the room amid chaos. "You could see his thick brows working, his eyes dilating as he surveyed the scene, as he moved from young artist to young artist, examining the work, and very soon a hush came over those of us who were working. We turned our heads and stared at him, waiting for the gavel of disapproval to drop. He had that aura of genius about him that only a few people have. We all wanted desperately to please him. He walked down the middle of the room beneath those huge arches, looking from side to side, craning his head this way, then gazing upon another area of work.

"I had been working with Bill Thompkins, a tall cowboy from Montana who could reach two feet higher than I, and I think when Bill looked around at Siqueiros, he nervously turned over a can of materials. The maestro said nothing. He stepped toward us, bent down, and turned the can upright. Bill sort of mumbled, 'Thank you, sir,' and Siqueiros glanced at him with what appeared to be a bemused, even playful look. But nothing was humorous to us. All of us were so serious. We wanted our images, our style, our view of Allende to be approved by the master."

Sterling Dickinson, who had been dismissed as an administrator of the *Escuela de Bellas Artes* by Campanella, only to be rehired at a higher salary and more authority after students voiced their disapproval of Campanella's heavy-handed management, said, "Siqueiros was using the students to point out essential fundamentals of mural-painting. First, there must be an undisputed leader. That leader must be the primary planner of a mural project. Second, the workers must be in tune with the leader. They all must not only agree to the theme and the overall statement of purpose as well as the basic design and color scheme, they must be prepared to work in unison as a team. What better way to illustrate the way a major mural is constructed than to leave the students to create on their own vision on the limited surface? In this manner, each sees his own mistake — and mistakes. Hopefully, the budding young muralist will have the ability to laugh at his own mistakes — see the error of his ways, if you will. Each will be able to see that it is not with regret that their work will be plastered over and prepared for the ultimate design.

"And that is what happened here."

"I think we were all hurt by his initial reaction," said Leslie Hampton. "Bill Thompkins and I got drunk at the Cucaracha that night. It was packed. There must have been twenty or more of us who swilled the tequila and cursed and criticized Siqueiros for all he was worth." Hampton, who after a few years in Paris settled in the Napa Valley in northern California and eventually had his work sold in galleries in San Francisco, Los Angeles, Santa Fe, New York, and even San Miguel, laughed at his recollection. "Of course," he said, "Siqueiros was not present when we cursed him."

Eventually he and Thompkins, who later found his way back to Montana and painted western landscapes until his death in the late 1980s, saw the humor in the work they and the others had done. James Pinto, who taught art and mural-making at the Instituto Allende when I first came there in the late fifties, thought the individual offerings were "a hodgepodge without direction, stick-figure drawings not yet even grasping for breath but struggling toward birth. But that birth was extraordinarily difficult. That is true for all creative artists. To be born we needed a capable midwife or surgeon. Siqueiros performed the Caesarean with a quick twist of his wrist."

When the maestro appeared, there was no mistaking who was in control of the room. "His words and actions hurt, but he was magnificent," said Thompkins. "He had become the center of our focus before. But this time, when he came back to the school and stepped into the convent, he was definitely the ruler of his world."

An expert from the Polytechnical Institute in Mexico City arrived to remove the plaster, resurface the walls, ceiling, and floor, and prepare the entire surface for the major project. A new plastic vinylite paint that dried fast and hard would be used to illuminate with brilliance the cave-like interior.

Like an actor preparing for his entrance onto a stage, Siqueiros stood outside the room and closed his eyes. The student-assistants gathered around him and watched eagerly. Others waited inside. All were silent. It looked as though he was praying.

The moment of truth drew near.

At the moment he felt appropriate, he stepped through the doorway and into the room. "The visitor who comes here will follow this path as he steps into the room," he announced.

It was the same door through which I stepped that morning with Roberto and Fernando. As I moved through it and gazed into the massive room, all of the history, the torment and the torture of a creative genius repressed by unwitting and unfeeling bureaucrats, filled me with wonder.

It had been less than a decade since his enthusiastic passion had filled this room, since it had caught like a fever the minds and hearts of the youthful artists surrounding him, showing them how the new vinylite paint made of plastic took on a life of its own when it was applied to a surface. During his absence from the convent and San Miguel, Siqueiros had dreamed the revolutionary dreams of Allende, and now he transposed his energy into the space. "All will be painted, including the floor; everything in movement: the forms, the volumes, the floor, the walls, and the ceiling vaults; bolts of lightning will rotate as though they were alive. This is life. Go onto the street, everyone is moving. Everybody moves with you. Death actually is the impossibility to perceive movement."

Scaffolds were built. The students climbed up, carrying heavy pencils and lifting after them the buckets of plastic paint. They followed the instructions shouted up to them, Siqueiros sweeping his arms from side to side, directing them as though living a role in an impromptu drama. "A bolt of lightning!" he called out.

The student muralists gazed down questioningly. "They were not sure what he meant," remembered Lyle Hampton. "We wanted to be sure," said Bill Thompkins. "His madness was contagious, but his meaning obtuse," stated James Pinto.

"Lightning will flash across at angles," Siqueiros said as he climbed up with them and took his crayon and made a sweeping stroke, almost falling from the platform. "It is the Revolution, the idea that sparked a nation, the storm that raged in Allende's brain, and struck the tree. Who is the tree?" he asked, his voice in crescendo. He stared into their youthful faces. "Padre Miguel Hidalgo, of course, who was totally captured by this mere mortal and his fantastic revolutionary idea of freedom. If you had been oppressed for more than two hundred years, would you not be a flash of lightning across a stormy sky?"

Most of the students felt deeply that when Siqueiros talked about "his fantastic idea," he was actually talking about the project that spread out before them in this large room. Siqueiros was mirroring his own work.

But behind the scenes, not all of the students and faculty members at the school shared in the master's enthusiasm over the project. Some of the students had had their artistic feelings hurt too deeply when Siqueiros returned to cast aside the work they felt they had accomplished in their allotted space on the wall of the convent dining room. Their egos had been so devastated, they felt, they could not be a part of this grand scheme. Others had been turned off immediately by the grand presence of the man whom they considered a braggart and a phony, and a ridiculous commie. Not all, like Hampton, Thompkins, Pinto, and Philip Stein, who later wrote an artistic and intellectual biography of Siqueiros, felt this was a work of grand international prestige. When the school's director, Campanella, attempted to extend Siqueiros's contract to include lectures to outsiders, even while he worked on *Monument to Ignacio Allende*, the artist balked. Campanella's business exploitation of the work was so audacious that it provoked Siqueiros to walk away, and many artists of renown immediately voiced support of Siqueiros, including Campanella's former friend Tamayo. After students voted 130 to 5 to stand with Siqueiros, the U.S. Veterans Administration cut off funding the G.I. Bill for students at the school. Those who had deemed him a "ridiculous commie" had gotten the attention of the bureaucracy in Washington, D.C.

Within a month, Sterling Dickinson, with help from the Mexican government and artists, organized a new school and the U.S. backed it and the faculty. But Siqueiros by now had returned to his home in Mexico City. When he was finally invited back to San Miguel, the Federal Bureau of Investigation in Washington had collected information showing that while he was employed at the *Escuela Universitaria de Bellas Artes* he attempted "to convert American war veterans to communism, and the school was removed from the U.S. Veterans approved list because of communist infiltration, stemming from the influence of Siqueiros." The new school moved to a location several blocks from the old convent, still owned by Campanella. Although Siqueiros continued to feel a passion for the unfinished work, he moved on to another project.

6.

Throughout his life his mind wondered back from time to time to those brushes, the lines against the concrete, and the unused plastic paint that he left sitting on the floor of the dining hall of the nuns. But he never returned to this place that became a school once again in the 1970s. When I revisited the site with my wife in the '70s, the room was open for visitors to peer inside from the roped doorway. Black and white photographs of the artist and his assistants were displayed on the walls beneath the large arches next to the neatly groomed garden with its fountain where water danced and birds sang.

On another trip to Mexico, nearly forty years after I had spent my first summer there, my wife Sally and I traveled to Cuernavaca where we found the seldom-visited last studio of Siqueiros. A small Indian woman with white hair spoke reverently of "*el maestro*" and showed us his single bed where he had died on Sunday morning, January 6, 1974. He was seventy-seven years old. His body was taken to the capital, where he lay in state in the lobby of the *Palacio de Bellas Artes*. President Luis Echeverria led the throng of hundreds who came to pay their respects, including fellow artist Rufino Tamayo, who stood near the coffin. Then his body was laid to rest in a place of honor next to Orozco and Rivera in the *Rotonda de los Hombres Illustres*.

Scotty

1.

For me, the Instituto Allende was the essence of two men: Sterling Dickinson, who embodied the quiet strength and the intellectual depth of an American in Mexico who understood the Mexican people and their complexities as well as any North American could, and Ashmead Scott, a veteran professional writer who tried hard to teach those who sat at his feet and listened. I never knew Enrique Fernandez. I met him and his wife briefly at a cocktail party at Dickinson's house one evening and I heard that he was a fine politician and businessman. But we never exchanged more than a few words.

Ashmead Scott was a big man, more than six feet tall, wide through the shoulders, with a huge head covered with thick gray hair, accentuated by matching eyebrows that swept upward over his forehead like streaked butterfly's wings, and a generous, gregarious mouth. He spoke in a flat baritone flavored with a Midwestern nasal drawl.

"When you sit down to write you bring with you the total of your entire experience," he told us as he leaned back and wrapped his long fingers around the back of his shaggy head. "Everything that you have ever done, every word that you have read up to this time, every sweet and sour experience you have had, every person you have known and every kiss you have ever received and returned, every ounce of your personality filters down through your head, through your heart, and into the hands that move the typewriter or the pencil. It is the path toward creativity.

"At that very moment when you enter a scene, you walk into it fully concentrating on the whole. As Hemingway said, 'Tell me what the day was like, how the sun was shining, how it smelled, and what the weather was like,' but I want to know more. Where has your character been? How did he or she feel when they left there? How *is* the sun shining? What is the time of day or night? If your character is approaching a house, let me know who, what, where, when, why, and how, all of the journalistic W's, and then some. Remember that you are creating life on the page, and to make that life live, fill out from the bones the way you see art students adding muscle, tone, shades of skin, and texture to the makeup of the anatomy. Like the artists whom you watch in the studios here at the Instituto, you the writer must know more than the measurements of your canvas. Your world must be larger than your knowledge. Your depth must reach deeper than you have ever thought possible. You are filling out the depth of your characters by your knowledge of those characters: his or her strengths and weaknesses, their desires, their wishes, their dreams. Once you've given your character life, give him or her a history. Where did he come from? Where has he been? How did he or she feel that morning when they awakened? Did his father beat him? Did his mother deny him? Why is he the way he is? Never be afraid to seek the truth about any character, no matter how sordid, no matter how hateful, no matter how romantic."

All of Scotty's rhetorical questions worked like fermentation in my brain. When I began to flesh out a character, I thought about some of the people I had known when I was growing up in rural Alabama. Granddaddy had been a carpenter whose expertise was building coffer dams to keep dry the area where the actual builders of the dam would work. That job became a metaphor for his life, for his strong belief in Christianity, or his love of my grand-mother, my mother, my uncle, me. He carried his family — Nanny, my mother, and my uncle — from dam site to dam site across the South. At places like Gant in rural Covington County, Alabama, Granddaddy guided his wagon, being pulled by a matched team of mules to a spot nearby, where they would have access to fresh water. He unhitched the mules over the rich meadow covering the sandy loam. He and Uncle Norris unfolded wooden platforms he had constructed with hinges. These platforms, unfolding like a large puzzle, formed sleeping areas over which a tent would be raised easily and simply over hinged wooden poles. Nanny and Mama set up a makeshift stove on the ground in front of their living quarters.

Until she graduated from high school, my mother, the former Myrtle Lee Able, never owned a store-bought dress, but she made straight A's and read Victor Hugo's masterpiece, *Les Misérables*, in the original French. No matter how smart nor how industrious, she was denied a university scholarship because she did not have the social credits necessary; she had not had time to participate in after-school club activities because she had to work to earn meager wages which she passed along to her parents. She worked as a clerk in a department store, attended business college at night, and met my smooth-talking daddy, a beauty-and-barber-supply sales-man, in the mid-1930s. She was a practical, God-fearing woman who believed her first son, born with a fever in February of 1940 and sentenced immediately to several weeks alone and untouched in an incubator, would make a preacher, until he grew up to live through six months of 1954 in a body cast to give his polio-wrecked frame strength to withstand the physical pressure of teenage growth, and read *The Grapes of Wrath* and dozens of other novels, including *Les Misérables* in English, and make the decision that he would become a writer and go to Mexico to study.

These were some of the real people who made up my world back home in Alabama. They lived a lifetime away, it seemed, but they breathed and laughed and cried and loved in my memory because a man named Ashmead Scott was a good teacher who tickled the imaginations of his students. Scotty had been a professional writer most of his adult life. He had moved from Indiana to New York and later the West Coast, where he wrote radio after World War II for comedians Fred Allen and Bob Burns. Over cups of black coffee during breaks in our classes, he told comic-tragic stories about the professional funny men. Bob Burns, for whom Scotty had invented the wildly erratic musical instrument called the Bazooka, had had a pet parrot whom he adored. Every morning the parrot sat on Burns's shoulder and chattered while Burns shaved. One morning the comedian was suffering a horrible hangover, was grouchy and grumpy, and growled at the bird, who flew away. When the bird repeated one of his funny lines, Burns swung around and slammed the bathroom door. Then he heard a pained squawk, looked down, and saw that he had caught the bird's head between the door and the jamb. Although he rushed the animal to the hospital, it was too late. "Poor Bob Burns was not the same for weeks, reading his lines that brought laughter from the radio audience but making him suffer a deeper and deeper depression," Scotty explained. "Finally his wife bought him a poodle, and he made a miraculous recovery."

2.

I had never experienced such a bright and angular sunlight as that that shone in San Miguel in midsummer. It shone especially light and bright upon the patio at the back of the Instituto, a flat paved place overlooking the town on the hillside, spreading out like a great panoramic canvas. And when we sat there beneath our awning, Scotty's words made the light even brighter. "Charlotte and I enjoy this town just as we loved Greenwich Village when we were first married, when the bohemians lived and partied there in the late 1930s, when we knew e. e. cummings and Edna St. Vincent Millay and the folk singer Woody Guthrie. They were all such wonderfully creative people, they worked hard, and their parties went on forever, it seemed. They talked. They all loved to talk, to tell about what had happened and was happening in their worlds. It was all very exciting.

"And when we moved to the West Coast, we got to know Woody even better for a while, and he introduced us to John and Carol Steinbeck, and we loved their sweet and gentle ways." I wondered how anyone could have been sweeter or more gentle than Scotty. I sat and listened to his words, feeling proud to know a person who had known the great Steinbeck.

He told us that he learned much about writing from Fred Allen, who could take a sentence apart, he said, and put it back together again and make something extraordinarily funny from the same words that had been serious a moment earlier. "He was a genius," he said of the comedian.

In class or at the outdoor table where we enjoyed coffee and delicious Mexican sweet rolls, Scotty was equally dramatic. When he was at home with his beloved Charlotte, he was gentle as a baby burro. And he was that way too when I read my first story in class, a sophomoric tale about two young people in love, running away from their parents in Alabama, and settling in Mexico.

In a voice so low I felt like the words were said to me and for me and could be heard by no one else, although the older students rimmed the long table and held their steady gaze on me like a line of vultures, Scotty asked, "Where's the tension? What's the theme?

What is it all about? Read your story to yourself and listen to your own words. Determine what it is all about before you begin to rewrite. Decide the question: What are Alma and Ferrell after? What truly are they trying to accomplish? Explore what they are all about, where they came from, where they want to go, and decide for yourself if they will ever arrive at their emotional destination. Dig down into your characters. Discover them. Not just what they look like, how they talk, the words they use, but *why*. That is the big question for the creative writer: *why?* Remember what I said about the bones, the tendons, the muscles, the skin, the complexion, the way the people move; it all tells everything about them. Then they come alive through your descriptions, your dialog, your plot, your words. There is a meaning beneath and beyond the words."

I nodded. Hurting inside with every word, thinking that I had written a stupid story about stupid people, I went home to Casa Jorado and took out my manuscript and my notebook with all of the scribbled notes. I began to peruse the geography of my creation. I followed his advice, remembering the people and what they were like, how I saw them when they stepped out of the '55 two-tone blue-and-white Chevrolet, Ferrell with his Vitalis slick-down look, his pompadour sweeping back just so, with each furrow of meticulous comb-stroke visible, and his full lips pouting, and the pimple prominent on his right cheek. I saw that glint in his dark eyes as he shifted his view to Alma, who hated her name and thought it should be Alice or Alicia, something she thought poetic and sophisticated, because she constantly teased her honey-blonde hair and painted her lips proudly and thought she looked like movie star Sandra Dee, especially how she looked in the moonlight with Bobby Darin in *A Summer Place*, which was *their* movie.

Reading over it, I felt hopeless. There was no irony in my people and their predicament. I saw them *too* clearly. I didn't have the tools to fix it. I didn't have the experience to hold my own with the students in the class. They were all years older. Some had been soldiers in Korea. They had killed. They had known death intimately. Several were married, some had been married, others had girlfriends or boyfriends. Feeling so lonely my insides ached, I left the manuscript and notebook scattered across my bed and walked aimlessly out of Casa Jorado.

With the slight whiff of an open sewer playing sickly at the edge of my nostrils, I climbed the hill up Avenada Mesones past the public market, turned a corner, and slowed as I neared Cholla's, a house like other houses in San Miguel, where I had been introduced to a way of life I had never known before. Behind these doors lived a little madam and her girls. Thoughts of one girl named Marena, gorgeous, mysterious, dark Marena with big eyes and melted-chocolate thighs, made me even sadder. She was a girl no older than I, with whom I'd lain and exchanged no more than a dozen words, some of which I didn't even understand. I picked up my pace and strode past, hurting with every solitary step.

3.

Higher on the hill I passed a little gray adobe hut built precariously off-square atop a stone embankment. From a cluster of red and yellow and green in a triangle of hanging pots, where brilliant rays of late afternoon sunlight burst onto the colors like a spotlight, I heard a high-pitched lilting sound. At first I thought it human, then — as it swirled up an octave, like I imagined a nightingale might sound — I knew it could not possibly be a person. I gazed up from the cobblestone street to the tiny porch. Beyond the triangle of stone pots draped with the colorful flowers was a small bamboo cage holding a yellow bird no larger than my forefinger. Perched on a miniature swing, its black beak opened, and a warbling yodel filled the atmosphere with rhythm. A streak of red across its throat vibrated like an instrument of percussion. I stood there in the middle of the narrow winding street and took a deep breath and felt a sudden renewal of strength and wonder. I watched and listened as the sun went down behind me.

When the small round face of a child appeared on the porch, looking down, a hint of embarrassment touched me, but I smiled and said, "*Buenos tardes*," and she gave a similar greeting as I strolled on my way to the top of the hill to look back on the sunset as — in the distance — the bird kept singing the wordless lullaby.

It was one of those late afternoons in San Miguel that could not have occurred anywhere else in the world. In my eighteen-year-old mind I felt the horror and wonder of a world just as confused as I in my deepest melancholy, a place that had known torture and upheaval both physically and spiritually, a country that in 1958 was still in its teenage years, less than a half-century away from its most brutal revolution ever, and I was less than four years away from major surgery that had totally disrupted and changed my young life. Standing on that precipice overlooking the immense valley of *El Bajío*, where God was pouring the last droplets of sunlight so red it was like fresh blood covering the earth as far as I could see, I felt as tiny as a flea in a forest.

Gabriela

When I met Gabriela, I was shocked. This six-foot-tall wide-shoul-dered black woman with African features, thick lips, broad nose, and high sloping forehead looked at me, grinned, and sidled close and asked, "Little white boy had any poontang lately?"

I pulled back, looked into her face incredulously, and she laughed with great vigor and vitality. Her large bosom shook with her laughter.

"You ain't, huh?" she said, trying to mimic a south Alabama sharecropper's accent with her own tinge of French.

I blushed, and she laughed harder.

"You have been to see Madam Cholla, sample a little señorita *puta*, enjoy the *lap-lap*," and she laughed still again. She had me backed into a corner and was enjoying every twist of her verbal dagger.

While we drank wine and the others around the table shouted conversation, Gabriela told about going home to Haiti to find her family being hounded by Papa Doc's henchmen. "They are horri-ble," she said. "If you do not worship them, they torture you. My father is a merchant. He sells this beautiful material." She fingered the red and yellow and orange and purple print that surrounded

195

her large body, wrapped in a big bundle with a sheath pinned in the front. Next to her smooth dark brown skin, I agreed honestly that the cloth was gorgeous. It felt as smooth as silk and displayed a rainbow of colors. "Now he cannot buy it from the natives in the hills without paying enormous taxes to the Ton-Ton Macout. It is ridiculous. I am very afraid that some day soon these evil men will do even more radical things to him and to all of my family." She shivered visibly.

"Like what?" I asked innocently.

"Like cut off their heads and drink their blood." She did not laugh. "Like strap them to a tree and whip the blood from their bodies. Like take the women and stretch their limbs in four directions and rape them like they were sows ready for slaughter." I cringed at her word pictures.

She told about stopping for several weeks in New York on her way back to Mexico, where she had lived for the past five years. "I got enough work to keep the rent paid and groceries on the table for at least a year." She explained that she translated books of New York publishers into French and French books into English. After her crude beginning, I warmed up to her, even when she started calling me "Billy Wayne, the redneck." She said it in such a way that she wasn't offensive, and within an hour she was telling me about the intellectual relationship between Satre and Camus and Existentialism.

At that time I had heard the names and the words, but I had no understanding of any of them. I felt so totally the Alabama farm boy that I am sure my awkward awareness of my own ignorance was obvious. I had read neither writer and was totally ignorant of Existentialism. Later we adjourned to Gabriela's apartment near the French Park. Most of her wall space was covered with shelves crammed with books, some in French, some English, some Spanish. Several abstract oils hung where shelves did not reach, and on her kitchen walls were several street scenes from the capital of her home country, Haiti. Each view was as colorful as her dress, and the miniature Haitian people seemed to dance on the canvas. "My mother did these," Gabriela said, pointing to the artwork. "She is very primitive, but very nice, don't you think?" I nodded as I gazed into the incredible detail, showing goat wagons, horses and buggies, shopkeepers, and women in colorful dress with baskets of fruit balanced on their heads. "Port Au Prince is a lovely place with so many nice people," she said. "But I cannot live there. It hurts me too much to see these naturally fun-loving people being horribly oppressed by our rulers. It is no democracy and probably never will be. It is terribly, terribly sad. Black people are horribly cruel to other black people." She threw up her arms. "But then, I come here. This is no democracy. Not really. They elect someone. But he is the only one running. It is all such a charade. It makes me so unhappy. I cry tears into my drink. My heart bleeds tears."

On walks up the hill on the road to Queretaro, I listened to Gabriela talk about the families she had adopted. Beyond the reservoir where the water for the town was captured and held and doled out to the houses on the hillside, a small compound of grass-brick houses sat on the edge of a rocky hill, atop which stood three crosses.

A little Indian woman as Aztec as Montezuma appeared from behind a tattered rag that sufficed for her doorway. Seeing Gabriela, she smiled widely, the deep friendliness exploding into the lines etched in her brown face. Gabriela took her in her arms and enveloped her little body into her own. *"Mi Gabriela, mi amiga, mi amor."* While they were hugging, four children scampered from behind the three square brown houses, the same color as the dusty rocks of the hill. Even the cacti that grew together so closely they formed a fence were coated with dust. And the children were the same color as the earth.

Gabriela introduced me to Tomasa and her children, Hector, Lucinda, Oleeta, and Tomas, all of whom gathered around their mother and held tightly to her long gray skirt. Gabriela handed out sugar candies she had brought from a confectionery store in San Miguel. From her oversized bag she pulled several sacks for Tomasa, who talked quickly and appreciatively in a dialect I didn't understand.

Later, as we walked away from them, all five standing next to the fire that was heating a black pot filled with soapy water, not unlike similar wash-pots I had seen all my life boiling in the yards of Negro houses in the South, Gabriela said, "Isn't she sweet? I love her and her children. Each is a jewel. Each shines in his or her own way. And Tomasa—she is the brightest gem of all. When she speaks to me, I hear the poetry of hundreds of generations of Indians that have occupied Mexico and have tried to eke a living from this damnable desert."

Then her face turned hard. Her eyes sharpened. Memory stung her from the inside out. "I wish I could take my hands to the throat of her old man. The sonofabitch comes around whenever he wants to pull up her skirt and enjoy himself with her. He is *el gato*, a tomcat, with the same morals. He's despicable, a pure asshole. He goes off and gets drunk and leaves her and the children. He tells her he works in the fields between here and Irapuato. Once he told her he worked in the mills there at the industrial town. She told me this, and that afternoon I saw him stagger out the doorway of a cantina with a filthy *puta* bitch on his arm. If I had loved Tomasa with the depth I think I do, I'd have cut out his nuts right there on the street and left them for the dogs to eat. But I didn't. My love was not strong enough."

"Why do they have so many babies?" I asked.

She stopped and turned to face me. Again, her face hardened. "What do you mean?!"

"It takes so much money—so much work, so much of everything she doesn't have—to raise four children."

"Only a stupid, idealistic, ignorant, uninvolved male whose knowledge of women could possibly fill a very tiny thimble, could say such a thing," she stated.

"But . . ."

"She has love. That little woman is overflowing with the capacity to love and care for human beings. You have no more sensitivity than Rudolpho the husband."

"Rudolpho?"

"A stupid name!" she spat. "He is the son of an ignorant woman who knew no better than to give him such a name. She raised him with no more care than went into the choosing of his name. She's a woman without heart and soul. It is perhaps the reason he is the way he is."

"Do you know her?" I asked.

"I have seen the product of her motherhood."

I walked slowly along the gravel side of the road. I tried to weigh what she was saying about the Indian woman and her family. My own prejudices were well entrenched from a life of growing up middle-class white in the South. We were Anglo-Saxon protestants; my mother's mother descended from Scotsmen who came to the Southeastern U.S. and intermingled with the Creek Indians; my mother's father came from Irish who sailed to South Carolina after their hard-scrabble land in southern Ireland was taxed to the hilt by a government that was as poor as the people, trying to gain economic stability from rocky soil and people who attempted to cultivate it. Also, both of my paternal grandparents were directly descended from pioneers who first traveled from England to Virginia in the early 1700s, then migrated southward and settled in the new frontier of Alabama in the early 1800s.

All were meshed together in a staunch conservative fundamentalist religion, my mother's people into the Baptist church and my father's Presbyterian. I grew up seesawing from one to the other. We basically believed that to win God's favor you must be good, do good deeds and treat people as you would have them treat you, but that Jesus, as the true son of God, saved us all by blessing us and giving his life in order to cleanse us, because we are all guilty of the original sin Adam committed with Eve in the Garden of Eden. Although most of my kinfolks believed black people were inferior to whites, I was raised to be kind to all people, and my mother taught me that black people were just as good as whites and the only difference was the pigment of our skin.

In late-night sessions at her *casa*, Gabriela and I discussed my history in the South, where my people came from and what they believed. "Are they all racists?" she asked.

"Most are, but not all. My mother's not. Her father, my Granddaddy Able, is and isn't," I said.

"You can't be both," she said.

And I told her that her statement was as stupid as my own about Tomasa. "It's difficult for Granddaddy to cast aside all the values of his upbringing," I said.

"Values?" she asked. "Those are not values, they're misgivings. They're false beliefs."

"He was taught that it was right to believe people of African extraction are dumb, that they do not have the morals of white people, and that they are slow and lazy."

"*I is just a little ol' nigger gal,*" she said in the worst-sounding dialect. She said that such teachings infuriated her and made her physically sick.

I said they infuriated me too, but more so. "Why?" I said, "Because I love him. He was my teacher, my mentor. I sat on his lap and listened to his words and hung to every one. He was the great person in my life. He taught me much of everything I know."

She said, "That's very little," sarcastically.

I shrugged, "Perhaps, but it's my own foundation. He was taught by a Southern system of education that was segregated. I was too. Schools in Alabama are still segregated. I couldn't go to school with you or your children, even if I wanted to."

"I wouldn't live in Alabama," she stated.

I said, "There you go again. Your statement sounds like something Granddaddy might say."

She shook her head. "You don't know what you're talking about," she said.

"You are condemning me, my state, my way of life, and the whole culture in which I grew up because you know only one fact about the whole society," I told her. "The more I live, the more I condemn it myself. But I condemn it with a knowledge and an understanding while you do so out of ignorance."

She exploded. "Get the hell out of my house! I don't want ignorant little Billy Wayne redneck uttering his racist nonsense here. Go! Out! Now! I do not wish to be contaminated with your venom."

As I walked away, up the hill toward the *jardín*, I felt as low as I had in a long while. All of my feelings about my homeland were mixing in a stew of new thoughts, new ideas, wonderings, questions that remained unanswered.

I felt almost as sad and forlorn as I had a year earlier when Lowney Handy chased me from the great novelist James Jones's house near Robinson, Illinois, and called me "a no-good little shit" and said I wasn't good enough to carry water for James Jones or any of the other members of the colony. She told me to hit the road and not look back, said I didn't have the courage, fortitude, or discipline to be a writer. As I stood in the harsh southern Illinois sunshine with my thumb out, I felt as low as I'd ever felt in my life.

Now, walking away from Gabriela's, I wondered if I would ever be anything but an ignorant Southern boy.

Finding little action at the Cucaracha and not wanting to venture to other places, I returned to my room, where I tried to read. I turned out my light and attempted to straighten my thoughts, compartmentalizing them and searching through them. I was too emotionally attached to my growing up in Alabama to separate it and intellectualize the emotions that were strongly embedded into my personality. I was so young that all of this new questioning from new people made me ill at ease with my Southernism. I did not even realize exactly what it was then. My God, in creative writing class, when I was reading a story I had someone "yelling," and the professor questioned my use of the word. I answered, "People 'yell' where I come from." Another student from Athens, Ohio, said, "I think you mean 'shout.'" I wanted to say, "No! Not at all!" but I did not. I made a note on my yellow legal pad and waited for the next criticism.

Now, I rolled over, wishing I had been born and raised in a simple easy place like the Midwest where people were not prejudiced and used precise, correct English that did not leap off the page as some aberration of the language, and people did not drown themselves in emotional turmoil as we tended to do in the South.

Late the next afternoon at the Cucaracha, Gabriela half-screamed, "The most mixed-up fool I have known came from Cleveland. That's Midwest, isn't it? Of course it is! He was so fucked up, he was a louse, an absolute, thorough-going louse. He hit me!"

"Was he a gentleman?" I asked over my third rum and Coke. I found myself drinking more and more, starting earlier and earlier.

"You're a damn louse too!" she spat. She squeezed into the large chair next to me, nuzzling her chin close to my face. "But you talk so pretty, I think I'll take you home with me."

That evening, after a supper of leftover chicken and *bolleta* hard rolls, we drank no more after leaving the Cucaracha; we entered into a pleasant conversation about the countryside of Mexico. She characterized central Mexico sarcastically as "the ass-end of paradise," and added that "simply being a part of paradise was better than never knowing such a place existed." She promised to borrow a car next weekend and take me to Dolores Hidalgo to buy some semiprecious stones and see Father Hidalgo's famous historical church and enjoy a picnic in the hills.

I TOLD GABRIELA about what I'd seen and heard at Casa Jorado between the girl and her father. She gazed into my eyes, then she shrugged and said, "Don't be surprised at anything you might find in this country. It is a wonderful country with wonderful people. They are my friends, most of them, but it is also a country filled with confusion and contradiction. If you explore the possibilities, nothing turns out as it first appears."

I wondered on her words. They were words that not only described Mexico. They described this town. They described Gabriela. They described many of the people—North Americans and Mexicans—that I had found here. In my life since those days, I have discovered that much of life is just as she described, especially in my home state of Alabama, which has always been filled with confusion and contradiction.

Gabriela and I went to Dolores, visited the church, and bought semiprecious stones.

After I returned to Alabama I wrote several letters to my friend but she never responded. The next summer, when I returned to San Miguel, Gabriela was gone. I was told that she was on a trip to visit her family in Haiti and that she would return by way of New York, where she would renew her business contacts in the publishing world.

In the next two years I too worked in New York with a big-time publisher. Once I thought I saw Gabriela from a distance. I trotted after her, called out her name, but the woman did not acknowledge my persistence.

When I returned to San Miguel in the early 1960s, I was told by a friend that the last few months had been tragic for Gabriela. She had suffered through a particularly painful and depressing pregnancy. She claimed she had no idea who the father was. She took painkillers, smoked marijuana, and drank excessively. The baby was born an addict. "Gabriela went crazy," our friend said. I listened, hurting with every word. "Rather than take the baby to a hospital, she became convinced that the little girl would live through her addiction. "She kept saying, 'She's strong. I know. She will live a good life. I know.' And when we told her, 'Gabriela, the baby needs medical help,' she'd pick her up and hold her to her breast, rocking back and forth, cooing." Within weeks of birth, the baby died. Still holding the tiny body in her arms, Gabriela took an overdose and succumbed to the drugs.

I took flowers to the graves where a friend's attempt at art—their names scratched into a makeshift concrete marker with a primitive curlicue decorative fleur-de-lis—was all that remained of the strange and erratic woman whom I will never forget.

*

Roy

*

1.

Of the many people I met during my first summer in Mexico, Roy
Calhoun touched me with his roughshod off-handed emotions.
Roy thought he had something in common with the movie star
Rory Calhoun. He did: his name and a thick shock of auburn hair
that curled up in a high pompadour at the top of his forehead. But
that was where their common ground ended. Roy was a good old
boy from Pine Bluff, Arkansas, who had gone off to World War II
after two years at a small Arkansas college. He went to boot camp
down in the swamps of Louisiana, was shipped in a slow boat to
north Africa, sailed on a troop ship to Sicily, and fought his way as
an infantryman up the boot of Italy, over the Dolomites, through
Brenner Pass, and was in the first wave of the liberation army to
open the gates of Dachau to free the horrible stench and the ema-
ciated survivors. "When we came up those railroad tracks out
through the Bavarian countryside, we got the first strong whiff of
rotten flesh and burned entrails about a mile or so away. At first
we had no idea what lay ahead of us, then we saw the most horrendous sight I'd ever witnessed in my life. And we're talking

about a man who had been through hundreds of miles of body-strewn, blood-soaked battlefields.

"This was worse than that, because these were civilians who never had a chance—captured because of their religions, their race, or their lifestyles. These poor bastards were piled high—human mountains—skin and bones—and now and then you'd see a movement and something inside you would catch and you crawled over all that people-debris with your insides growling and grab an arm and pull, hoping with all your heart that you'd found one of 'em alive, but most of the time the movement'd just be a mechanical twitch, some kind of separate sense that made 'em twitch—even in death. The feeling of desperation caught inside you and held on and squeezed tighter and tighter—and you prayed to God you'd never ever see anything like that again. And the next Nazi you saw, you'd *rare* back with your rifle and haul off and knock that sorry-ass sonofabitch off his feet. He'd grab his jaw or his shoulder or whatever and would look at you like you were crazy, but you knew you had to hit the bastard again just to keep from going crazy." When Roy recalled that time in his life, tears came to his eyes and rolled down his cheeks. He didn't move to wipe them away, like he was proud of them, wore them with dubious honor.

Every morning at five till ten, Roy Calhoun paced the sidewalk outside of the Cucaracha. If the night had been especially bad, or the goblins had invaded his little room at Hotel San Miguel too early and made too much noise in his brain at night, Roy sought solace at one of the cantinas near the central market. But if it had been just an ordinary night when he was visited only by the usual myriad of ghosts, like the battalion of goose-stepping stormtroopers who periodically marched into his memory, then he waited until Chucho opened the inviting door of the Cuc, where he had a charge account after his pension check gave out, usually by the last week of every month. He stepped into the sanctuary of Chucho's

206

place, sighing with relief as he left the outside world behind. With a shaky hand, he held the glass to his flaccid, trembling lips and swallowed fast the first drink of the day. Bringing it down, his skinny body gave a little twitch, his eyes sparkled as though the day had just begun, and he'd push his glass toward Chucho, who knew the routine.

Almost every afternoon Roy could be found crumpled in one of the Cuc's cushioned chairs in the front room, taking his siesta. He snored and grumbled in his sleep, now and then striking out at some imaginary demon. He changed positions as he slept fitfully. No one ever disturbed him. And very occasionally he slid out of the chair onto the floor where he rolled into a ball and finished his nap in a corner, in peace.

2.

After World War II, Roy Calhoun attended Ohio State where he studied art on the G.I. Bill. He heard about the Instituto and came to Mexico, where he drained the rest of his supply of G.I. Bill money and learned to live on the medical disability he was paid each month by Uncle Sam. He cussed the U.S. government every day while he lived and drank from its handouts. "Damn ol' Ike," he said. "Look at that sorry sonofabitch up there in the White House, playing golf and living high on the hog. All he did in Europe was ride from country club to country club, screwing his way from one high-class whorehouse to another, with the biggest whore of all driving him from place to place, eating first-class gourmet food and drinking the best wine in the world, a dozen aides at his beck and call, and now he's the biggest cheese in the whole world. You know how much retirement he gets?"

He stood five-seven, weighed about 120, or less, and both of my hands could reach around his scrawny waist. His bony face was pockmarked from some illness he'd contracted on the march through Europe. He was hospitalized for a month near Baden-Baden and recuperated at an old posh hotel that General George Patton, his hero, had turned into a spa especially for wounded and sick soldiers. "I got more pussy in those weeks in the Black Forest than I ever had before or since. It was wall-to-wall. Ol' Blood and Guts sent a passel of pussy in there to tend to us boys, and he told 'em, 'Treat those boys good, girls, cause they've been through total hell to get here,' and they did. I'd soak myself in those hot baths and a little blonde from Buffalo'd give me a massage, and I mean it was a sure enough massage, not just a little rubbing here and there; the sure-'nough thing."

He still talked like a hillbilly. He had a head full of hair. Not a speck of it was gray. It was dark auburn, and he pampered it with a perfumed oil and combed the high pompadour at his widow's peak exactly like Rory Calhoun of movie fame. "I thought at times I'd go back to the Ozarks and settle down, find me some little ol' Arkansas hill-country girl who didn't know no better and have us a two-bedroom house in the suburbs, then my brain'd start to ache and my stomach'd act up; I'd start smelling tequila way back up in the roof of my mouth, and I'd get all sour and fussy. Shit, boy, I knew that wouldn't work. Not for me. Hell, some day I'll light out for California and talk my way into the movies. I'd make a helluva star. Don't you think?"

When he was first into the juice in the morning, drinking Oso Negro vodka with tomato juice or orange or grapefruit juice, Terry or Peter or Donald started in on him. "Where you going, Roy? What you going to do? California? What's in California for you?" They asked him about the movies, which on his better days he would verbally dream about becoming a western movie star, riding horses, shooting Indians; always play-like shooting. Not the real thing, like in Europe, like in his worst dreams.

3.

There was one person Roy Calhoun could better, and he did so every chance he got: a farm implement salesman from the nearby town of Dolores Hidalgo named Chico Alonzo Gonzalez. A slight man with a dark brown bald head, Chico always wore colored dress shirts, either stripes or checks, with wide patterned ties and slick gabardine trousers with pleats on both sides and wing-tipped shoes. Chico was very nervous, and the more nervous he became the faster he talked. Most of the time, after only a few minutes in the Cucaracha, I could not understand a word he said.

After he called on a half-dozen customers around the central market area, he strolled down to the *jardín* and into the Cucaracha. When he came to town, he usually showed up at the Cuc by 11 A.M. Someone would see him coming and skip ahead to warn Roy and the boys that their prey was on his way. If I cut classes or decided to nurse a hangover, I would join in the fun, with Chico as the goat.

One time Roy had purchased a rubber spider about the size of my thumb. He tied it to a string just long enough to fall exactly in front of Chico when he approached the rear bar. He always walked past the outer room, speaking to the drinkers, and going back, raising his voice in welcome to Chucho. Roy and his pals were on the balcony above the rear bar, a twenty-by-twenty room where we watched bullfights on Sunday afternoons on a small black-and-white snowy television set balanced on a shelf high in the far corner. With a rail along the open end above the bar, it made a perfect spot for us to prepare to scare the wits out of our friend.

As Chico entered, he talked loudly to Chucho. It was the best Wednesday he had ever had, sold plows for John Deere tractors, hay rakes, combines, and other instruments for farming. Chucho poured a tequila neat. Chico raised his glass in a friendly toast.

When the glass was almost to his lips, Roy dropped the rubber spider that bounced at the end of the string not three inches in front of Chico's nose.

209

Chico threw his glass skyward. *"Ey, yeh, yeh, yeh!"* he shouted. *"Besa mi culo,* hombre of *sheet!"* He balled his fist and shook it toward Roy Calhoun and the rest of us, who were laughing out of control. He cursed more, calling us every foul name he could find in his vocabulary.

As soon as Chico managed to swallow a fast set-up of tequila and follow it with a cold *cerveza* (because he had so many North American customers through the years, Chucho learned to keep his beer on ice), the salesman grinned and spouted pleasantries. He even bought Roy a drink and hugged him. Invariably, Roy would have a child's buzzer between his fingers to frighten poor Chico one last time before he said, *"Adiós,"* and headed out to finish his rounds before comida.

One Sunday I borrowed a car from Gabriela and drove with Roy to Dolores Hidalgo to take comida with Chico and his family. He and his wife, Marisa, and their four children lived in a very modest *casa* on the edge of town. It was a relatively new place, built since World War II, a square block of yellow plaster. He proudly pointed out that it was not adobe, it was built of reinforced concrete. A chin-high wall with a wrought-iron extension with several artistic curliques made it distinctly different from the other houses of this suburban housing project. The house had a tiny courtyard between the wall and the front door. Three bougainvillea plants bloomed a bright red. Two jacaranda trees, one on each side of the walk, had bright orange blossoms. The yard was spotless without one sprig of grass. Marisa explained the details, such as the pot on the far side. It had been found by their oldest child, Hector, on a field trip to the ruins at Tula. I didn't ask if it came from the government-guarded archaeological land there. In those days most people were deaf and blind to such things. She was very proud of it, because, she said, it was a reminder of their Chichimeca ancestry. Both she and Chico had Indian ancestors

210

who lived in the land of north-central Mexico hundreds of years ago when the Spanish missionaries first came to the area.

Little Marisa, who was twelve, brought Roy and me vodka tonics into the living room that smelled of fresh plaster, furniture polish, and garlic and peppers roasting in the kitchen. The room looked as though it were a display area from a Mexican department store. A painting of a beautiful damp-eyed Jesus hung over the mantel above the small half-moon fireplace. A small statue of the virgin Mary sat on bookshelves filled with two-year-old set of World Book Encyclopedia. The books reminded me of my parents' home in suburban Tuscaloosa. Later, Marisa told us Hector studied the World Book and could speak very good English. The fourteen-year-old, scrubbed like the furniture to a shiny polish, was asked to say the blessing in English after we had had three vodkas. Other than one slip on thanking God "for all inordinate vices," which pressed a smile onto Roy's bowed face, the youngster made it through the ordeal like a true World Book scholar.

Before the meal, Chico and Marisa gave us a guided tour through their home. In their voices was a deep-seated pride in the success that Chico had obviously brought to the family. He was a good honest hard-working salesman who attended mass every Sunday morning with his family. Marisa did not have car-pool duty like similar moms in the U.S., but she was a Brownie scout leader for her daughters and was a regular attendee of PTA-type meetings at the local school, and she went to Mass more than once a week to pray for her husband and children and their continued success.

Over a cinnamon cake and a taste of brandy, Chico said, "We are the new Mexico. There are few of us now. But there are more and more each year. In the years to come, people like me and Marisa and our children will be the majority. At that time there will be more democracy. It is heresy to say it today, but there will be much more than the one Revolutionary Party [the PRI, Party of

Revolutionary Independence, was the legacy of the Revolution of 1911 and the politicians who were the heirs to the victory over the longtime dictatorship of Porforio Diaz]. There will be two or more political parties that will grow out of the various factions, the agrarian farmers from the capital to the U.S. border and the angry Indians who have been oppressed for decades in the southernmost states such as Chiapas." He was very proud of this knowledge he had picked up from the conversations in the offices of the feed stores, the mill houses, and the farm implement stores across his territory. I noticed that Hector sat nearby, listening to every word spoken by his father. I could not help but wonder if Chico's experiences among the merchants in his world was not indeed an extension of Ignacio Allende's Literary Study Clubs nearly 150 years ago.

I sat back in my half-drunken slumber, teetering on the edge of sleep and exhaustion, my stomach packed and my head abuzz. To hear this little Aztec great-great-great-grandson of some chieftain talk about the intricacies of the complex political system was more than I could quite comprehend at the moment. He was far removed from that clown-like figure in a dark suit with wide lapels and pleated pants and four-inch-wide tie that always stopped several inches short of his bellybutton. In this house he was not afraid of flying rubber bugs. Here he was king of the castle. He was husband, father, provider and protector, political prognosticator and pronouncer of eloquent prayers.

After the living room, darkened behind drawn drapes, grew quiet, both Roy and I dropped our heads. We probably snored. The children of Chico and Marisa probably giggled at us. We rested. Some time later I awakened. It was late afternoon. The house was very quiet. I looked across the room at Roy, who was still asleep. I stretched and tiptoed to him, shook his scrawny shoulder, and his eyes flew open, startled.

I put my finger to my lips.

He looked around and realized where we were. He wiped his eyes and followed me quietly outside. I drove us home over the hills and through the valleys while Roy sank back into sleep.

4.

Three weeks later Chico traveled to San Miguel with his valise filled with catalogues. After his first round of regular calls, he headed down the hill toward the *jardín* and the Cucaracha. Roy had purchased a rubber snake, had it poised at the railing over-head while Chico innocently and ignorantly ordered a drink. Roy dropped the snake that bounced at the end of the string in front of Chico's face. As usual, the nervous salesman dropped his glass onto the bar. It bounced. Ice cubes slid toward Chucho.

We all giggled and waited for Chico to raise his eyes toward us and begin his cursing.

Instead, we heard only silence.

Chico reached out slowly toward the front edge of the bar. He slid his brown fingers across the wet surface. His face never turned up toward us. His words caught in his throat as his body crumbled forward and he fell in slow motion.

"Chico?" Roy said, and I heard the touch of a cry in his sound. He rushed down the stairs.

At the bottom, in front of the bar, Chucho knelt over the body that lay unmoving on the floor.

Chucho took care of the details of taking Chico's body home to his wife and children. A few days later we all rode together in Chucho's long Oldsmobile to the church in Dolores Hidalgo. Neither Roy nor I could look Marisa in the eyes as she wept and lifted her black veil and kissed our cheeks and called us "Chico's American amigos." In her thick accent, she told us that Chico talked about us often to her and to his children, and that he was very proud that we had come to his house and accepted his hospitality. I told her that we were the ones who were honored.

Roy was silent all the way back to San Miguel. Whenever anyone in the Cuc remembered the little salesman from Dolores Hidalgo, Roy silently moved out of hearing range.

When I returned to San Miguel a year later, I was told that Roy had left for Hollywood one morning. "But he never made it to the border," the mutual friend said. He died in Mexico and was buried in a little town south of California.

*

William Spratling:
Alabama's Mexican Connection

*

1.

Early on the fog-shrouded morning of August 7, 1967, William Spratling drove his new Mustang at his customary top speed over the still-wet blacktop of rural southwest Mexico where he'd lived for decades. He rounded a hairpin curve on the familiar highway to Iguala and ran head-on into a tree that had fallen during a storm the night before. He died at a local hospital and was buried with great ceremony in the public cemetery at nearby Taxco, where he had become a legendary figure.

Several months later, two of his friends visited Spratling's gravesite at precisely 5 P.M., his cocktail time, and placed an icy martini straight-up on the stone. To honor their old compadre, the friends hoisted several strong drinks, toasting his memory. After a while, they noticed that the glass on Spratling's grave was now only half-full. "It was eerie," the friend recalled, "but we felt that we had indeed had a last drink with the great man."

Spratling inspired that kind of loyalty — and that kind of story. He was a man whose presence and power was felt by many, whose memory is still felt years after his death. A heavy drinker, a tireless self-promoter, a world-renowned artist and architectural genius, he was also recognized as an authority on pre-Columbian art. Author of a half-dozen books and illustrator of that many others, Spratling's reputation spanned the globe, yet he chose to live in rural southwest Mexico where he had almost single-handedly created an industry from the natural riches of the land.

Friends did not merely like him, they adored him, but he infuriated many with his unabashed arrogance. He spoke out abruptly and loudly, passionately promoting pet projects such as historical preservation.

In the introduction to Spratling's rambling autobiography, *File on Spratling* (Little, Brown and Company, 1967) — by all accounts a sometimes creative, often forgetful remembrance — his friend Budd Schulberg, author of the classic novel *What Makes Sammy Run?* and screenplay *On the Waterfront*, described Spratling as "the only truly Renaissance Man I know" and "not only My Most Unforgettable Character, but My Five Most Unforgettable Characters."

Spratling defied conventional mores in order to live life as he wished. He was a master at publicity and public relations, surrounding himself with brilliant and interesting people, all of whom he used ultimately to promote himself and his causes, but he chose to share his life on a permanent basis only with his large menagerie of animals. He inspired numerous articles, a short film, and books about himself. Over drinks, he was an autocratic raconteur. "I loved to listen to him talk," recalled his old friend Danny Branman, "but if you did not agree with his every opinion, he could be a total bastard."

By the time he died at age 67, he had been awarded an honorary doctorate from Auburn University, had a street named for him in Taxco, and had received presidential honors for his work with Indians and Eskimos. After his death, an annual celebration in Taxco attracted thousands from around the world, to participate and view the presentation of the Spratling Award to the finest example of silver artistry of the year.

2.

Born in upstate New York in 1900, William Spratling was the third of four children to Anna Gorton and William P. Spratling II—an Alabama-born medical doctor who specialized in the treatment of epilepsy. Young Billy, named after his father and grandfather, seemed set for a comfortable life in a well-to-do family when tragedy struck quickly and repeatedly. Never comfortable discussing his childhood, Spratling, in his autobiography, gives short shrift to his early years, often confusing dates and glossing over the more painful memories.

According to recent biographers, Taylor D. Littleton in *The Color of Silver* (Louisiana State University Press, 2000) and Joan T. Mark in *The Silver Gringo* (University of New Mexico Press, 2000), Spratling's mother and an older sister, Wilhelmina, both died of tuberculosis in 1910. But things were not steady in the Spratling household even before these two untimely deaths. Forced by her deteriorating health to a warmer climate, Mrs. Spratling found herself isolated with her children in Summit, New Jersey, while her husband tended to his private practice in Baltimore, even as his own mental state—and the marriage—deteriorated.

After his wife's death, Dr. Spratling suffered a mental breakdown in 1911 and took his children to his father's home in the east Alabama community of Gold Hill. Unable to tend to his children, the senior Spratling retired to Florida, leaving Billy and his siblings to the care of the family. The children were soon separated, dispersed to relatives. For a while, Billy was sent to stay with his uncle, Edgar Johnson "Johnny" Spratling, also a doctor, in Atlanta.

217

In a strange, tragic twist befitting the drama swirling around Spratling's life from then on, both his father and his uncle Johnny died of gunshot wounds within eight months of each other in 1915. William Spratling II died at his own hands in what was called a hunting accident, though many regarded it as a suicide. Less than a year later, Johnny Spratling was killed by a deranged patient.

In the wake of these tragedies, young Billy went back to Gold Hill where he was surrounded by his extended family. In the wooded hills and hollows, he settled into a more normal life, free to lose himself in the world of boyish things. It was here that he first heard romantic stories about the magic of mining. As an adolescent, Spratling explored shacks said to have been a tavern and a company store, roamed ghost-shafts deep into a ridge known locally as Devil's Backbone, and stored a wealth of lore in his active young imagination. A budding artist, he was never without his sketchpad.

A few years later, Spratling moved in with a cousin who ran a boarding house in the small town of Auburn, Alabama, and in 1917 he entered Alabama Polytechnic Institute (Alabama's land-grant college, later renamed Auburn University). His architecture professors were impressed by the young man's drawing skills, which showed signs of enormous creative energy and prowess, as well as an individuality they had seldom seen in someone so young. While still an undergraduate, he was asked to become a part-time student lecturer, teaching classes in anatomy and the history of architecture.

In the summer of 1921, he and several Pi Kappa Alpha fraternity brothers worked their way to Europe aboard a freighter. Spratling made his first watercolors of castles and other classic structures on that trip. That fall, his work became the centerpiece for a major layout in *Architectural Forum*, considered the top architectural periodical of its day. Shortly after his return to Alabama, Spratling sent copies of the *Forum* layout to administrators in the architectural school at Tulane University in New Orleans, where Spratling—still a few hours short of graduation from Auburn—was offered a position as an instructor.

3.

In New Orleans, Spratling quickly caught the attention of the artsy crowd that orbited around famed novelist and short story writer Sherwood Anderson, an older man of letters whose *Winesburg, Ohio* was already considered a classic. At the time, the French Quarter set was as filled with talent as any outside Paris or Greenwich Village. Introducing him to the group was his landlady, Natalie Scott, a handsome and intelligent woman who wrote a society column for the *Times-Picayune* newspaper.

Younger than most of this group that included writers Roark Bradford, Oliver La Farge, Hamilton Basso, and John Dos Passos, Spratling made friends with a writer near his own age—a Mississippian named William Faulkner, who also rented a room from Miss Scott at Number 264 Pirate's Alley. It was Faulkner who took Spratling to meet Lillian Marcus Friend, publisher of the small literary magazine *Double-Dealer* that soon began publishing Spratling's line drawings.

In a now infamous incident that offers a glimpse into the sort of ridiculous and sublime existence this bohemian crew enjoyed, Anderson rounded all of them up to tool around Lake Pontchartrain in a rented yacht. It was the spring of 1925 and the occasion was a party in honor of best-selling author Anita Loos, who was then finishing *Gentlemen Prefer Blondes* (1925). The revelers sailed out into the huge lake and were immediately encapsulated by a thick blanket of fog. Gusty winds blew up and rains came. The group, all in various stages of intoxication, was forced to sit uncomfortably for several hours in the dank interior of the boat, drinking more and more, trying to relax and enjoy the party.

The famously irreverent Faulkner teamed up with Spratling in 1926 to produce a booklet satirizing their self-satisfied intellectual friends. They called their slim volume *Sherwood Anderson and Other Famous Creoles* and dedicated it "To All the Artful and Crafty Ones of the French Quarter." The booklet, featuring Spratling's caricatures and Faulkner's wry words, infuriated Anderson, who ranted about it for weeks. Not satisfied, an impish Faulkner later wrote about the Ponchartrain excursion in his satiric novel, *Mosquitoes*, where even his friend Spratling was not immune to parody: he is depicted as the self-centered poet Mark Frost, who groans aloud every time Dawson, the Anderson character, began another long-winded tale of recollection.

While Spratling enjoyed himself immensely in the social set, he also worked hard. By now his work was receiving national attention on a regular basis. At Tulane, where his lectures were widely touted by local architects, Spratling found time to write *Pencil Drawings*, published in 1923 by Pelican Bookshop in New Orleans and praised as "masterful" by critics. He also published *Picturesque New Orleans: Ten Drawings of the French Quarter* (Tulane University Press, 1923) and, with N. C. Curtis, *The Wrought Iron Works of Old New Orleans* (1925), with the American Institute of Architects.

On off-days from Tulane, he accompanied Natalie Scott as she motored the backroads along the Mississippi River. While she interviewed people who lived mostly along the levees, he sketched the places they visited. This work was first appeared in the pages of *Architectural Forum* in November 1927, where readers could again admire his simple yet magical drawings. That same year, *Plantation Houses of Louisiana*, featuring Spratling's drawings and Scott's text, was published by William Helburn, Inc., of New York. Spratling followed up with an April 1928 publication of "Cane River Portraits," which he wrote and illustrated for *Scribner's Magazine*.

4.

As his time at Tulane wore on, however, he felt the creative juices in New Orleans starting to run dry. His active imagination was on the lookout for a new world to explore and conquer. He found it in Mexico. Among his friends at Tulane was archaeologist Frans Blom, who had written a well-received two-volume work on the Mayan tribes and temples. Spratling listened intently as Blom recounted his time in the jungles of southern Mexico, particularly Chiapas, on the Guatemala border. Spratling was an eager student, asking questions, enchanted and enthralled with the new subject.

Soon Spratling had sold his *Forum* editors on sending him to Mexico to sketch the country's colonial buildings. In the summer of 1926 he sailed to Veracruz, then traveled by rail through the jungles, past the snow-peaked Orizaba mountain, and through the valleys of Puebla, and up again to the capital at Mexico City. Sitting in the rear observation car of *Her Majesty's Special* train, he was impressed by the natural beauty of the landscape. In Mexico City he walked the streets of downtown, across the 40-acre concrete square of the *zócalo*, sketched the *Catedral Metropolitana* on one side and the National Palace on the other, and captured the heroic faces of the peasants who sold tamales, tortillas, and tacos. He fell in love with Mexico and the Mexican people. He knew that he wanted to find a way to live in this country.

As always, when he traveled, Spratling searched out the most influential people. He knew they could give him the best help in a strange land. His friend Frans Blom had listed six names and addresses, and Spratling sent a card to each, telling a little something about himself. As an introduction, he never told too much, making a mystery of himself and his art. "If there are still questions to be answered," he told a friend, "people will want to know more about you. If you talk too much about yourself, they will know you so well, you will become a bore. I wish to be entertaining, never boring."

He was introduced to Gerardo Murillo, widely known as the famous "Dr. Atl," an artist, writer, teacher, and revolutionary who was already a legendary figure here. Dr. Atl considered himself the preeminent expert on the architecture of convents and churches in Mexico. Atl heaped praise on Spratling's work while serving him a five-course comida, or afternoon lunch, at the *Convento de la Merced*, an ancient building that Dr. Atl had himself seized during the Revolution little more than ten years earlier. At the end of the meal, Atl presented his guest with a gift of his six-volume work on Mexican religious architecture. Spratling, very pleased, pored over the drawings and descriptions, and grew even more enamored with the prospects of living in this fascinating country.

His enthusiasm mounted when he met the giant of a man and artist, Diego Rivera, who took him to view his newly completed murals in the National Ministry of Education only a few blocks from the *zócalo*. Six-foot six-inch, 300-pound Diego towered over the tall and slender figure of Spratling, who expressed his appreciation for the quiet power of the Mexican artist's portrayal of his country's history. Here were rich and varied pictures of simple brown-skinned people living in simple adobe huts, working the land, struggling against great odds, dreaming of precious freedom and the opportunity to be educated. As the two men strolled from panel to panel, discussing each piece, they became fast friends: Spratling admiring Rivera, Diego regarding Spratling as an American equal, a generosity he seldom shared. In this case, both recognized that each was larger than life. Spratling wrote that the sophistication of the murals worked well with the institutional architecture of wide porticoes open through high arches to the broad patios.

Back home in New Orleans, Spratling began publishing his drawings of Mexico and writing with emotion about the buildings and countryside he had seen. In 1928 and 1929, his text and sketches appeared in *Scribner's Magazine*, *Architectural Forum*, and *Travel*, a widely read national magazine. "I have never encountered a city like this before," he wrote of Mexico City. "Somehow in parts, it is European . . . But there is always that in the air which belies these suggestions of cosmopolitanism. There is something savage here that lies just beneath the surface."

As a member of the Fine Arts Committee of the American Institute of Architects in New York, Spratling insisted that Rivera be awarded the group's gold medal for the most distinguished work in the fine arts for 1928. He showed them photographs to support his argument, and the committee agreed. Diego thanked the committee but said he was too busy painting to travel to New York. The AIA sent the medal to Mexico, where Spratling would make the presentation in person. However, Mexican customs held up delivery, demanding an entrance fee of 1,980 pesos, which Rivera refused to pay. After months of haggling, Spratling retrieved the award, a golden eagle weighing a hundred grams, which Spratling then ceremoniously presented to the artist during an elaborate comida.

5.

By 1929 Spratling had arranged to move to Mexico City as distinguished lecturer at the National University of Mexico's summer school. Spratling soon became a close friend of U.S. Ambassador Dwight Morrow, who asked him to organize a Mexican art exhibit for the Carnegie Institute, which he did with gusto, reacquainting himself not only with Rivera but artists David Alfaro Siqueiros, Jose Clemente Orozco, and Dr. Atl. Spratling wrote a major article bringing these names and their work to the attention of the American public in *Scribner's Magazine* (January 1929). In the article, "Figures in the Mexican Renaissance," he praised the talent of the artists, all of whom returned the favor by seeking him out, becoming his friend, and publicly praising his own talent.

Spratling was never short on advice. When Ambassador Morrow told Spratling that, at the end of his tenure, he would like to leave the Mexican people something of lasting value to be appreciated for years to come, Spratling suggested that he commission Rivera to do frescoes in the Cortes Palace at Cuernavaca. Rivera's position as head of the country's Communist party presented a twofold problem: Morrow did not want to appear too friendly with a Communist and Rivera did not want to lose face with his party by appearing too friendly with the American Ambassador. To solve the problem and to isolate the incident from Embassy or government, Spratling suggested that an invitation to tea be extended by Mrs. Morrow. She would be the hostess. Rivera would be visiting her. No one would wish for him to be disrespectful to a lady. Then Mr. Morrow could just happen to appear.

To give the occasion an appearance of social grace, Spratling accompanied the artist, who wore a wide-brimmed white Stetson, was dressed in a new sharkskin suit, and had a .45 revolver strapped around his waist. At five sharp, they were greeted at the door by Mrs. Morrow, who escorted them into the residence. Mr. Morrow appeared and guided Rivera into a side room where the two talked about art. Later they joined Spratling and Mrs. Morrow for tea. In the days ahead, Diego sketched his proposal but told Spratling he was unsure what to charge for his work. Spratling suggested that Diego measure the walls to be painted, then charge by the meter. "Mr. Morrow is a businessman," Spratling said. "He will understand such a proposition." But this worried Diego, who said it would be a very large mural. "If he pays $12,000," Rivera said, "I will insist you accept $2,000 commission." Several months later, after Morrow had happily paid, Diego sent Spratling his commission.

When not lecturing, Spratling explored the countryside south and west of Mexico City, riding out on horseback and wandering over the hilly terrain. On one trip into rural Guerrero he happened upon a gorgeous little village. Crisscrossed with ancient cobblestone streets and dotted with adobe houses with red tiled roofs, the town of Taxco spread out on the hillside across a *barranca*, or gorge, like a huge colorful canvas. He followed a zigzag street up the steep hill, entered the tree-lined *zócalo*, and gazed up at the twin towers of the magnificent Santa Prisca church built hundreds of years earlier. Finding the place *simpático*, he decided this was where he would live.

Spratling's tenacity would be challenged. Such a remote village offered a professional few opportunities to earn a living. There was no school here where he could lecture. He could write here, but about what? He talked with editors in New York. His editors at the *Forum* assured him they would continue to use his work. *The New York Herald Tribune* agreed to pay him fifty dollars a month for columns on Latin American literature. Then he approached book publishers Jonathan Cape and Harrison Smith, with whom he signed a contract for a book "to picture normal life in a small Mexican village" and was sent an advance of two hundred dollars. Leading a pack mule loaded with his belongings, he rode horseback to Taxco, where he purchased a small house on a narrow slanting lot within a stone's throw of the plaza. The roof leaked and there was no bathroom, but he started renovating the house and working the garden. Although in his autobiography, *My Art, My Life*, Rivera wrote that Spratling would not accept a commission for his services, Spratling told his old friend Ted Wick many times that without Rivera's commission he would never have been able to afford the house in Taxco.

Spratling began writing his book, *Little Mexico*: "The houses of the town are shining and compact, a study in red and white and green. The poverty and simplicity of it goes all unsuspected. Each house, resolving the problem of an odd corner, the sudden declivity of a *barranca* or a spur of virgin rock, has resulted individually. Yet the whole has that same unity of growth that exists in plants." In the foreword, Diego Rivera stated: "You have made a portrait of Mexico composed of many small portraits of people and things. Your portraits have the acuteness and grace of those painted by certain masters in my country who died before I was born. Those portraits were made with precision and tenderness and contain irony and love."

Little Mexico was published in 1932 by Cape and Smith to poor sales, because the publishers closed their doors shortly after the book was released. Years later, it was republished as *A Small Mexican World* to greater sales. In both instances, reviewers praised the book and its author, but in neither case did the volume make Spratling much money, and finances in Taxco were beginning to be a problem.

7.

Once when Morrow was visiting, the Ambassador declared it a shame that the vast amount of silver still in the mountains surrounding Taxco was not being mined. Years before, the Spanish had mined millions of dollars worth of silver here. Now it lay dormant beneath the earth. The thought stayed with Spratling, who remembered fondly his Alabama background. His grandfather had told him about the riches in the earth around Gold Hill and Goldville in Lee County, where entire towns had thrived before the rush to California in 1849. When his grandfather talked of gold, his voice rang with a thrill of possibilities. Spratling turned to his own

artistic talent and began drawing designs for jewelry, but he needed a silversmith to turn his art into reality. "The local people could
not imagine why anyone should want to buy silver," he said.
"Besides, who would want a silver belt buckle if a gold-plated
brass one cost less?"

Spratling's imagination soared with the idea that the craft of
silversmithing and the art of jewelry design could be successfully
executed and marketed—even from a small town in Mexico. He
searched the back alleys of Taxco and found several silversmiths
working with ancient tools, making beads and spoons, rings and
earrings. Eager and enthusiastic, Spratling convinced these men to
work with him.

He rented the old customs house, *La Aduana*, and began to
design jewelry, oftentimes using the basic curls and angles of classic Mayan or Aztec symbols. With his shop, which he called *Las
Delicias* (The Delights), expanding, he wrote in *File on Spratling*: "I
decided to attempt to smelt ore the way they used to do it centuries ago. Silversmithing is learned best firsthand. Thus, as only
man can produce man, you need silversmiths to produce silversmiths."

Spratling became skilled at the craft. He developed a unique
style and made jewelry—with his special Spratling Silver mark—
that was more than simply a decoration for a woman's evening
wear. He knew instinctively that to stand out in the market,
Spratling Silver had to be sold as something very special. To provide status for himself and his products—just as he had with his
art—he was a relentless self-promoter. On a New York trip, when
he befriended industrialist-politician Nelson Rockefeller, he sold
the millionaire a necklace and earrings, and told a friend at *The
New York Times*, who happened also to be an editor in the culture
section of the world's most prominent newspaper. And when the
editor happened to write that Mrs. Rockefeller was wearing
Spratling jewelry from Mexico, the designer showed the printed

words to influential buyers for luxury department stores Saks Fifth Avenue, Tiffany and Company, and Neiman-Marcus, all of whom were impressed.

8.

The 1930s were heady years for Spratling, as his reputation as a design genius soared. As usual, he filled his life with interesting people, but he could not abide fools or bores. When someone stayed too long at his house, as poet Hart Crane once did, staying up late, drinking into the night, repeating story after story, Spratling opened his door and told him to take his tales elsewhere. One day, after he had been in Taxco only a short while, his old friend from New Orleans, Natalie Scott, showed up. She had missed him so terribly, she said, that she had ridden hundreds of miles from the border on horseback to find him. Instead of admiring her gallantry, he chided her for not being more practical. In front of friends at Paco Bar on the plaza, he told her he did not love her. He made it clear that he did not love any woman. But she stayed and bought a house near his, and they remained close friends.

Soon he was joined by another female friend from his days in New Orleans. In 1931, Spratling bumped into Elizabeth Anderson, who was on an indefinite excursion in Mexico City. Newly divorced from Sherwood, Elizabeth had received a letter from Natalie Scott raving about the wonders south of the border and decided to explore the possibilities. Following their chance meeting on the streets of the capital, she became Spratling's "willing captive" as he drove her through the countryside to Taxco, to the delighted surprise of Natalie Scott.

Eventually, the two expatriates—Spratling and Scott— implored Anderson to relocate to Taxco permanently. When

Spratling went so far as to purchase a small strip of land adjoining his garden and build a cottage for her, Anderson agreed. Eventually she began designing clothing made under her supervision by local Indian women. With Spratling engineering her publicity, her designs caught the eye of editors at *Vogue*, where her work was displayed with flare. Spratling and the older woman remained friends for life, and she remembered the time warmly in her memoir.

Ms. Anderson wrote: "Taxco was no sleepy little town in the sun; an air of vitality and purpose permeated everything. Even at the parties, people set out to have a good time and did so with great gusto. In Taxco, none of us were young, but we felt young and we behaved young. There was a rebirth of youthful enthusiasm and we felt that valuable things could be done in this vibrant country that was still shuddering from a violent and bloody revolution. We wanted to impart the quality and intensity of Mexico to our lives and our work."

It was Spratling, called "Don Guillermo" by his Mexican friends, who was the centerpiece of this scene, socially and professionally.

One of his early famous guests was historian Stuart Chase, whose bestselling *Mexico: A Study of Two Worlds*, published by The Macmillan Company of New York in 1931, credited Spratling as being one of the few *norte Americanos* schooled in the history and culture of the country. In a radio interview following the book's publication, Chase talked about Spratling being "a great influence on modern art in Mexico." Chase's history, illustrated by Diego Rivera, was praised in the U.S. and Mexico for its clear understanding of the very complex land.

9

He loved Taxco. He had discovered an original: a gorgeous old primitive colonial town with narrow winding cobblestone streets perfect for pack mules but not conducive to auto traffic. He wanted to keep it as he found it and promised to make the entire town a national monument. Not everyone liked his idea. Young entrepreneurs wanted to widen some streets. New industrialists wanted to expand business interests. Developers of tourist attractions also saw possibilities. But Spratling fought back. Determined to establish an architectural review board to oversee building and restoration within the historical perimeters of the old city, he went to Mexico City and visited lawmakers individually. His ideas were so radical, he was invited to address the entire Mexican Congress, which voted overwhelmingly for his proposal and added the towns of San Miguel de Allende and Alamos. With this success, Spratling became the champion of colonial Mexico, and the historical sites he helped save are today among the country's leading tourist attractions.

10.

As the decade progressed, Spratling's factory or atelier, *Taller de las Delicias*, became big business, and he eventually changed the name of his company to *Spratling y Artesanos*. By 1938 he had nearly fifty silvermakers at work, plus a number of other artisans, including weavers, carpenters, and tinsmiths. To meet the needs of expansion after signing contracts for jewelry, rugs, furniture, and ceramics with Montgomery Ward, Tiffany's, and Lord & Taylor, Spratling incorporated his business to raise capital, and found fourteen partners to whom he sold controlling interest. He also moved the factory to larger quarters at the spacious *Hacienda del Florida.*

In 1939, famed travel writer and novelist Henry Albert Phillips wrote in his book *New Designs for Old Mexico*, published by the National Travel Club of New York: "Sooner or later, every visitor to Taxco comes to William Spratling's Atelier. On first mention, it sounds suspiciously like an Atlantic City souvenir shop raising its ballyhoo in Mexico's Number One show town. The discerning one will soon dismiss this idea. Personally, I consider Bill Spratling's Atelier an institution unsurpassed in merit by the best that the Government has done on similar lines and with equally fine spirit. Spratling has succeeded in organizing and stabilizing the fine arts and crafts in the state of Guerrero into a single profitable unit, without disturbing the more delicate framework of Indian native moods, modes and materials. Each visit to the Atelier reminded me more and more of the *souks* of Morocco where the native fine arts craftsmen carried on their ancient trades in the same primitive manner, and with the same inimitably lovely results, as that of their forefathers, dating back perhaps to the time of Christ."

Spratling obviously delighted in creatively engineering "details" of his own myth to Phillips, whose *White Elephants in the Caribbean* had been a best-seller. He told the writer about existing in Taxco on three pesos a day for a year, until he opened his little shop "with fifty pesos capital." Spratling told Phillips that when he saw Indians bringing beautiful serapes into town, he asked them, "How would you like to bring your loom and work with me?" At first they shook their heads, he said; they brought their looms to the factory. "I pay weavers fifty pesos a week, or more than twice as much as a good secretary earns in Mexico City. Four of my silversmiths are making more than four hundred pesos a month," Spratling stated. "My great problem is avoiding novelties. Always simplifying and possibly improving on the old. I have done much for Mexican labor by raising wages, but already the

231

unions are after my people to demand more. The Mexicans are after my business! You know — 'Mexico for the Mexicans'? Radio, unions, and the tourists are going to spoil this place someday!"

Time magazine reported on July 7, 1941, that Spratling was doing some "$381,000 worth of business a year, selling to customers all over the Americas, and sixty percent of Taxco's income now comes from the metal handicrafts he revived." Spratling enjoyed his newfound wealth immensely. He bought a plane which he flew cross-country to Mexico City or to Acapulco, where he purchased a bayside *casa* and bought a yacht, which he sailed to California, spending nearly two weeks lost at sea on the return trip. In Acapulco, where his name and photograph appeared often in the gossip columns, he became friends with movie stars John Wayne, Errol Flynn, and Dolores Del Rio. Once again, he used these friendships to his own best advantage, selling them Spratling jewelry, then publicizing the sale in the West Coast press. "If there was a famous person near, he'd find them," said Danny Branman. "He thrived off celebrity."

My old professor of creative writing at the University of Alabama, Hudson Strode, himself a world-class name-dropper, wrote in a 1941 article in *Harper's Bazaar* magazine and later in his book *Now in Mexico*, published by Harcourt, Brace, and Company of New York, that Spratling had become the most famous silver artist in the country. "When we got back to Acapulco, we drove to Bill Spratling's new villa by the sea for cocktails. He had acquired the house and the trim yacht moored in the bay with profits from his famous silversmithy in Taxco. We knew the place was within an arrow's flight of Lord Morley's house, but we couldn't find it. We passed it, we were redirected to it, we passed it again. At last there on the roadside appeared Spratling himself, bronzed and hospitable, scouting for us with a highball glass in his hand.

"His house was down, not up. Even its roof was ambushed in greenery. We descended steep winding stairs through towering

232

shrubs and arrived at the doorstep. It was a spreading house of a warm color between oleander and brick dust. It seemed to rise straight from the water. There were no walls, only a cool tile floor and a spreading roof. Yet it was as private from the road and neighbors as if it were encased in windowless masonry ten feet thick. The whole villa seemed planned to minimize such things as cooking and sleeping.

". . . as if the superlative view out of the open veranda–drawing room–dining room were not enough, at the southwest corner there was a mirador ascended by winding stairs. Here aloft, stretched out in long chairs, the men had highballs . . . while the sun went down behind a promontory. All our eyes were magnetized to the islands across the inlet, which the unearthly rose-violet glow from the setting sun had turned into heaps of carved amethyst set in silver. 'I see now,' Andree said to Spratling, 'where you get inspiration for some of your workshop creations.'"

The 1943 *Terry's Guide to Mexico* detailed offerings from the famed Mexico City department store, Sanborn's. Its jewelry section had "Spratling silver better than sterling."

In 1944, *Mexico: Magnetic Southland* by Sydney A. Clark, author of two dozen travel books published by Dodd, Mead, and Company of New York, praised Spratling and his work. Later, in an article in *Esquire*, Clark described Spratling as an artist "of the world-class variety." His jewelry "is exquisite, and temptation demolishes the last vestige of sales resistance."

But while Spratling polished and magnified his own celebrity status, he ignored the factory and its operations. When he did return to Taxco, he found that several large orders had been canceled because they had not been filled on schedule. At the end of World War II, the factory went bankrupt and closed its doors. Spratling refused to accept responsibility. He pointed his finger elsewhere, saying, "My little company had been used as a sacrificial goat for [his U.S. investors'] tax interests." At the final board meeting, Spratling, in a characteristic devil-may-care attitude, told them, "I'm going to Acapulco tomorrow. I may be back in a month—or it may be six."

While he had failed as a businessman, he had succeeded as a teacher. Many of the young men he had trained—Antonio and Jorge Castillo, Enrique Ledesma, Antonio Pineda, Felipe Martinez, and others—opened their own factories and shops in Taxco, Iguala, Mexico City, and Acapulco, and all of these achieved success as artists in their own right. Among the original silversmiths Spratling found in Taxco was Guadalupe Castellanos. Like the other older smiths, Castellanos was accustomed to making trinkets and costume jewelry. He became one of the most accomplished of the primitive artists, allowing his personality, dark and brooding, to show in his finished work, just as Spratling had taught.

Spratling wrote: "The element of design is the most precious element and a designer's style is not something that may be developed overnight. It is no accident. A style is molded by a sensitive person's own convictions, or tendencies, which he has expressed and experimented with over a period of months, or even years."

Of his artistry and his contributions to the silver industry of Taxco, two leading experts, Mary L. Davis and Greta Pack, wrote: "The combination of an artist, a craft, and a congenial environment can be seen in his workshop where some of the most beautiful and unusual jewelry in the country is made."

11.

Soon after the factory closed in 1945, Spratling bought a chicken ranch at *Taxco-el-Viejo* or Old Taxco, ten miles southwest of town. Next to the highway to Iguala, he built a sprawling hacienda including a miniature version of his former factory. Each year he taught several young workers the skills of silversmithing.

Spratling let each know he had been chosen because he was very talented. One trainee said of Spratling, "The workers respected him. If a piece [of jewelry] was not done perfectly, he would become angry, and the worker did not want to see Don Guillermo's anger or hear such words from him. They worked hard, wanting to impress him with their skill." Nearby was Spratling's own workroom, the blue alcove, where he worked alone, drawing new designs and creating intricate jewelry.

On the land between the road and the small river lived the creatures dear to him: twenty-three Great Danes, seven Siamese cats, and various other animals, including otters, several macaws, deer, a pair of large boa-type snakes, and a small wild boar. Hidden behind thick hedges was a swimming pool where his friend Ted Wick, a writer who came frequently for comida and drinks, found him frolicking in the nude one day with movie star Paulette Goddard. That evening, Ms. Goddard showed up wearing a Spratling silver necklace. The next week a photograph, identifying the jewelry, was featured in a Hollywood newspaper.

Elizabeth Anderson wrote: "Girls . . . would fall for him in droves. He had a dynamic, mesmerizing personality and knew so much about so many things that girls could not resist him." While he enjoyed their company for a while, he made it obvious that he loved no one. It was also rumored that his favorites among the Mexican boys who worked for him also became his temporary lovers.

Now in his forties, Spratling kept to the rigid schedule he had maintained for years. He awakened early, took breakfast at 6 A.M., especially enjoying *chiliquilles*, a Mexican egg dish with tortillas, peppers, and onions, and began work at his desk in the blue alcove. Later his workers joined him in the *taller*, where he oversaw the actual making of the jewelry. Work stopped in early afternoon. He greeted his guests, had drinks, followed by a multiple-course comida. After the meal he retired for *siesta*, then drinks began again—usually martinis straight up—promptly at five. He was generally ready for bed by nine.

12.

Even though he had little money after his factory folded—and could not legally use his name on silver jewelry for a while— Spratling never stopped promoting himself. Any time a famous person came to Taxco, they would eventually—usually through careful planning on Spratling's part—find their way to his *hacienda*. When then–U.S. Senator Lyndon Baines Johnson and his wife, Lady Bird, visited, he took them into the blue alcove. From a drawer he extracted what he said was, "One of my latest pieces," fastening the beautiful silver necklace around the neck of the future first lady. He guided Johnson aside later and asked if he would "talk to the President" (Harry Truman). Several months later, Truman asked Spratling to travel to Alaska and teach Eskimos how to make artifacts from materials indigenous to that region. With great flurry, Spratling accepted the challenge, flew to Alaska in his small plane, and taught Eskimo artists to make items they could sell to tourists. As a result, Spratling was invited to the White House, where President Truman praised his efforts on behalf of the government.

Later, when then–U.S. Senator Richard Nixon and his wife, Pat, visited, Spratling repeated his earlier performance. Later, President Dwight Eisenhower asked Spratling to travel to the Southwest U.S. and teach Indians there. Spratling did so, then attended ceremonies at the White House, where he presented First Lady Mamie Eisenhower with a Spratling necklace.

All of these instances received wide publicity. His fame spread through the world when *Reader's Digest* published "Silver Bill" by journalist J. P. McEvoy, and that article inspired Warner Brothers to make a short-subject film for release in theaters with feature-length movies. Spratling feigned disbelief that anyone could call him "Silver Bill" and said he would not approve the film if that title was used. Instead, Warner Brothers called it "The Man from New Orleans." Picked to play Spratling was Enrique Breceda, a tall handsome mustachioed young Mexican remarkably resembling Spratling. Breceda had married an American girl who was a Bennington College student when she vacationed in Taxco with her mother. He spoke splendid English and had actually been head salesman for Spratling's now-defunct company. Although Spratling displayed unaccustomed humility at the film's first showing in Taxco, friends said that he secretly delighted in its heroic portrayal, although it exaggerated more the myth than the man.

13.

Through the years, Spratling always hated to waste time. Whatever he did, he did it with purpose. He kept his single-engine plane at an airfield near Iguala, thirty twisting miles south of Taxco—a trip he bragged about making in twenty-one minutes. On at least four different occasions, Spratling crashed his plane and walked away unharmed. He took an Indian friend for a pleasure flight one afternoon when the plane struck and killed a bull on takeoff. After an hour of sightseeing, he managed to land the plane without wheels. When he was flying to Mexico City with a box of fresh strawberries for a friend, he headed directly into a thunderstorm, disregarding the danger, and found himself being swept down into thick jungle-like trees, where he crashed and was knocked out. He awakened to find himself covered in red. He raked his fingers across his chest and tasted the sweetness.

Knowing it was only strawberry juice, he climbed down and caught a ride into the city. He wrote later: "I have always felt that to be able to drive a car well or fly a plane is somehow integral with the same sense of line which produces a good draftsman. These things—plus my feeling for three-dimensional form—have given flavor to my life and have filled it with adventure."

14.

When his friend Diego Rivera gave him a small stone figure from an early classic period of Mexican history, Spratling regarded it as the beginning of another phase of his life. Again, he saw purposeful drama in a simple act of generosity. From earlier evenings in New Orleans, listening to Frans Blom talking about Chiapas, Spratling had been interested in archaeology. Rivera's gift renewed that interest.

Spratling set out on adventures he would personally publicize to add to his already considerable mystique. He flew his plane south to San Cristobal de las Casas to visit Blom, who took him into the Lacandon rain forest and showed him the temples of Bonampak. High on the banks of the Rio Usumacinta the two men climbed the steep stone stairs into the Mayan towers at the temples of Yaxchilan. Here Blom introduced Spratling to Indians who gave him a treasure of artifacts that he brought home to Rancho Spratling.

In Mexico City, he befriended George Vaillant, whom he called "the most brilliant American archaeologist ever to work here in Mexico." Vaillant, then writing his classic *The Aztecs of Mexico*, took Spratling to meet his aunt, Zelia Nattall, who had tracked down the Mixtec Codex known as the Nattall Codex. Her gathering of picture-writing and its phonetic pronunciations and meanings were considered the greatest and most complete in the world.

238

At Dona Nattall's home, *Casa de Alvarado* in Coyoacan in the southern suburbs of Mexico City, she took Spratling through her fabulous garden, showing him her Aztec herbal plants used for various medicinal purposes. When he expressed interest in each of the herbs, she presented him with cuttings, which he took back to Taxco-el-Viejo and cultivated with care. From that moment on, according to his self-promotion, he was an expert in medicinal plants.

On his afternoon with Dona Nattall—a time he later recalled as one of the most important of his life—Spratling sat in the chair where British novelist D. H. Lawrence had sat years earlier. With vibrant intensity, she recounted her trips into the jungles of Tobasco, Chiapas, and Veracruz, where she had discovered the hidden language of the ancient people. As he said good-bye, she held out to him a small clay figure which, she said, was made by the Olmecs in southern Veracruz during a classic period.

"He did not simply collect," said his old acquaintance Danny Branman, "he bought and sold. He had a large number of pieces from the state of Guerrero, but he did not think as highly of them as he did the classic works from other parts of Mexico. It was illegal to sell outside the country. But he had buyers fly in from New York, London, Paris. He would sell to them. What they did with the pieces, he did not know, or care." However, at various times, he gave important pieces of pre-Columbian sculpture to several Mexican museums, always followed by headlines and photographs.

After publishing numerous articles on pre-Columbian art, in 1960 he put together a coffee-table-sized book on the subject, *More Human Than Divine,* with black-and-white photographs by Manuel Alvarez Bravo, whom Spratling called "the Edward Weston of Mexican photographers." Again, Spratling spread the word of his own mastery, writing: "I have become increasingly interested in certain types of ancient art, the so-called 'primitive arts,' a misnomer, since the works executed by these ancient people tend to be far more sophisticated and more sensitively executed than the works of our contemporary eclectics. The enduring qualities of their art result in a solution to a design problem which could only have been solved by one single individual, sometimes resolved again and again over many centuries, always toward a greater perfection in a given culture."

15.

At age 62, Spratling came home to Alabama. In December of 1962, Auburn University bestowed upon him an honorary doctorate in humane letters—a gesture that, in Spratling's mind, validated his entire professional life. After the ceremonies, he was whisked off to his grandfather's old farm where "bourbon flowed and there were intimate memories dredged up out of the past."

When he returned to Taxco-el-Viejo, he lived a quieter, more sedate life, still creating his jewelry but socializing less and less.

After Lyndon Johnson became President, he invited Spratling to Washington, and the First Lady appeared at dinner wearing her Spratling jewelry. Again, the fact somehow found its way into print.

When John Palmer Leeper, director of the Marion Koogler McNay Art Institute of San Antonio, Texas, visited the Rancho, he suggested a retrospective to be entitled "The World of William Spratling." The show of twenty-three pieces of fine sculpture and Spratling's books and illustrations was so successful it inspired a six-page article in *Architectural Digest*. After the show traveled to other museums across the U.S., Spratling himself engineered the expanded opening at Mexico City's *La Escuela Nacional de Artesanos* "with considerable pomp," as he described it.

After his death in 1967, the award for the country's leading silver artist of the year, given at the end of Silver Week every November, was named the Spratling Prize. Each year, thousands of tourists walk along Calle Guillermo Spratling, one of the many winding little streets protected by the Act of Congress that he had sought and won. Tourists stand before the handsome bust of the man and study his finely wrought features near the buildings where he once lived and worked. Then they parade through the small *zócalo*, past the Santa Prisca church, to the William Spratling Museum where many of the pieces from his vast collection of pre-Columbian art are on display.

I FIRST WROTE about Spratling as "Auburn Man, Mexican Hero" in the *Alabama Magazine* in the early 1980s. My friend Ted Wick in Taxco talked with a number of Spratling's friends and former students about the maestro. Wick, who had known Spratling very well in his last years, was quite a character in his own right. As publicist for Frank Sinatra and later his daughter, Nancy, and her then-husband, singer Tommy Sand, Wick first discovered Taxco in the early 1960s when he visited "the perfect little Italian town for a movie the newlyweds planned to make together." Wick fell in love with Taxco, and after he suffered a heart attack while working in Hollywood, he decided to move south of the border. He bought a great old hacienda on a ridge opposite the town.

When the great recession of the early 1970s hit Mexico and the peso was devalued, Wick lost much of his savings, forcing him to sell his beloved home that later became the Hacienda del Solar, a fine hotel where my wife, Sally, and I stayed a number of times. Once we awakened in one of the casitas, stepped onto a balcony, and found ourselves overlooking a sunlit hillside covered in magnificent red poinsettias. I told Sally it looked like the earth was on fire. Wick, who for years wrote a Taxco gossip column for the

English-language *Mexico City News*, invited us to comida at his house on one of the up-and-down curving cobblestone streets of Taxco. Guests with us were Enrique and Nora Breceda, who told us about his starring in Warner Brothers' short subject film about Spratling, and about their romance that blossomed in the early 1940s. Nora, a teenager who'd accompanied her parents to Europe every summer while growing up, came to Taxco because the fighting of World War II kept them from crossing the Atlantic. She met the tall, dark, and handsome Mexican, fell in love with him, and they raised a family in Taxco.

I met with Wick and many of his friends from time to time in Acapulco and Taxco, and we had extended correspondence about the famed silver designer. In 2001, *Alabama Heritage*, a history quarterly published by the University of Alabama and the University of Alabama at Birmingham, ran my article "William Spratling." It was condensed slightly from the version that appears here.

Juan Quezada: Feeling the Heart of the Earth

With the exquisite touch of fingers that have grappled in the dirt floor of the desert where he lives in rural Chihuahua in northwest Mexico, Juan Quezada first felt the magic within the earth as a boy of twelve. He picked up shards of pots made by ancient prehistoric Indians. He gazed upon the intricate designs still vibrant after more than a thousand years. His fingers felt the smooth texture of the clay, and deep within he felt the throbbing pulse of artists of yesterday.

During the next dozen years, he listened to elders in the tiny community of Mata Ortiz, which stretches several streets deep along the railroad tracks where once upon a time General Francisco "Pancho" Villa and his revolutionary troops captured trains that ran through the desolate valley, where the Indians once made their home in this arid atmosphere.

Juan Quezada, an intense, compact man whose masculine persona matured as his art developed, wears a fine white-felt Stetson with a wide brim that shades his sharp Indian features: a prominent eagle's beak, deep-set chocolate brown eyes, chiseled high cheekbones shaded the same patina as the tan earth. His sand-colored jeans fit snugly to his wiry frame. His green western shirt and snakeskin boots fill a color scheme. He spoke in a Spanish as weighted with thought as the complex, intricate drawings on his pottery.

"I felt the strength of the ancients in the earth," Juan Quezada said. He was without English and I have little Spanish, but I depended on friends to translate, although his eyes and his gestures spoke as strongly as his words. "I felt the earth come alive in my hands." He cupped his hands below his chin. His fingers quivered. "*Es poderoso!* Powerful."

As a youth in this town of Mata Ortiz, Juan Quezada heard the call of the earth and felt it tremble under his fingers that were beginning to understand — as his mind was just beginning to comprehend the history that surrounded him. For both the earth and the history were complicated things, and he knew he would need help to bring the two together to join within himself. He started school at age nine and quit three years later. Instead of attending class, he took the family burro into the hills in search of firewood to sell to neighbors.

After summer rains, which left the dust of his world a sea of mud, he reached down and picked it up. With movements as natural as his rolling country-boy gait, he began shaping the mud. Into the mud he crumbled the fascinating shards of old Indian pots he had collected from the arroyo, to the north of the railroad tracks at the place where the ancients once lived centuries earlier.

As the mud hardened into clay he held it up to the sun and felt its warmth and recognized the difference between the raw product of his land and the makings of a pot that now rested in his palms. But his piece of art was not finished. It broke too easily. It did not have a unique design and it did not hold the sheen that he envisioned.

In his walks near the river to the south he found shards of the ancient pottery colored with various dyes. He studied the makeup of the shards, rubbing them between his fingers, staring at the shaded surface beneath the sunlight in the morning and in the late afternoon. In the distance, toward the mountain called El Indio, because it resembled the profile of an Indian looking skyward, he found hardened chunks of yellow and red and black and even blue, all natural materials that had developed over time within the earth. He brought the materials back to his yard at the little adobe house next to the Palanganas River. By now the rustic patio was beginning to be transformed into a workshop. He ground the colored material into dust to be worked into the mud to add color and design.

He investigated various methods to form and to shape his pots. He explored the traditional, adding his own inventions, twisting and turning, dreaming. One form melted with another. His dreams began to sharpen into frozen images. He never worked with a wheel as other, more traditional potters did; he felt the necessity to physically and emotionally feel the clay. He came to know that the work had to be shapened by his fingers, in the turn of his hand, and in the rhythm of his fingers working together to squeeze power into and out of the raw materials. He built a cup-shaped base from a hard substance, then fitted a tortilla-shaped, thin and round piece of clay inside this form to use it as his base, then he rolled out one coil of clay from which he would form the shape of his pot. Out of this single coil he would create the entire thin-walled pot. As he worked it with his fingers the colors flowed together, blending—iron oxide deposits making vibrant reds and others turning the clay black as midnight.

For the visitors from the U.S., Italy, Germany, and Spain, he showed how he sanded a pot's surface after it had been shaped, how he applied a thin layer of vegetable oil with a soft cloth, then rubbed it lovingly with his bare hands, covering all of the surface several times, then rubbing it again with another cloth, until the surface was so smooth it could take one line of paint, if that was his desire.

He tried various ways to strengthen the walls of the pots and to give them a special, individual hue. To decorate, he cut the hair from his head and built brushes which he used to etch designs, the most intricate of which was formed with strands of hair to paint a tiny line going around and around and around the exterior of a pot.

"Design is a dream," he said, pointing to his head. "It takes shape in the imagination." He pronounced the word *imaginación* with emphasis.

For many elaborate designs, he draws in his mind, picturing the scheme completely before he actually begins work on the still-damp pot.

Unlike other potters who paint their pots while still wet, Quezada learned to let the clay dry completely before painting it. After painting the pot, a process that takes upward of three to three-and-a-half hours, the artist covers the design with a protective layer of clear liquid, then he rubs this layer with a polishing stone to give the pot surface sheen. A slick round river-tumbled agate is used to cover every inch of the surface, the artist barely touching the exterior, using his sensitive touch to guide his fingers.

At this point, Quezada tried various techniques of firing, to bring about the final exact temperature to burn into the center of the pot and make it a living, breathing, pulsating piece of art, and not merely a vessel. He discovered that if he built a wire cage to hold the pot, then stacked half-dried cow dung around the pot, building a shell, and he set fire to the dung, it would burn quickly, and when it fell away the pot was perfect.

Through the years, Juan Quezada changed and refined each step of the process. As Walter P. Parks points out in his 1993 book, *The Miracle of Mata Ortiz*, the artist no longer uses slipping or painting with a light beige clay as a base for design and he no longer paints and polishes a pot while it is still wet. However, in the spring of 2001, Quezada said that he has changed his work significantly. "I am always changing," he said. "I am always seeking perfection."

"I learned from the ancients," Juan Quezada said. "I learned by feeling the soul of the clay, by carrying the shards from the pots a thousand years old next to my heart, by feeling the heat burn into my body. I use only the materials that were available to the ancients, when they lived here and worked here and made their pots here."

When he worked, he worked in a concentrated rhythm, as later observers realized as they watched, photographed, and tried to draw his attention away from the business at hand. Once he had begun the process he was into it all the way. Once while doing a demonstration at Wichita State University, rain began pouring down while Juan prepared his firing, piling the dung from grass-fed cows around his pot in beehive fashion, lighting it, and burning. Upon completion, Quezada, soaking wet, lifted the glowing pot with a poker, set it down before his audience, and they gazed in amazement at the perfect results.

EVEN AFTER he began making pots, however, life was not easy. As a young man — the sixth of eleven children — he had traveled to Chihuahua City and Ciudad Juarez and into Texas and Arizona looking for work. In 1964, when he was 24 years old, he met 19-year-old Guillermina Olivas Reyes from the farming community of Namiquipa. Visiting friends and looking for work, she met and fell in love with the handsome potter. After they were married they moved to Namiquipa, where Juan worked raising beans as a sharecropper. But he was not making enough money to feed his fast-growing family. He and his wife, Guille, would have a total of

247

eight children. They moved back to Mata Ortiz, he went to work for the railroad, and they lived in a boxcar. It was during this time that he finally learned his firing technique and began selling pots to traders from nearby towns. At first, unsigned pots were sold as prehistoric work.

By 1976, anthropologist Spencer MacCallum, who had had a long love affair with Mexico, the country's history, and Latin American art, found several interesting pots in a New Mexican junk shop. He was so impressed by the work he decided to track down the potter. In his exuberance, he discovered Juan Quezada in the tiny dusty village of Mata Ortiz. By that time Juan had been free from railroad work for a year.

With MacCallum buying all of his pieces, guaranteeing him $300 a month, and arranging for shows and publicity at museums and galleries throughout the Southwest U.S., Quezada was free to work. For years the two men enjoyed a relationship that worked for both. MacCallum, who visited Mata Ortiz frequently, was genuinely taken with Quezada's enormous talent, and he publicized it with gusto. However, after Quezada's fame and popularity grew and the prices of his work reached new heights, others expressed interest in his art and planted seeds of skepticism about the arrangement with MacCallum, and soon thereafter the two parted ways.

In the summer of 1982, Quezada was invited to teach at the Idyllwild School of Music and the Arts (ISOMATA) in the San Jacinto Mountains of Southern California. There, he met fellow artist Tom Fresh, who acted as his interpreter, and the two became friends. The following year Fresh made his way to Mata Ortiz, became enchanted by the Quezada family of potters—by now Juan had taught two of his brothers, his sisters, and several of his children the art of pottery—and Fresh returned many times. Such began a new personal and business relationship.

Joining Fresh on a trip to Mata Ortiz was an associate from ISOMATA, Walter P. Parks, a fellow Californian who had displayed a deep interest in art and especially Quezada's pottery. For a while, he too helped sell and distribute Quezada's pottery to dealers.

After the bishop of the Diocese of Nuevo Casas Grandes commissioned Juan Quezada to make a pot especially for the Pope, who visited Ciudad Chihuahua in May of 1990, several Japanese businesspeople became interested in his art. And when a Japanese conglomerate began buying Quezada pots at much higher prices, the artist left both Fresh and Parks behind—sometimes promising pots and not delivering them, sometimes obviously selling them at higher prices to the foreigners.

An El Paso newspaper quoted Mrs. Reiko Horiguchi, a major art collector and owner of a Tokyo gallery, saying that Juan's work had "natural purity." She spoke with respect for his aversion to modern techniques and compared his work to the honored simplicity of the ancient tea ceremony in her native country. And after she spent several days at Mata Ortiz, watching Juan shaping and firing his pots, she told the press that she planned to recreate his workshop in a museum in Japan.

Shortly thereafter, however, the Japanese buying spree proved fickle. Some continued to purchase pots, but not with the overflowing enthusiasm that they once exhibited. The contractual arrangement became cluttered and confused. For a serious artist, business problems created disastrous delays in his work schedule and cost him money to boot—once being stuck with a $3,000 shipping bill for rejected pots returned from the Orient.

When Juan approached Walter Parks about being his exclusive agent in the U.S., Parks explained that Quezada was *"un hombre muy independiente"* and should not require a contract but should simply sell on "a first-come basis."

In 1993, Walter Parks's book *The Miracle of Mata Ortiz* detailed the long and arduous story of Juan Quezada and his art. The author was careful to include numerous other potter-artists whose fame had not reached the heights of the master. One was Andres Villalba, who also made a pot that was presented to the Pope in 1990 and whose work has been chosen for exhibition by the University of New Mexico Art Museum. Villalba died in May of 2001.

By this time the Quezada family had purchased the former Hotel Colon, a multiple-room single-story ancient adobe building opposite the railroad track on Calle Ferrocarril, with living room space that could easily become a gallery and display area for Juan's awards that he had been presented through the years. In the rear was a spacious patio and beyond that a workshop area. At last he had ample working room where he could stretch his talents skyward.

When I visited in the spring of 2001, also aimed at the sky was the Direct TV antenna mounted on the roof. Inside, around the large kitchen table, sat several members of the Quezada family and several neighbors, watching a soccer match, cheering for their team.

Juan Quezada not only began an ambitious printmaking program, which he marketed through a gallery in Albuquerque, his larger pots became more expansive and expensive. In 1998, he was chosen to be included in *Great Masters of Mexican Folk Art*, an illustrative collection sponsored by Fomento Cultural Banamex. By 1999, when he was honored with the enormously prestigious National Prize in Sciences and Arts in the field of Arts and Popular Traditions, the Mexican government's highest award, he had reached a pinnacle beyond his wildest dreams. He became the only artist from the state of Chihuahua ever to have won this accolade.

With a winning, playful smile on his sun-brown lips, Juan Quezada spoke of being an ill-educated country boy from a little village in the middle of a great desert. Listening, deciphering his Spanish tongue in my Southern mind, I thought about many others I'd heard throughout the years in Alabama and across Mexico, men and women of world-class talent and intelligence, talking about themselves and their universe in the same tone, delightfully playing a game: matching demonstrated talent with a humble front, his persona filling a room with his grace and affable manner. He wore his wide-brimmed white Stetson the same way Paul W. "Bear" Bryant wore his red-and-white baseball cap or his black-and-white houndstooth hat: with a comfortable look of deep-seated self-confidence.

As the *Great Masters* described Juan Quezada's art: "Stirring up the earth and the past. Giving form and life to the clay. Trying to discover and understand the creative and artistic techniques of one's ancestors, their forms of working in pottery, this art that gives the clay concept, image and beauty. Seeking and finding the ways in which the hands can form, emit and diffuse. Achieving an expression that transcends time and space."

The Death Mask of Frida

It leaps up,
full of life,
flaming,
red as blood,
lingering,
branding life
on a dead society.

Tortured pupils
reflect suffering
of Mao's mother,
Trotsky's lover,
without regret,
and it is called
a political statement.

Her insides
erupted
onto canvas,
breathing
delicate
rhythms
of a wounded deer,
and showing
a sweet toughness
to an insincere
universe.

Honey dripped
alcohol tears
and Demerol sweat
without regret
while demons dance
and big-eyed girls
work
and love
with parted thighs
for the world to see
through a blood-stained
telescope.

She bounded up
from the flames,
grinning
beneath the torch
reaching out,
grimacing coyly,
a shy doe,
a battered whore,
reaching out,
for her darling
Diego.

Written after I visited Casa Azul, Frida Kahlo's house in the suburb of Coyoacan in Mexico City, and after I returned home to Alabama and read her biography, *Frida*, and discovered that during her cremation her body bounded upright as if to fight death. I not only felt great empathy for this woman who had lived much of her life in agony with a tortured spine much like my own—spending much of her time in a body cast as I had experienced when I was fourteen years old—but I was so taken with the multiple images of her that I wrote this poem. Then I sent it to my friend Sue Walker in Mobile and she published it in *Negative Capability*, Volume XII, Number 1 & 2, 1992.

*

Diego Rivera & Frida Kahlo:
Gentle Giant, Tortured Soul

*

1.

His birthplace is a simple house on a narrow, winding street in the town built on the hills of the frogs. Perhaps it was with a purpose that the great artist Diego Rivera had eyes that bulged, like a frog's, from his enormous head. The four-storied house where the Rivera family had an apartment on the third floor is painted red and has a small brass plaque next to the entrance proclaiming it Museo de Diego Rivera on Calle Pocitos in Guanajuato.

The first floor is furnished with period furniture like that used in 1886 when Maria Rivera, who had given birth to three stillborn babies in the first three years of marriage to schoolteacher Diego Rivera, lay in the throes of childbirth. On the morning of December 8th, she gave birth to twin boys and named them Diego Maria Rivera and Carlos Maria Rivera. It is not without interest that Diego's birth is shrouded with as much mystery and controversy as his adult life. Later, as a young art student in Paris, he told his friend Pablo Picasso that at birth his heartbeat was so weak that the midwife attending his mother actually threw his tiny body into

253

the slop-jar or dung-bucket before his grandmother retrieved him. She killed several pigeons and wrapped his little body in their warm entrails, keeping his blood circulating.

Little Carlos, who had always been sickly, died during his second year. As soon as little Diego could grip a pencil in his tiny hands, he began drawing. When I visited the Museo in the winter of 2000, the second, third, and fourth floors of the red house on the narrow cobblestone street near the Church of San Diego were lined with paintings and drawings by the greatest painter in the history of Mexico.

Although these paintings change from time to time, in November of 2000, the first that I saw was a small picture of a bust of Julius Caesar. Probably done from a photo or a painting of the original bust, it showed perfection in its most minute detail: every crack and crevice a sure representation. It was finished in Diego Rivera's twelfth year. Nearby was a perfect farm scene from central Mexico: a pastoral of a rural house, a pasture, cows standing near a pleasant stream. It was painted when he was fourteen.

After the family moved to the bustling capital at Mexico City, ten-year-old Rivera was sent to San Carlos Academy of Fine Arts. It was there that he trained in drawing, first copying the masters, tuning his hand at draftsmanship under the tutelage of a master. Among his first finished works were images of the streets of the city with the snow-capped peaks of the two volcanoes, Iztaccihuatl and Popocatepetl, looming in the background. At the school, Rivera doubtless heard much heated talk of liberal politics. He had been exposed to such talk early in life from his father, who felt betrayal by the heavy-handed regime of dictator Porfirio Diaz. While others around him grew wealthy, the elder Rivera never made much money as a teacher. Having heard the liberal tone of his father's conversation, young Rivera moved easily into *El Grupo Bohemio*, a group of young art students who revolved around the teachings and personality of Gerardo Murillo, the revolutionary who called himself Dr. Atl. This was the same Dr. Atl whom William Spratling years later befriended and learned about classical Mexican architecture.

Rivera, eager and enthusiastic, sat for hours and listened to the one-eyed Atl tell of his European experiences, how he had been influenced by Post-Impressionists Cezanne, Gauguin, and others. He also talked passionately about politics of anarchism. And while Rivera later claimed a lifelong commitment to revolution and communism, as a student he worked diligently at perfecting his art. In 1906, the twenty-year-old lost a fellowship for a year's study in Europe to his number-one competitor, Roberto Montenegro of Guadalajara. Rivera's father, who had by now begun to work within the system of Diaz's government and had cultivated a friendship with Teodoro A. Dehesa, governor of Veracruz, talked to the politician on his son's behalf. Dehesa granted the youth an audience. He was so impressed by the young man and his work that he offered three hundred pesos a month to allow Diego to live and work in Europe.

First in Spain and later in Paris, Diego Rivera studied the masters, spent hours and days in museums, then rubbed elbows with the finest of the moderns, including Picasso. His work during the next few years showed strong patterns, shades of colors, views of the universe, and visions expressed by other artists he deemed his superior.

2.

While traveling in rural France in 1909, Rivera met a young Russian named Angelina Beloff from St. Petersburg. Three years younger than Diego, she too was an apprentice artist who'd undergone training at the Russian Academy of Fine Arts in the same tradition of San Carlos Academy. Angelina was traveling in the company of fellow artist Maria Blanchard, a Mexican who had also attended San Carlos. They went to the port town of Burges, where they met Diego. At first the beautiful, petite, blonde Angelina was turned off by the large, boisterous, dark, ugly Diego. He conversed with Maria Blanchard in fever-pitched Spanish, a language Angelina barely knew. When Maria and Angelina spoke French, Diego was left out. Finally he spoke to her in the language he knew best: making a charcoal sketch he called *Night Scene of Burges*, dedicating it to "Mademoiselle Angelina Beloff as a sign of my affection." Through art, he could speak to her without words.

While they soon adored each other and began an affair, Rivera later stated that he made her life miserable. In 1910, he returned to Mexico to visit with his patron, Governor Dehesa at Jalapa, the capital of Veracruz. Angelina returned to Russia. According to several of his biographers, Rivera years later manufactured stories for his autobiography showing that he returned to his home an impassioned revolutionary with plans to overthrow the Diaz regime. He told about smuggling explosives into the country to give to a friend who planned Diaz's assassination. In fact, at a November exhibition of his paintings he was proclaimed "a great artist" by the president's wife, Dona Carmelita Diaz, who not only opened the show but bought six of Diego's paintings. However, he did travel south to Morelos to find Emiliano Zapata, the charismatic rebel leader. Diego, who later dressed in all black with matching wide-brimmed sombrero, and who later painted Zapata in several of his murals, admired Zapata's audacity and verve as well as his revolutionary spirit. But when the movement appeared doomed, Rivera decided in 1911 to return to Europe and his art and Angelina.

The two young artists moved into an apartment in Paris as husband and wife. During the following two years, most art experts agree that Rivera's work matured enormously with large canvases such as *The Old Ones* and *View of Toledo*. During this time he became friends with Picasso. Both were being influenced strongly by the Cubist movement. Picasso was known as a notorious thief of other artists' ideas, and Diego was convinced that the Spanish artist copied his *Zapatista Landscape* in Picasso's *Seated Man*, done later the same year. Today a visitor to Mexico City may peruse *Zapatista Landscape* or *El Guerrillero* in the Museo Nacional de Arte. In it, the artist believed he captured the heart of his country's spirit: the warrior clothed in the various colors of the countryside, armed, with the snow-capped peak of a mountain in the background.

Although the revolution in Mexico was raging and Diaz was overthrown, the government of Francisco Madero continued Rivera's fellowship. Then Madero was murdered by Victoriano Huerta, the country was thrust into a civil war of revolutionary against revolutionary, and Rivera found himself having to support his lifestyle solely with his art.

3.

According to biographers, while Angelina was giving birth in 1916 to their son, Diego, Rivera began an affair with Russian artist Marevna Vorobev. In the midst of emotional turmoil, he lashed out verbally against leading Cubists, including his old friend Picasso. At age fourteen months, the baby died. Later Rivera stated that he broke off his affair with Marevna after the baby's death, but nearly two years later she too became pregnant. While he worked hard painting portraits, at the same time studying Italian Renaissance masters, Marevna gave birth to his daughter, Marika. Rivera moved from one woman to the other, then left both in 1920 for a trip through Italy to study paintings there. It was in a small chapel in Florence that biographer Patrick Marnham wrote that, while standing in front of a fresco by Masaccio, the true artist in Diego Rivera was born. Rivera, Marnham wrote, "was not looking at the painting. His attention had turned to a muralist's scaffold by his side. It was a wooden pyramid, five ascending platforms, connected by ladders and mounted on wheels. Rivera made a detailed sketch of the platform." The whole idea of working on a project larger than life, larger than his own six-feet six-inches, appealed to Rivera.

Indeed, the incident, happening when it did, changed Rivera's life. Soon, after another murder of another Mexican president, Venustiano Carranza, when General Alvaro Obregon took over the reins of government, Rivera left Europe and the women with whom he was having torrid love affairs. He returned to Mexico to find Jose Vasconcelos in the position of Minister of Education. Long a friend of the arts, Vasconcelos was close to Rivera's old compadres from the San Carlos Academy, Dr. Atl and David Alfaro Siqueiros.

Rivera showed Vasconcelos examples of his work, but the educator was not impressed. However, he did manage to give Rivera an appointment to teach in the university's fine arts department at a meager salary. In the meantime, for the magazine *El Maestro*, Rivera explored the country's artistic and cultural world. He wrote: "On my arrival in Mexico I was struck by the inexpressible beauty of that rich and severe, wretched and exuberant land. All the colors I saw appeared to be heightened; they were clearer, richer, finer, and more full of light." It is what other artists found through the years, when Europeans moved west and North Americans moved south, struck by the same conflicting elements and the light that shone so brightly.

In time, Vasconcelos turned over to Rivera a wall in the National Preparatory School that included a broad archway. He would paint *Creation,* began making full-scale drawings and studying the various techniques of mural-painting. The artist positioned himself on a scaffold and surrounded himself with a team of technical assistants. He surveyed his space and prepared to work within the limits of the blank wall.

Rivera drew on his entire scope of training, brought into play his travels and education, and gathered his knowledge into that room where he stood tall on the scaffold and made his broad strokes. Today, in the Amfiteatro Bolivar, the rainbow of colors shows twenty figures in *Creation,* figures with bowed heads, closed eyes, eyes beholding the sight of wonder, a creation that is itself a sight to behold. When he painted it, there was a huge organ with high pipes that thrust upward from the floor, and Rivera tried to incorporate the organ into his vision. Now, the organ is no longer present and there is a hole where the trunk of the tree of life once sat. Nevertheless, the mural is still a feat of great accomplishment—especially when one considers that it was his first attempt at the new technique.

During the time of his painting *Creation* two events occurred that again changed his life. He met the tall, gorgeous, black-haired Guadalupe Marin, whom he found "a strange and marvelous-looking creature." In his studio he immediately began drawing her portrait. He wrote later: "Her green eyes were so transparent she seemed to be blind. Her face was an Indian's, the mouth with its full, powerful lips open, the corners drooping like those of a tiger . . . her long muscular legs made me think of the legs of a filly." And he joined the Mexican Communist Party. In late 1922, while he was finishing *Creation,* Lupe posed nude as the woman in the bottom left corner of the mural. Soon thereafter, he and Lupe were married.

Another of the female figures in the mural, representing the virtue of prudence, was beautiful young Maria Dolores Asunsolo, who later became the film star Dolores Del Rio with whom Diego had an affair.

His mural opened to the public in March of 1923. It was immediately criticized by fellow muralists and the artistic community, saying that—rather than applying his own creative talents—he was merely following the dictates of Vasconcelos, who was not himself entirely satisfied with the work, saying that Rivera had "too much Picasso in his head."

Rivera persisted, assuring Vasconcelos that he had only begun as a muralist, that he had a far greater vision with which to celebrate the revolution and the entire country. After returning from a trip to Tehuantepec in Oaxaca near the Pacific, where he witnessed Zapotec Indians with their colorful costumes, he painted a simple but elegant portrait entitled *The Bather of Tehuantepec*, which caught Vasconcelos's eye. Not long after, Rivera finally persuaded the minister to allow him to paint 128 panels on the walls of three floors of the Ministry of Education building in downtown Mexico City, within several blocks of the Zócalo.

4.

On March 23, 1923, Rivera began work on another of his many masterpieces. Today, as the visitor walks slowly through the patios of the Ministry, usually hundreds of school children from across the city and the country sit on the floors staring up into the faces of their ancestors.

Using the technique of fresco-painting which he'd seen on the walls in Italy, applied by the Rennaissance artists, Rivera began to outline the history of his country through its people. He found in the faces of laborers the heart and soul that he sought to embody in his work. Overcome with joy and amazement, his brushes danced across the space, filling it with an emotional and intellectual splash of colors. His heart was in the earth where his subjects worked: the silver miners of Taxco and Guanajuato, the farmers of Sonora and Chihuahua, the foot soldiers who followed first Hidalgo and Allende and later Villa and Zapata, the street vendors of small towns and huge cities, the mothers caring for children, and the teacher in a classroom. Where he had previously been eager and anxious, a student of art, now he felt a burning in his brain with the same intensity he felt when his loins caught fire at the touch of a beautiful woman.

For the next year he worked as hard and long as he'd ever painted, until Vasconcelos resigned and his fellow artists insisted that Diego also stop. Just as his wife gave birth to their daughter, Rivera resigned from the Communist Party and took another mural assignment in the National Agricultural School in a former hacienda at Chapingo, outside the city.

Diego had already met and become infatuated with a lovely young Italian-American actress who had begun modeling for his assistants. In 1923, Tina Modotti started an affair with famous photographer Edward Weston, whose nudes of her quickly gained wide recognition. She confided in Rivera that she too was interested in photography, and he asked if she would record his work at the Ministry. She took photos that he praised as perfect. When he chose to paint an eruption of sexual forces in the frescoes at Chapingo, explaining that he felt the need to explore the imagery of his and Lupe's sexual harmony, it was actually Tina Modotti who accompanied him as his new model and lover.

Although the message of his Chapingo mural is convoluted with socialist doctrine, the painting itself is a uniquely powerful representation of the nude female form in several beatific poses that many years later would be idolized by many of the Beatnik and Zen poets and philosophers. In the two distinct panels he attempts to blend his distrust and even hatred for the church and its priests with his obvious sensual fascination with Tina's luscious and even voluptuous body. The result is a confusing yet forceful message.

While he was finishing his work at Chapingo, Rivera met a young visitor from the north named William Spratling, who was impressed with Diego's new work. They became friends, and in the next few years, Spratling wrote glowing pieces about the magnificence of Rivera's art in influential magazines in the U.S., and Rivera introduced Spratling to the elite of the Mexican art world.

In Rivera's politics, which for a while overpowered his art, he showed even more confusion. He traveled to Russia, where in Moscow he became so embroiled in anti-Soviet politics that he was asked to leave. Even so, his European journey was a success. He had become an international celebrity. Modigliani's *Portrait of Diego Rivera* sold for six figures in Paris. Rivera was wined and dined by the royalty of the art world.

5.

Back in Mexico, where Lupe had divorced him, he lived the life of a successful and much-sought-after playboy. Although he was a huge man — six-feet six-inches tall and three hundred pounds, with eyes that bulged from a gigantic head — many women obviously found him sexually attractive. Consorts said that while he seldom bathed, he was full of humorous exuberance, brilliant conversation, and tender, even sensuous charm. Although he was seen at the most popular spots around the city almost every night with a different woman — some of them visiting *norte Americanas* who came south to flirt with promiscuity — his art did not suffer. He finished several canvases and the Ministry of Education panels on which he'd been working off and on for six years. In one of the final panels he painted his former lover Modotti as a nun and used one of her young friends, Frida Kahlo, as a revolutionary. They had met at a party at Modotti's apartment when, full of drink and fun, Diego pulled a pistol and shot a phonograph Tina had been playing. Frida wrote, "I began to be very interested in him in spite of the fear I had of him."

Later, Kahlo added that she had met the artist years earlier when she was still a teenager. She was recuperating from injuries received while riding in a bus that was in a collision on a downtown street. When the bus to the suburb of Coyoacan reached the corner of Cuahutemotzin and Cinco de Mayo, preparing to turn onto Calzada de Tlalpan, a trolley from Xochimilco slammed into it. Frida Kahlo was thrown forward. "A handrail pierced me the way a sword pierces a bull," she wrote later. Her friend, Alejandro Gomez Arias, who was accompanying her, remembered that her clothes were torn from her body that was bleeding profusely. Another passenger spilled gold onto her, and when people saw her, "they cried, 'La bailarina, la bailarina!' With the gold on her red, bloody body, they thought she was a dancer.

"I picked her up . . . and then I noticed with horror that Frida had a piece of iron in her body. A man said, 'We have to take it out!' He put his knee on Frida's body, and said, 'Let's take it out.' When he pulled it out, Frida screamed so loud that when the ambulance from the Red Cross arrived, her screaming was louder than the siren. Before the ambulance came, I picked up Frida and put her in the display window of a billiard room. I took off my coat and put it over her. I thought she was going to die."

Her spine, already suffering from congenital scoliosis, was broken in several places. Her collarbone and several ribs were broken. Her right leg was fractured in eleven places. Her right foot was crushed. Her left shoulder was out of joint and her pelvis was cracked in three places. The rail had entered her abdomen in the left side and came out through her vagina. Later, she said, that afternoon "I lost my virginity."

In the hospital, where she underwent numerous surgical procedures and was encased in a body cast, she told Alejandro, "Death dances around my bed at night."

While recuperating, she found that drawing and painting helped take her mind away from the physical agony. Back on her feet after months, she showed her works to artist friends, including Orozco, who liked them very much. Then she went to the Ministry of Education where Rivera was working on a high scaffold. Kahlo wrote that she called him down and said, "Look, I have not come to flirt or anything, even if you are a woman-chaser. I have come to show you my painting." He looked over her work and announced, "I am very interested in your painting, above all in this portrait of you, which is the most original. Go home, paint a painting, and next Sunday I will come and see it and tell you what I think." She ended, "This he did and he said, 'You have talent.'"

In his own autobiography, Diego remembered that a girl of about eighteen visited him at the Ministry. "She had a fine nervous body, topped by a delicate face. Her hair was long; dark and thick eyebrows met above her nose. They seemed like the wings of a blackbird, their black arches framing two extraordinary brown eyes."

He remembered going to the home of her parents at 126 Avenida Londres in Coyoacan, where her paintings "filled me with a wonderful joy" and she "became the most important fact in my life. And she would continue to be, up to the moment she died."

However their courtship started, it was a tempestuous relationship. In August of 1929, they were married: he a rotund forty-two-year-old giant and she a petite twenty-two-year-old Indian princess. She knew he was a woman-chaser, as she'd put it. He knew that she was far more rabid in liberal politics than he. Although her internal organs had been battered and torn apart in the wreck, Frida desperately wished to get pregnant and have a child.

6.

The same year they were married, Diego began work on a major mural on the walls of the National Palace. While working on the drawings for his new masterpiece, his friend William Spratling, who by then had become enchanted with the mountain village of Taxco, introduced him to the American ambassador to Mexico, Dwight Morrow, who commissioned Diego to paint another major mural in the Cortes Palace at Cuernavaca.

These two murals on which he worked simultaneously are considered by many Rivera's crowning achievement. At Cuernavaca he recreated his version of a battle between iron-plated Spaniards and Jaguar Indians. In a panel called *The New Religion and the Holy Inquisition*, Rivera continued his retribution against the Catholic church. Again, he showed the Spanish priests as cruel masters who lorded over captive Indians. Morrow asked Rivera if he could paint "at least one kindly priest" and the artist included Fray Toribio de Benevente, a priest known as the "one in rags," who befriended Indians; but Diego still suggested that the church taught kindness to Indians in order to exploit them. Retelling the history of the Spanish Conquest, Rivera again chose a gigantic theme to fill his walls. His new wife, dressed in her long colorful Tehuana skirts, her Indian beads of semiprecious stones, and rainbow-shaded hairpieces, not only posed for his new work but talked with him long into the cool mountain nights about the project. She soon became a very strong influence on his art.

Another panel over an arched doorway portrayed *Revolt*, showing the artist's impressions: Zapata and his white horse, farm workers fighting with their implements, the same Indians being hanged, then, once again, the church taking over the lives of the *compesinos*.

However, while Frida stayed in Cuernavaca, where the Morrows had turned over their villa to the couple while the ambassador and his wife were in Europe, Rivera traveled weekly to Mexico City to work on the massive murals in the National Palace. On those trips he was continuing an affair begun long before with Iona Robinson, one of the young women from the U.S. whom he'd met through Tina Modotti.

Still, Frida became pregnant. Although she stayed under the close scrutiny of a doctor, within several months she suffered a miscarriage—the first of several that would continue to damage her already battered internal organs. Her struggle throughout life was both physical and emotional. Each time she got pregnant, one doctor would prescribe abortion, another would say abortion was too dangerous. As much as she wanted to have a baby, she knew the chances of a successful birth were slight. Her miscarriages became the subject of her most powerful paintings. One entitled *Henry Ford Hospital* showed her naked body hemorrhaging on a suspended bed, a six-pronged umbilical cord attaching her to a fetus with male genitals, a pink torso representing her own twisted frame, two spinal columns showing her scoliosis, a snail, a piece of metal machinery, and a lavender orchid. Another entitled *My Birth* showed a female body naked with knees raised, the upper body covered with a sheet, a baby who resembled her own face, bloody and inert, entering the world from between the mother's spread legs. Both paintings show pain and suffering, a heart that has been battered, a body that has suffered, a soul as lonely as a single butterfly.

Again, at the National Palace, Diego set his sights higher than ever before—so high, as a matter of fact, that he never actually finished the entire project in more than twenty years of work. Perhaps this was by design; Diego Rivera never liked to believe that he had actually finished any mural; he spoke always of "the continuing process" as though it kept him and his art alive with hope for another wall, another chance to tell more of the history about which he felt so deeply.

At the National Palace, new panels showed *The Aztec World, from the Conquest to 1930* and *Mexico Today and Tomorrow*, the first showing the hard-working Indians and their gods of the sun and the moon, then with the conquest of the Spanish, once again the church took power, rendering the Indians helpless, then revolution and violence. In the third panel he painted Frida and several of their friends mixed with images of more than a thousand faces.

Late in 1930, Rivera accepted a commission to paint a mural at the San Francisco School of Fine Arts. This became a huge self-portrait of his work, *The Making of a Fresco*, showing the scaffold and the artists painting: a huge laborer in the center and various aspects of building a city on each side. While in San Francisco, the Pacific Stock Exchange commissioned another, which became *The Allegory of California*, telling the history of the state in fairly simplistic images.

With more money at his disposal—and with the promise of even more rich commissions in the U.S.—Rivera and Kahlo returned to Mexico City and contracted with Mexico's premier architect, Juan O'Gorman, to build their new house and studio in the suburb of San Angel near the famous San Angel Inn, a former mission where Zapata and Villa met face-to-face for the only time. It later became one of the finest restaurants in Mexico City.

Diego and Frida traveled to Detroit, Michigan, where he painted two gigantic murals, then on to New York, where he was commissioned to decorate the lobby of the new Radio Corporation Arts (RCA) building in Rockefeller Center. In March of 1933 the Riveras were among the most popular celebrities in Manhattan. Frida, who had not matched Diego lover-for-lover, had had several male and female lovers, including Georgia O'Keeffe. She also painted: smaller than her husband, on canvas, tin, plates, pottery, whatever she found handy, and her subjects were usually very personal from the point of view of a tortured soul that knew and had known dreadful pain. Critics began to view her work as significant. In a newspaper interview, she was asked how she spent an average day, she answered, "Make love, take a bath, start again . . ."

But it was still Diego who stole the spotlight. When his mural *Man at the Crossroads Looking for Hope and High Vision of a New and Better Future* began to draw attention, first in the *New York World-Telegram* in a story under the headline "Rivera Paints Scenes of Communist Activity — and John D. Jr. Foots Bill," the Rockefellers were outraged. Before the work was publicly unveiled, Nelson Rockefeller ordered the mural destroyed. The reason for its destruction, according to art critic Carla Stellweg, was because "it incensed a public who found it anti-capitalist." As Rivera and his workers, including artist Ben Shahn, were escorted out of the building, others began destroying the mural. That evening about three hundred people gathered to demonstrate against the destruction. They were dispersed and Rivera was told he could return to finish his work. However, when the artist ridiculed Rockefeller at a public meeting, Nelson Rockefeller paid him the rest of his commission and again ordered the mural ripped apart. The entire drama later became a part of the prize-winning Tim Robbins film, *The Cradle Will Rock*.

Upon returning to Mexico, Rivera was given a wall in the *Palacio de Bellas Artes*, where he repeated the work that had been destroyed in New York. Now entitled *Man, Controller of the Universe*, the work never reached the scale and scope that the artist desired. Some critics stated it was like a retold joke, it had lost its punch in the first telling. Overall, Rivera's Marxist theme was too worn and overwrought, his images too blatant.

The Riveras moved into their new Cubist-style house and studios. Diego began drawing Frida's younger sister, Cristina, whose husband had abandoned her. Shortly, they began an affair. Frida, depressed after suffering another miscarriage, moved into an apartment of her own, then traveled to New York, where she sold a number of her paintings at a major show. Reacting to Diego's affair with her sister, Frida cropped her long black hair; later, she painted *Self-Portrait with Cropped Hair*: below a pink sky splotched with billowing clouds, she sat alone on a bright yellow chair in the middle of a red-brown earth scattered with the clipped strands of her once-lovely hair. To me, in this poignant painting, her heart, lonely and tortured, is in the earth. Several months later her divorce from Diego became final.

7.

Through the 1930s they continued their promiscuity. Each took several lovers. When Diego discovered Frida was having an affair with another muralist he threw a fit, shouting and cursing, throwing objects across the floor of his large studio. When Leon Trotsky came to Mexico City, after parting the Soviet Union, Frida moved him into her family home at Casa Azul in Coyoacan. It was there that she took the Russian leader to bed, and their affair began.

Trotsky moved into a nearby house with his wife but continued to see Frida at Casa Azul whenever he could break away. One

Friday night a gunman broke into the new house and riddled the place with machine-gun bullets. Diego learned about the shooting the next morning while he was painting his new lover's portrait at the studio in San Angel. Movie star Paulette Goddard, who was still married to Charlie Chaplin, had traveled to Mexico to meet the great artist and pose for him. They quickly became lovers.

Diego, who had strongly defended Trotsky against his detractors in the Mexican Communist Party, and who had opposed the Soviet pact with Nazi Germany and Italy, rushed to Trotsky's aid. He and Frida moved Trotsky to a more securely barricaded fortress nearby. It was there, some weeks later, behind heavily armored doors, that assassins found Trotsky and bludgeoned him to death with a pick-axe.

Diego fled to San Francisco, where he started a new mural for City College. In Mexico City, Frida's house was searched by *federales*, and she was arrested and questioned for two days. Afraid and despondent, she telephoned Diego, who suggested she come to San Francisco and be with him. Nevertheless, he was still seeing Paulette Goddard. Frida was hospitalized soon after arriving in California. At first, her doctor planned spinal surgery. Then he changed his mind, put her on an alcohol-free diet, and suggested that the two artists remarry. After surgery was canceled, the two remarried on December 8, 1940, Rivera's fifty-fourth birthday.

Returning to Mexico, Rivera decided to build an Aztec palace for himself as his home and studio. He and Frida met with his old friend William Spratling, who advised on the planning of the huge dwelling in a volcanic lava plain on the edge of the city at Anahuacalli. It would be a place to live and work with his art and his pre-Columbian sculpture and artifacts, molding together all that had become a part of his tempestuous and complex personality.

Stone pillars form an entrance, rising out of the earth. A stone bridge crosses a moat, leading to the structure with high, slanting granite walls. The feeling of an Aztec temple persists, like one has entered the Temple of the Sun. Stairways move down, down, down into the cavern-like structure with its opaque onyx slits as windows. The light is felt, rather than seen, as it seeps through the walls. Serpents' heads and snake bodies have been sculpted into the high stone ceilings and passageways. On the first floor a door opens into a massive room where light expands like the sun itself, an entire wall of glass facing north. Here, even the huge A-frame-like wooden easel, built especially for his larger-than-life canvases, is dwarfed in the great room.

In smaller rooms above, his collection of pre-Columbian stone idols were placed on exhibit. At the top of the highest stairway is an opening onto the roof terrace looking out over the valley of Mexico.

While Anahuacalli was being built, Rivera began work on the pre-Columbian murals in the National Palace, reconstructing the great civilizations of ancient Mexico and how they converged into modern Mexico. The large central panel showed the vast, rich and peaceful valley with the Aztec capital at Tenochtitlan, a place that in later panels, after the Spanish conquest, becomes a slave market lorded over by Cortes, now "a hunchbacked, syphilitic, micro-cephalic imbecile."

8.

Frida lived with her menagerie of dogs, cats, a monkey, and several tiny deer at Casa Azul, where she brightened the place with blue and yellow tiles, yellow chairs, and white walls and ceilings. When Diego came for comida, she cooked him vegetables. She too continued to paint between spells of agony, when she was in such pain that again she had to be encased in a body cast and sedated with drugs.

In 1948, Rivera was commissioned by the owners of the new Del Prado Hotel on Avenida Juarez, facing Alameda Park, to paint *Dream of a Sunday Afternoon in Alameda Park*. The work would measure fifty by sixteen feet. In the center, Diego put himself as a fat little boy holding an umbrella and a vulture's head, wearing knickers, striped socks, and a straw hat. A frog sits in his breast pocket. Behind him stands Frida with her hand on his shoulder. He is holding hands with lady death with a boa around her shoulders. The entire painting is peopled with famous persons of Mexico's history and its society, both past and present. He did not simply mirror the times, he created surreal satire. Into his work he painted "*Dios no existe*," or God does not exist, infuriating the Catholic hierarchy. Religious students burst into the hotel and mutilated the mural. The owners of the hotel were heaped with criticism and were threatened with arson. It was covered with a curtain. Nine years later, Rivera removed the words and the painting was unveiled. Still, it was very controversial.

When I first came to Mexico City in 1959, I was having a drink in the Del Prado lobby. Behind the bar was a huge wall covered with wood and curtain. I asked the bartender why. He explained that behind the wood was the mural which angered "church people and politicians." I asked why they didn't simply paint over it or rip it down. He looked at me incredulously and said, "Because, Señor, in the future there will be other church leaders and other politicians who might think differently." I considered his explanation as good as any — not only for the situation with the painting but for the entire country and its history. When the hotel was destroyed in the earthquake of 1985, the mural was rescued, reassembled, and given its own museum: Museo Mural Diego Rivera near the original site.

Rivera continued work on the National Palace murals into the early 1950s but spent afternoon hours with Frida, when she was able to enjoy his company. Still, he entertained numerous women

272

friends at the San Angel house, often taking them across the street to the Inn for comida or dinner. These included Paulette Goddard, who kept returning even after he was remarried to Frida; movie actresses Dolores Del Rio, whose portrait he painted again in the 1950s, and Linda Christian, Maria Felix, and Pita Amor.

In 1951, Frida developed gangrene in her right foot. Two years later her leg was amputated. Once, in a jealous rage, she threatened to send her amputated leg to Dolores Del Rio, who had been seen leaving the San Angel house in the middle of the night.

On July 13, 1954, Frida died. Diego wrote that it "was the most tragic day of my life." As her body was being pushed into the crematorium oven, it sprang upright, as though attempting to defy death. When her ashes returned, Diego took a pinch in his hand and ate them.

He painted no more frescoes. In November, Rivera gave the Mexican government both Casa Azul and Anahuacalli. The following summer he married art dealer Emma Hurtado, who had become successful selling his work.

A doctor had diagnosed Rivera with cancer of the penis in 1952 and had recommended amputation. The artist wryly commented that the cure would be far worse than the condition. When it recurred in 1955, he and his wife flew to Moscow for the latest cobalt treatment. Once he was declared cured, they returned to Mexico, where he soon fell in love with Dolores Olmedo, with whom he'd had an earlier affair and whose nude he'd painted in 1930. It had been rumored that Olmedo had been the mistress of several Mexican presidents. She was a lovely woman who had a beach home in Acapulco as well as a home in Mexico City. In 1955, he painted her barefoot in her native Tehuana dress with a basket of fruit. However, unlike most maidens from Tehuantepec, she wore a jeweled necklace, a gold bracelet, and her toenails were painted red.

On November 24, 1957, Rivera, who was still trying to paint even after a stroke paralyzed his right arm, died in a bed off his studio at San Angel. Although he asked to have his ashes mixed with Frida's and buried in his small temple at Anahuacalli with his collection of stone statues, the political establishment decided he should be given a state funeral and be buried in the Rotunda of Illustrious Men in the *Panteon Dolores*.

The Mayan Quartet

1.

Deep in the lush green valley of the Lacandon Rain Forest, named for the Maya who live there and cultivate the land, fish the streams, hunt the game, and weave the wool, are the ruins of Bonampak, the city of painted walls. Ravaged by the growth of two-hundred-foot-tall mahogany trees with massive root systems, the temples—first discovered by the outside world in the 1940s—have cracked, and some have not yet been excavated.

Bonampak is one of four Mayan ruins in the Usumacinta Valley in the southernmost region of Mexico. Nestled in the wilderness in the heart of the state of Chiapas, the ruins, if viewed on an aerial map, form a triangle shaped not unlike a great pyramid of the Classic Period, A.D. 300 to 900, when they were ceremonial centers. The Maya were the last of the four great Indian nations to rule parts of Mexico. The three others were the Toltecs, the Aztecs, and the Olmecs.

Of the four ruins—Bonampak and Yaxchilan, about twenty miles apart to the east; Chinkultic to the south, and the gigantic Mayan capital of Palenque in the north—Palenque is the most visited. With a paved highway giving it access from Villahermosa or San Cristobal de las Casas, Palenque is popular with people interested in the Mayan world and its history of opulence and violence. However, the more adventurous may wish to rent a four-wheel-drive vehicle with a driver-guide in the village of Palenque during the dry periods of late fall, winter, and early spring for a visit to Bonampak or Yaxchilan, two of the most mysterious and controversial ruins of Latin America. In the wet seasons of late spring, summer, and early fall, boat trips down the Rio Usumacinta can be arranged. And since I first visited in 1991, chartering a plane for a bumpy, stomach-wrenching ride into the thick and uncompromising bush, a highway has been cut through the jungle to the locations, making it even more accessible.

At Palenque, beyond the gates, the first sound that fills the jungle atmosphere is the screaming chatter of howling monkeys in a tree somewhere up on the first hillside. Beyond is the great Temple of the Inscriptions sitting high on the top of a steep series of stone steps. There, as you wander through the columned facade, a staircase leads downward into the mysterious bowels of this gigantic pyramid. The discoverer, Alberto Ruz l'Huillier, an archaeologist with few equals, worked at this site for years before finding this stairway one morning in 1949 filled with earth and rubble. It took him three more years to dig his way down to a large opening where he found pottery, shells, jade jewelry, and a pearl. Workers had to tear down a wall to find a slab of stone in the shape of a triangle standing upright against the opposite wall. In front of the triangle lay the skeletons of six children.

On June 15, 1952, Ruz's workers rolled back the stone and he entered a small dark room where he found a crypt twenty-three feet high, thirty feet long, and thirteen feet wide. On the walls were nine stucco reliefs of gods or priests. On the floor were two stucco heads. Along the center of the floor was a sarcophagus. Carved in relief on the 12.5-foot-long and 7-foot-wide slab was a figure whom Ruz later identified as Lord Shield Pacal, who reigned over Palenque from 615 to 683 A.D. For six months longer, Ruz and his people worked painstakingly with each and every detail of the small room, sifting dust and uncovering every detail. On November 28, 1952, the workmen lifted the five-ton slab to reveal Pacal's skeleton draped with precious jewelry and other necessities to assist him on his journey into another world. His death mask was made of jade and gold mosaic. Other jade ornaments were found on his fingers, neck, and arms. He held a piece of jade in each hand and had another piece in his mouth. His teeth were painted red. This was the first time archaeologists discovered a burial within a Mayan pyramid the same way rulers were buried in the pyramids of Egypt.

From the precipice of this temple you can look out over most of Palenque. The closest ruin is the Palace, a huge trapezoid structure spread out to the north. I climbed down and skirted the ballcourt surrounding. On the opposite side I found a relatively easy climb onto the Palace and up into its four-story tower, an observatory from which archaeologists believe the Mayans made astronomical calculations. On the winter solstice, while the viewer stands in the tower, facing south, the sun appears to drop directly into the Temple of the Inscriptions.

To the east, over a slight ridge, is the Temple of the Sun, with its roof like a honeycomb. In the center of the main room is the sun god and a pair of figures thought to be gods of the underworld.

Climb back down and cross the Rio Otulum that flows through the site, cross the flat grass-carpeted ball court, and visit the Temple of the Court, which appears to have been a series of apartments for the early Mayas who lived here. To the northeast is the museum filled with stone heads, jewelry, pottery, and other artifacts found in the temples as they were uncovered.

2.

Flying into the jungle at any time of the year can be exhausting. It is always hot and humid. The plane in which I rode sat on the narrow landing strip with little difficulty. The visual effects, a kaleidoscope of shades of green emblazoned by bright sunlight, as well as the quick drop in altitude, made me gasp. But within minutes we were over mahogany roots beneath a solid chorus of birds and insects, a never-ceasing sound that crescendos with the arrival of a plane or some other outside disturbance. Otherwise, it remains a loud eerie chirp that eventually seems to fade into the background.

A visitor should allow one full day at Palenque, another for the ruins of Bonampak and Yaxchilan to climb atop temples and explore palaces. With an added day of travel to Chinkultic, four full days would be adequate for most travelers. By boat add another full day.

3.

From the river, I made my way along a path beneath thick jungle growth, skirting rock walls and climbing steep stairways. At the top stood a giant stele: the rock carving of Hatach Huinic, victorious in battle, a tall and proud symbol of the Mayan warrior. Another, smaller stele showed Chac, the god of lightning and rain, a recurring figure in Mayan culture.

There are a dozen or so semi-uncovered buildings at Bonampak, about one hundred miles as the crow flies, or about forty-five minutes by bush plane, or half a day by boat from Palenque. None of the buildings are named but most are numbered in a Spanish-language brochure. The main three are the largest, famous for their interior murals showing vivid scenes of Mayan warfare. Prior to their discovery it was believed that the

Maya were a peace-loving people who avoided tribal warfare. The washed-out and aged scenes on the walls have changed that belief.

Sylvanus G. Morley, who directed the Carnegie Institution's excavations at Chichen Itza on the Yucatan Peninsula, first wrote of Bonampak's paintings in *The Ancient Maya*, completed in 1956. "The murals stand in sharp contrast to the sculpture of the stelae, where the principal figure remained styled in attitude and accouterments for over five hundred years," he wrote. "The scenes are narrative in a forthright yet sensitive style. Naturalism was held so important to the artist that the faces of certain of the participants in the murals can be recognized from room to room as they recur in parts of the story. The moods of the scenes vary: postures and facial expressions are relaxed during the preparations, ferocious in the raid, cold and forbidding during the judgment and sacrifice. The naturalism is stronger and the drafting more skillful than in any Old World art of the same period."

Amid the symphony of birds and insects one gazes up at scenes of high-browed, strong-chinned warriors. Musicians, warriors, prisoners, noblemen, dancers, women, and children total 270 human figures, each between thirty-three and thirty-six inches tall. The scenes lead up to a climax wherein the ruler and his family participate in a violent bloodletting, killing their enemies, who have been conquered in preceding battle scenes.

It was not until 1946, when the American photographer Giles Healey, hired by the United Fruit Company to produce a documentary about the Mayan culture, persuaded a Lacandon to lead him to Bonampak, that the outside world learned of these art treasures.

4.

Even more overgrown than Bonampak, about five miles to the northeast through thick jungle, or an hour of steady hiking, is

Yaxchilan, meaning *place of green stones*. Built on the cliffs above the Rio Usumacinta, forming the Mexican-Guatemalan border, the ruins are practically invisible to the traveler standing on the river bank. As I climbed through a maze of paths up the rugged terrain, I discovered a hodgepodge of temples, walkways, stone monuments, and ceremonial courts, all abandoned by the Maya in the ninth century.

Along the zigzagging stone stairs, at the end of dark passageways connected by cavelike hallways, the British archaeologist Alfred P. Maudslay found in the 1880s sculptured lintels that impressed him so much he wrote, "We have here the most marvelous monument ever to be offered to us by America, and we can be daring enough to present it as a work of art." Although he took much of the stone artwork back to the British Museum, many stelae and lintels remain.

Among the most outstanding lintels is that of a tall, heavy-nosed priest with a high, plumed headdress, making a penitent kneel while he pulled the rope barbed with thorns through the penitent's tongue.

Until recently, in the plaza where a stone crocodile and jaguar stand guard on gigantic stelae, the remaining five hundred Lacandon Indians celebrated ancient rites each season. They made pilgrimages to worship before the stone altar of Ach Bilam, lord of Yaxchilan, the great feathered god carved in the facade before the temple, where according to legend all of the Lacandons will gather at the end of time. Then the gods will behead all single men, hang them high by their heels and gather blood to paint their houses. This will be the final resting place of the Lacandon souls. Afterward, the gods will rebuild Yaxchilan to its former splendor.

Unlike Palenque, neither Bonampak nor Yaxchilan is huge. Their importance to Maya culture lies in their ceremonial significance. They are so buried in jungle growth, and inaccessible, that part of their beauty is in not knowing exactly how many buildings exist. Looking around through the jungle shadows, I was amazed at building on top of building, like a gigantic wedding cake, partly covered with dirt, frosted here and there with green moss and laced with a veil of stringy vines.

Today, archaeological students from the University of Mexico dig near the cavelike chambers of the great pyramid known to English-speaking visitors as the Labyrinth. It is a high climb. By the time I got to the top my calves were aching and I was covered with sweat, but it was worth the effort. High in the passageways of the tallest ruin, bird watchers gathered to peer over the tops of the jungle trees, searching for scarlet macaws, white hawks, and other birds.

At Yaxchilan every turn of the head is a visual adventure. The piers along the Rio Usumacinta, where those who arrive by raft tie up, deserve exploring, and visitors can rent a rope hammock for about a dollar-fifty to relax, close their eyes, and listen to the symphony of the jungle and dream about the days of Mayan past.

5.

Chinkultic, meaning *cave of the steps*, is the southernmost and least sophisticated of the Chiapas ruins. Built at the beginning of the Christian era, Chinkultic reached its height as a ceremonial center in the Late Classic Period but was abandoned in the thirteenth century.

Chinkultic rises out of the flatlands near the main highway traveling south from San Cristobal de las Casas and Comitan toward Guatemala. Turn left onto a secondary road, following the signs to the archaeological site. Although little of Chinkultic has been excavated, for me it is the most exciting because it presents a challenge in exploration. There are no guides.

Just inside the gate, I turned left on a path to discover a series of stelae amid thorn bushes. On these are carvings of various gods, particularly the jaguar god and Chac. Several have fallen and broken.

Down the stone-paved Mayan road between two smaller pyamids, neither of which has been uncovered, I stopped. Ahead, across a stone bridge, I saw an enormous mound. Although it was not as high as the Labyrinth at Yaxchilan, it seemed gigantic because there were no two-hundred-foot-high trees and no dense jungle growth. At the top, stone steps had been swept clean by wind and rain.

I climbed to the top and stood where the air was so clear it seemed as though I could see forever. The breeze was clean and cool, not half as humid as the jungle, and below, at the bottom of a steep stone cliff, a blue-green *cenote*, or sacrificial pool, glistened in the sunlight. This was the beginning of the Lagos de Montebello, lakes that are deep blue in early morning and that turn green later in the day. They are known as Las Encantadas (the enchanted lakes).

Looking south from atop the pyramid, I gazed at the purple mountains of Guatemala and thought about all the smaller temples below as stages on which Indians were dancing in splendid costumes.

Published in the travel section of *The New York Times* on Sunday, January 5, 1992, as "Mayan Treasures of Chiapas," this article stimulated thought and conversation among those interested in the temples and Mayan culture. Since then, a road has been cut through the jungle to a spot near Bonampak and Yaxchilan. More excavation, discovery, and study has continued at Palenque. I am told that Chinkultic is still splendidly natural.

In Love with Mexico

1.

When I first visited Mexico City in the late 1950s, it was a glorious city with wide boulevards and sidewalk cafes, and life was centered around the old historical downtown area. Today, it is a sprawling monstrosity with more than twenty-five million inhabitants, perhaps the largest city in the world. It is huge, and in many quarters unsafe. People who travel there should not be afraid but should be alert and use common sense, as they would in any large metropolitan area in the world. The old city is still my favorite part of the city.

Life and history in Mexico City revolve around the 792-foot-wide concrete square known as the Zócalo in the heart of the historical district. At the end of Avenida Juarez, named for the patriot leader who overthrew Maximilian in the mid-nineteenth century, I stood on the edge and watched as the daily morning ceremonies concluded when a group of brown-uniformed Mexican soldiers hoisted the huge green, white, and red flag to the sound of bugles and drums and the rhythmic step-and-slide march. I looked in all directions, getting my bearings, shifting my carrying case—

an old navy-blue canvas Land's End bag with ALABAMA stitched across the side. A smiling policeman, Eduardo Romorez, who had partrolled the Zócalo for more than thirty years, stepped to my side and warned: Make sure the strap of my bag was fastened around my neck and my right arm guarded the zippered top. "Not all of the people are as friendly as I." Then he asked if he could be of assistance.

When I told him I wanted first to go to the National Palace, the long four-storied government building constructed in 1521 by Hernan Cortes, he smiled and nodded. "The Diego Rivera murals are excellent."

In the National Palace I found Rivera's vast portrait of his country, detail after detail following the course of history as interpreted through the artist's idiosyncratic vision: The busy Aztec marketplace, Tarascan fishermen swinging butterfly nets on Lake Patzcuaro, the principal Spanish conqueror, Cortes, depicted as a syphilitic hunchback. The murals cover an entire entrance wall up a stairway to the second floor where more panels tell more history.

To the north of the Zócalo stands the ornate *Catedral Metropolitana*, the country's largest cathedral. Begun as a Baroque design in 1573, it took more than 250 years to reach completion.

Following a passage past a model of the great Aztec capital at Tenochtilan, complete with water showing the massive lake that once covered most of present-day Mexico City, I stepped down into the ruins of *Templo Mayor* or Great Temple. Here, in 1978, the site of the twin temples to the gods of rain and war — Tlaloc and Huitzilopochtli — was uncovered.

I continued through the maze of exterior stonework, noticing the intricate carving, all of the designs coming together in an elaborate motif. In the museum eight rooms were filled with more than three thousand pieces of Aztec treasures: sculpted stone goddesses, decapitated heads of prisoners, knives and other weapons.

Hot and tired, I exited and found a seat and watched as half-dozen energetic Indians, relatives of the original Aztecs, I imagined, balanced colorful headdresses and began a dance to the beat of handmade drums.

Refreshed, I moved north again along the crowded street in search of more murals. At the Ministry of Education, only several blocks from the Zócalo, on Republic of Argentina Street, I moved among hundreds of elementary school students, all in their uniforms, their eager faces gazing at the walls covered with the early murals of Diego Rivera.

Not as complex as the panels in the National Palace, these depict the simple life of the Mexican peasant: poor people eking a living from the soil, women grinding corn to make tortillas, men riding burros into cities where they work in the new industries.

On the third floor, Rivera's panels show the country's heroes: Ignacio Allende, youthful rebel of 1810; Padre Miguel Hidalgo, who issued his *Grito* or call to arms the same year, and was executed along with Allende only a few days later; handsome warrior Santa Anna; stern-faced Juarez; jovial gunman Pancho Villa, and angry-eyed Emiliano Zapata.

Around another block on Republic of Brazil Street, I found the Custom House. Tucked beneath the X of a large stairway is the modernesque mural *Patricians and Patricides* by avowed Stalinist David Alfaro Siqueiros. His sweeping lines leap from the walls. He shows an angry world in turmoil, man and animal crying out together for freedom, every inch a passionate wail.

A half-dozen blocks to the west I climbed the steps into *Palacia Nacional de Bellas Artes*, where the colorful dancers from each region of this immense country perform *Ballet Folklorico* every week. On the morning in 1998 that I walked into this world of Art Deco, there was a reverence held over from the previous day, when Mexico's Nobel Prize poet and novelist Octavio Paz had lain in state in the immense marble lobby. He was mourned by a nation before he was laid to rest in *La Rotunda de Los Hombres* in the Dolores Cemetery, where other major political and cultural personalities are buried.

At the top of the stairs I gazed at a wall covered with the subtle images of Mexico's greatest living artist, Rufino Tamayo. Purple on purple on purple, all shades separate yet flowing together, they blend as a soulful moan for all who behold it to hear.

On the next two floors Rivera, Siqueiros, and Jose Clemente Orozco present one gigantic image after another. Here Rivera recreated the famous Rockefeller Center piece that was destroyed at the direction of American businessman Nelson Rockefeller, after he felt he was ridiculed by the artist and his images.

After I walked through Alameda Park, where once-white, somewhat erotic statues have turned gray and impotent with age and pollution, I crossed Avenida Juarez to Museo Mural de Diego Rivera, where the work *Sunday Afternoon in the Alameda Park* gave a particular surrealistic view of the same place I had strolled only moments before.

At 2 P.M. on that spring afternoon, I hiked a block east of the Bellas Artes to the Bar L'Opera, an ornate corner with twenty-plus-foot ceilings with carved wood decorations and a forty-foot bar backed by Victorian mirrors. The maitre d' seated me at a table near the front and told me the story, passed down to him from an elderly bartender, of Francisco "Pancho" Villa riding into the bar on horseback, leaning down and shooting a *caballito* of tequila, firing his pistol into the ceiling, and riding out into the street. The tall man in the severe dark suit pointed out Villa's "signature" notched in the wood overhead.

Beneath photographs of recent celebrities — Mexican novelist Carlos Fuentes with American writer William Styron, movie stars Jane Fonda and Gregory Peck, who starred in the movie version of

Fuentes's novel *The Old Gringo*, and others—I enjoyed a leisurely afternoon comida. At a table nearby were two Mexican couples from a southern suburb. They'd come into the city to shop and enjoy the day. They had been taking comida at L'Opera on their leisure afternoons for years. I asked about the National Pawn Shop where I had found the doors locked. They informed me that workers there had been on strike for more than a year.

The Pawn Shop building near the Zócalo was where people who had fallen on hard times could hock their worldly goods. I had visited it years ago and found the variety of merchandise astounding—from pure junk to glittering jewelry to hand-tooled saddles to gun collections. One of the women told me she had bought an antique vase from Michoacan at the Pawn Shop. "It is a wonderful piece of art," she said, her voice a combination of sorrow for the people who had to part with the piece and joy for her own good fortune. When I perused it in the 1980s, each and every stall held story after story of families hit by natural and manmade disaster, sisters against sisters, children against parents, earthquakes and droughts. It was organized and funded as a charitable venture more than two hundred years ago by the owner of a silver mine to help those who found themselves facing financial ruin.

The next morning I rode a hotel taxi to Chapultepec Park where I spent three hours in the National Museum of Anthropology. After the Smithsonian in Washington, D.C., it is my favorite museum in the world. Every time I visit I find something new and different. And this time, not only did I relive old exhibits, I lingered and studied the lifestyle show of the living Maya—the Zinacantan, Chamula, and Lacandon, all of whom live in the state of Chiapas near the border with Guatemala. The exhibit showed the dwellings where the Indians live, their religious temples, ways of worship, and political ceremonies, showing how they blend into the world of the tropical rain forest. Several years earlier I had visited that mysterious place at the time of their *Fiesta de San Sebastian* and found it strange and powerful in its symbolic rituals—men dressed as monkeys climbing barkless trees, young men riding bareback with spears jousting a small round object suspended from poles, and evening rites of song and dance and drink around a blazing fire.

Also in the park I visited the modern Rufino Tamayo Museum. The building itself is worth the visit. It looks as through the steel and concrete juts up naturally from the gray earth. It twists and turns against the elements, the lines strong and abrupt, like a great piece of sculpture. Inside are some of the artist's finest paintings and sculptures—including his most famous rendering of *Watermelons* and his *Portrait of Olga* with its suspended watermelon. At the time I visited, there were also paintings by Picasso, Miro, and Warhol.

Across the Paseo de la Reforma is the Museum of Modern Art, where I viewed more art by Tamayo, including his Picasso-like *Woman with Pineapple* and his amazingly primitive *Two Dogs*. I found power and drama in his 1954 work *Cosmic Terror*, at once frightening and overwhelming. Here too is the Frida Kahlo self-portrait masterpiece, *The Two Fridas*, showing her haunting mirrored image. Gazing into it gave me goosebumps, thinking about the history of the tortured woman who painted pain better than anyone.

Other museums, a zoo, and many other monuments are located in the sixteen-hundred-acre Chapultepec Park, but the castle itself on *Cerro del Chapulin* —Grasshopper Hill—is a place of wonder. The castle, first built in 1783, became the home of Emperor Maximilian, sent by his cousin Napoleon in the 1860s to rule Mexico for France. He lived there with his Belgian princess wife, Carlotta. It was he who planned and started the Paseo (or wide boulevard) from here to downtown. And before he left his native

Austria to take his throne here, he demanded that his cousin provide a German brewmaster and a French baker for each battalion
of soldiers accompanying him to the new world. His legacy lasts
in modern Mexico's outstanding beer and breads.

Near Chapultepec, in the area known as Polanco, I took comida in a small Italian restaurant near the Hotel Polanco, a comfortable seventy-seven-room hotel on Calle Edgar Allen Poe. At La
Bottiglia, tucked into several rooms of a cellar, I sipped icy
Verdicchio and enjoyed melt-in-my-mouth paper-thin slices of
beef carpaccio on toast. After a tiny but tasty salad with capers and
vinegar and oil, the waiter brought forth a steaming platter of osso
bucco. The perfectly seasoned veal shanks, slow-cooked for hours
with herbs, onions, garlic, and tomatoes, were served with a side
of pasta with a smattering of underflavored pesto sauce.

After such a meal, the only item on any agenda should be a
siesta—a long, deep, reviving sleep—before awakening to more
sights and scenes of a dirty-aired but delightful experience in one
of the world's most interesting cities.

2.

When two U.S. movie stars of the 1940s, Johnny Weissmuller and
John Wayne, discovered the fishing town of Acapulco on the
southern Pacific coast of Mexico, they immediately began spreading the word among their Hollywood friends about this tropical
paradise.

Although it has grown to a city of a million, you would never
know it if you bury yourself in the delights of historic downtown,
Caleta beach and the environs of La Quebrada with its cliff divers,
the secluded *Pie de la Cuesta* (on a peninsula jutting westward
toward the setting sun) or the south-of-town resort hotels at the

Acapulco Princess or Vidafel Mayan Palace. Each area is unusual and interesting unto itself.

Only a few minutes from the Acapulco International Airport is the Vidafel, a sprawling resort that rises up from the beach like a gigantic thatch-roofed temple. The lobby with its huge Mayan sculptures greets the visitor with a feeling of immensity that spreads out among the acres under roof. A thousand luxury rooms are scattered around the tropical garden, that may be seen from a small train that runs from one end to the other. A long free-flowing swimming pool parallels the beach, then moves between big boulders and splashing waterfalls and under a half-dozen bridges.

Several miles to the north is the Acapulco Princess in the shape of three Mayan pyramids. From the moment I first stepped into the open-air lobby in the middle building, with its constant breeze bringing immediate freshness to the lungs, I felt like I had moved into another world. I have stayed at the Princess a half-dozen times, and each time was a unique and valued experience. Not only are the rooms comfortable and the grounds glorious, the professional staff makes you feel completely at home.

One of the most wonderful weeks at the Princess was in the mid-1980s when my wife Sally and I attended cooking school there. The main chef, Xavier, was a delightful showman, demonstrating everything from making melon water to slapping out a tortilla, to stuffing chiles rellenos to baking *huachinango* (red snapper) Veracruz style with tomatoes, bell pepper, olives, capers, and jalapenos.

The executive chef, a stern but dry-witted German, gave us a tour of the hotel's kitchens, showing the largest ice-maker we had ever seen and explaining the process of making thousands of delicious meals every day.

Our last day, we were awakened at 4 A.M. and transported to the public docks downtown, where we were allowed to pick out our own fresh catch of the day. The fish had been caught that morning. We carried them back to the Princess, where we prepared them under the watchful eye of Chef Xavier. That afternoon we enjoyed immensely our comida and our final siesta.

Several years later, my friends from the Mexico Writers Alliance, Bob Brooke and Marita Adair, thoughtful aficionados of the Mexican scene, took me to a terrific seafood restaurant in *Acapulco viejo* or old Acapulco. We enjoyed shrimp, salad, and fish for mere pennies. Another of my MWA friends, columnist and prize-winning photographer Reed Glenn from Colorado, and I had a wonderful breakfast under a laurel tree on the zócalo near the *Catedral Nuestra Sonora de la Soledad*, a gleaming white church built in 1930; then we hiked through the narrow cobblestone streets on the hill overlooking the harbor. As far as we were concerned, we were not even close to the Costera Aleman, the main curving boulevard that parallels the bay, lined by the huge hotels. We were in the world of old Mexico.

I have been attending an annual conference for travel writers and tourism professionals at Acapulco for nearly twenty years. I usually stay at one of the high-rise hotels along the beach because that is where the Mexico Government Tourism Office puts us. Then we begin looking for out-of-the-way places to visit.

Not long ago, my friend Ron Butler, one of the most knowledgeable people I know on the art and lifestyle of bullfighting, and I found a pleasant bar in a shopping center near the Acapulco Plaza hotel. Ron lives in Tucson, has traveled across the border for many years, and has written some poignant poetic pieces about the country, especially in his book, *Dancing Alone in Mexico*. Of it, I wrote in the *Montgomery Advertiser*, "Butler begins his story with a personal vision of the place, remembered beautifully and sadly, when he and his wife enjoyed a *simpatico* time together in the hills of Acapulco. It is a time broken in memory, a time and a place that resonates for him, and the reader is brought into his world and is shown how he becomes a man left to dance alone in Mexico."

I first came to Acapulco in 1959 while a student at the Instituto Allende at San Miguel de Allende. A friend and I drove three Texas businessmen first to Mexico City, where they ate, drank, and partied, then to Taxco, and finally to Acapulco. As we crossed the last hill after the six-hour drive, we had to stop while several men dragged a dead burro from the road. Back then, we stayed at the Papaguyo Hotel, which has long since been razed. Today, there are literally dozens of hotels lining the bay.

Back then, the fanciest resort on the bay was Las Brisas. It is still one of the finest. For honeymooners, Las Brisas is the ultimate resort. Each casita has its own private thumbnail-sized pool with fresh red, pink, and yellow hibiscus blossoms floating on the surface every morning. If you are not assigned your own pink-and-white Jeep, call the desk and ask for transportation, and the large chauffeur-driven Jeep will arrive at your front door in seconds.

Every morning a breakfast of fresh warm rolls, jellies, fruit, juice and hot coffee appears like magic in a two-way box in the wall of your sitting room.

Each guest is given a membership in La Concha Beach Club, built on the rocky terrain next to the lapping water of the bay. Here, the freshest drinks, salads, and heaping sandwiches may be enjoyed next to the large round saltwater pool.

The Costera Aleman, named for a former president of Mexico who always sang praises of Acapulco's tourism potential, parallels the edge of the bay that was picked by conquistador Hernan Cortes to be the main Spanish port on the Pacific. Stone-and-mortar Fort San Diego, built in 1776, was rebuilt in 1800 on a hillside overlooking the bay.

Within the walls of the fort is *Museo Historico de Acapulco*, with exhibits showing how the Spanish used Acapulco as a base of operations after trade routes were opened to the Far East. Displayed here is a model of the eighteenth-century sailing ship *Galeon de Manila* that sailed from the Philippines to China to the Mexican coast.

A short taxi ride from the fort takes the visitor to Caleta and Calletilla beaches off Avenida Lopez Mateo. Here again is the delightful essence of old Acapulco, beach style. Nestled between rocky cliffs where the movie stars from Hollywood cavorted from the early 1940s until the early 1960s, the beaches still have thatched-roof huts where fish, shrimp, oysters, and seafood soup may be enjoyed.

William Spratling's beach house was located on Caleta, where the silver artist hosted many parties for movie stars Dolores Del Rio, Paulette Goddard, Johnny Weissmuller, and artists Diego Rivera and David Alfaro Siqueiros.

From Caleta, take a boat to Isla la Roqueta, a hilly island that separates the beaches from the open sea. Spend a day on the island, hiking up to the lighthouse. Visit the small zoo or laze around on the beach, swimming or snorkeling.

A giant thatched-roof *palapa* covers Palao's Restaurant on the beach, where mariachis accompany coconut drinks and grilled shrimp. It is a truly laid-back Margaritaville atmosphere.

Back on the mainland, continue northwest on Lopez Mateo to the Hotel Las Glorias El Mirador, high above the rocky cliffs where the world-famous La Quebrada divers have been working their daredevil magic for many years.

Guillermo Garcia, one of the younger divers of the late 1990s, insisted that he learned by doing. "I started on some of the smaller cliffs, where the other, older divers told me the waves and tides matched the way the water acts here."

Garcia pointed to his head. "It is all in the vision. If you do not see so well, you can make a deadly mistake. If you do not know the rhythm of the water, you are putting yourself into a treacherous situation."

The dives begin daily at 12:45 P.M., but it is best to wait until sunset and after for the best show. Sitting on the La Perla terrace at the El Mirador, arrive an hour early for the 7:45 or 8 P.M. dives. Then they continue every hour until after midnight. After the sun goes down, the divers kneel at the tiny altar and take torches in their folded hands. They cross themselves, stand on the precipice 130 feet above the water that crashes against the rocks below, then thrust their bodies out, looking as though they are flying. The body extends, arching against the sky, then knifes down through the water's surface. When the head bobs up, arms high, applause breaks through the night.

About ten miles northwest of Acapulco, on the road toward Zihuatanejo, Pie de la Cuesta sits on a peninsula jutting into the Pacific. Numerous tiny outdoor restaurants dot the beach, where sitting and sipping and watching the sun go down provide another ending of another perfect day in paradise.

3.

The state of Jalisco spreads from the highlands north of Guadalajara, where the song of the same name is often heard in its after-midnight mariachi clubs, to the small village of Tequila, where the famous distilled liquor is made from the blue agave plant, down to San Pedro Tlaquepaque, with its pottery and antique shops, and west to the Pacific resort of Puerto Vallarta, otherwise known among the jet-set as P.V.

The old city of Guadalajara spreads out like a grand mural painted to perfection by one of Mexico's numero-uno artistes. It is broad and long, with an expanse of colonial architecture amid modern gardens that thrill the observer.

Although it is the country's second-largest city, it is truly an overgrown cattle town. On a Saturday night the revelers at downtown nightclubs are likely to be rancheros or cowboys from the surrounding countryside looking for a good time. It totally lacks the worldly sophistication of Mexico City.

I stayed downtown at the oldest hotel in the city where the Mexican hat dance was actually invented. The Hotel Frances is a four-story wonder opening onto an atrium lobby filled with leafy colorful plants.

Breakfast in the atrium garden is a major experience with friendly waiters and pleasant Mexican guitar music. *Huevos rancheros* are sunny-side-up atop a layer of refried beans mixed with peppers spread over a lightly fried tortilla. Or you may choose *chiliquiles*, a casserole mixture of scrambled eggs, spicy chorizo sausage, pulled chicken, strips of tortillas, chopped white onions, melted cheese, sour cream, and chiles with crumbled white cheese over the top. Served with a mug of *café con leche*, heavy black coffee with cream, either dish is a hearty start for a full day of walking and sightseeing.

To begin, turn north on Mestranza at the front of the Frances, then left on Calle Morena and continue down *Plaza de Armas*, a park lined with wrought-iron benches along a walkway to a raised ornate bandstand.

To the north is the cathedral consecrated in 1618. Its exterior is an interesting mixture of Baroque, Churrigueresque, and neo-classical designs. Twin towers pierce the sky above the remains of St. Innocence, removed from the catacombs of Rome and placed to the left of the main altar. The reverent quiet of the cathedral is made more majestic by the full rich chords of its nineteenth-century French organ.

Across Avenida Alcalde at Plaza Guadalajara sit ample benches where the weary walker may rest before reaching the *Palacio*

Municipal or city hall. Since I have grown older and somewhat crippled I pay more attention to resting places on my travels.

Nearby is *Museo Regional de Guadalajara*, built in 1701. In these halls the geographical and cultural history of the area is illustrated with artifacts and anthropological findings from prehistoric times to the Spanish conquest.

Outside, along the *Plaza de la Liberacion*, which gives way to the five-block *Plaza Tapatia* with spraying fountains and modern sculpture down its center, visit the Palacio de Gobierno, housing the office of state government of Jalisco. On the walls are two rousing murals by the city's most renowned artist, Jose Clemente Orozco. One shows Padre Miguel Hidalgo in 1810 opposing slavery and announcing his Grito of Revolution at Dolores. The other shows Presidente Benito Juarez from the mid-nineteenth century.

At the far end of *Plaza Tapatia* is the *Instituto Cultural Cabanas*, a huge domed building designed by famed architect Manuel Tolsá. In the central chapel, you can best view Orozco's finest work by lying down on benches and looking up at the magnificent ceiling, where the artist painted a series of murals entitled *The Man of Fire*. The scenes show man's spirit fighting against the engulfing power of flames. Take your time and let the powerful images soak in. In the smaller buildings surrounding the chapel are hundreds of smaller paintings and drawings by Orozco.

These are a mere taste of the full-course cultural offering served up by Guadalajara, where on numerous nights world-class opera is performed at *Teatro Degollado*, built in 1866 to copy the plans of Milan's La Scala. On the stage beneath the red-and-gold balconies, the Jalisco Philharmonic and Ballet Folklorico of the University of Guadalajara perform regularly.

Less than five miles southeast of Guadalajara is San Pedro Tlaquepaque, a village of artisans known for exquisite hand-painted pottery. Along the shaded, narrow, pristine streets, the visitor will find shop after shop with hand-tooled leather goods, hand-woven cloth and clothing, and hand-carved furniture.

About thirty-five miles northwest of Guadalajara is the small village of Tequila. Here, the *Herradura* or Horseshoe tequila distillery, in the old family hacienda in the middle of perfectly manicured gardens, offers simpatico hospitality at its finest. Huge vats bubble as the juice from the hearts of the blue agave plants is extracted, beginning the distillation process, the fumes heavy with an intoxicating aroma.

In a dark, wood-paneled saloon with a long mahogany bar and a rear mirror framed in ornate hand-carved wood, a member of the family demonstrated the proper way to drink tequila: a dust of salt on the top of the left fist to lick first, a quick suck from a wedge of lemon, and then a sip from a *caballito* or shot-glass neat. If you wish, have a swallow of *sangrita* or spicy hot lemon-orange-tomato juice served on the side. The Mexican expert advised that it is always best to sip good tequila: only shoot or knock back *cheap* tequila or mezcal in one quick gulp. "The idea is to have all of the flavors mixing strongly and perfectly in your stomach," our host explained. "For perfection, never mix good tequila with any other liquid." He shrugged. "But, of course, the margarita is not totally bad."

According to Tomas Alzarez, the Herradura *blanco* or white aged tequila is the best in the entire world. Then, if you move on to another distillery in Tequila, you will hear the same proclaimed of another brand from another hacienda factory.

A thirty-minute flight south from Guadalajara will take the visitor to the Pacific coast town of Puerto Vallarta, which was a sleepy little fishing village without a paved street until its most celebrated resident, film director John Huston, brought famous actors and actresses here to make Tennessee Williams's *Night of the Iguana*. Since then, it has grown into a town of more than 200,000 and celebrity-sighting has become a pastime.

In a bar near the *Malécon* or concrete walkway along the beach, it is said, best-selling author Robert James Waller sat every afternoon for more than a week and outlined his novel *Puerto Vallarta Squeeze*, set in Mamma Mia's, where the bartender named Pedro tells stories about people named Lobo and Willie Royal and Luz and Danny, characters Waller made famous.

Tequila's, near the famous bronze statue of a boy riding a seahorse, was the hotel that once was home of Elizabeth Taylor, Richard Burton, Deborah Kerr and others involved with the shooting of *Iguana*. It was the site of the wedding of Miss Taylor and Mr. Burton, and today, beneath photographs of the wedding, the shrimp cocktail and other fruits of the sea are scrumptious.

South on the *Malécon*, turn east into Gringo Gulch, named for the hundreds of U.S. expatriates who bought homes here, including the Burtons. Their homes, together called Casa Kimberly, include a small bridge over the road connecting his with hers. It has been turned into a bed-and-breakfast and a mini-museum of Taylor-Burton memorabilia on Calle Zaragosa.

Continue south and cross a small bridge onto Cuale Island. Here, in a small but colorful little garden, sits film director John Huston in bronze, his bare feet in sandals, his callused fingers holding a cigarette.

Near the statue are chic restaurants, bars, and shops.

A short drive south of P.V. is the Playa Mismaloya, a half-moon bay that was secluded with its tiny spit of a beach until Mr. Huston brought his cameras and actors and actresses. Now it is the site of La Jolla de Mismaloya, a luxurious suite hotel amid the lush jungle growth. If there is any better place to watch the sun set over the Pacific than the Pie de la Cuesta north of Acapulco, it is the Night of the Iguana bar at Mismaloya. Here, sitting in one of the highest alcoves, look out over the Pacific past Los Arcos, a great rock formation about a half-mile off shore. The rock forms a huge arch of pocked stone where birds nest, play, and sing. Often, especially in spring or fall, the sunset is often as dramatic as the movie from yesteryear. When the sun turns orange on the horizon, Los Arcos rock is backlit to cast mysterious, elongated shadows that play in one's memory long after the sun has dropped into the ocean.

After nightfall, the hillside on the opposite side of Playa de Mismaloya opens to show the restored set that Huston built for the action of his film. It was here that Ava Gardner ran an off-the-beaten-path hotel for wayward travelers. This is where Richard Burton brought his tour of church ladies after their bus conveniently broke down on the road nearby. It is where Deborah Kerr and her father, the world's oldest practicing poet, stayed amid the jungle growth. Today you may walk where they walked, through the rooms and across the patio where the characters enacted the dramatic scenes. Standing on the edge of the patio and looking down through the jungle toward the beach, you can almost see the lovely Miss Gardner romping with her beach boys. If you concentrate, you can hear the sound of her giggling voice mixed with the waves lapping onto the shore far below.

A slightly different version of these articles first ran under the headline "In Love with Mexico" in the Arts & Leisure section of the *Mobile Register* on Sunday, June 21, 1998. Another version of the piece on Tequila was published in *The Montgomery Independent* in the fall of 2000, and about Puerto Vallarta and John Huston in *The Montgomery Independent* in the spring of 2001.

❋

See Y'all Later or *En la Manana*

❋

Every time I drive down a country road into the wilderness of my home state, and every time I ride through the hillsides of Guanajuato or the jungles of Chiapas, I feel at home with a history and a people I admire. As far as I am concerned, my heart is in the earth of both places. With each passing day, I hope that I will have the opportunity to visit more sites and to learn more about the history and the people.

—Wayne Greenhaw
Montgomery, 2001

*

Acknowledgments

*

There have been so many people who have affected my life in Alabama and in Mexico, I could never list them all and thank them properly.

For all those people no longer with us — my parents, Harold Reed and Myrtie Lee Able Greenhaw, who had the courage to allow their son to leap from the nest and experience an amazing adventure south of the border in the late 1950s; my stepfather, Andrew Brown, a wonderful person; my teachers, Hudson Strode, John Craig Stewart, and Yewell Lybrand in Alabama, Sterling Dickinson and Ashmead Scott and others in Mexico, all of whom instilled in me an eagerness for travel and the learning experiences; my writer-mentor Borden Deal who had had his own Mexican experience, and his wife Babs who gave literary nourishment to a kid who was trying; fellow writers both in Alabama and in Mexico, especially Jeanie Thompson and Bart Barton with the Alabama Writers Forum and Bob Brooke and Marita Adair with the Mexico Writers Alliance; all of my writer friends who were always willing to share, I love them and appreciate them.

I want to thank my friends in Alabama and in Mexico. In Alabama, I have been blessed to have wonderful friends in high places, especially Governor Jim Folsom, who appointed me to his cabinet as director of the Alabama Bureau of Tourism and Travel, and Governor Don Siegelman, with whom I have worked closely and who appointed me to the Alabama Humanities Foundation and Andy Brittion with the Montgomery Area Chamber of Commerce. In Mexico, Teresa Villarreal Saitcevsky with the Mexico Tourism Office, Jaime Fernandez and Lou Christine with the Instituto Allende, Desmond O'Shaughnessy Doyle, the director general of tourism promotion for the State of Guanajuato, Sarah Hoch DeLong with the tourism public relations office at San Miguel de Allende, Alicia del Villar de Blanco with the Hotel Nikko in Mexico City, Oscar Veiliz Quiroga and Octavio Venegas Nakaturo with the Secretaria de Turistico de Gobierno del Estado Chihuahua, for introducing me to Juan Quezada and Mata Ortiz, and numerous other tourism professionals and people who simply love their country. All have been enormously cooperative, sharing stories about its history and culture.

I would also like to thank my friends and associates, Dr. Alfred Newman and his wife, Carolyn, two wonderful people who operate River City Publishing like it belongs to the authors and artists who work hard to provide the manuscripts they make into books. My editor, Jim Davis, is a true gentleman, and I want him and all the others at River City — Lissa, Tangela, Tina, Tony, and William — to know how much I appreciate their work. Also, thanks are due my friend Adriane Butterfield for meticulously checking my dubious Spanish.

And not least of all, my wife, Sally, whom I cherish, who has shared in good times in both places.

— Wayne Greenhaw

About the Author

Wayne Greenhaw has had a career most authors only dream about.

In his teens, he studied writing at the Instituto Allende in San Miguel de Allende, Mexico. Later he studied writing under the legendary Hudson Strode at the University of Alabama. Greenhaw's first article, about traveling in Mexico, was published in the early 1960s.

As a columnist and reporter, he has published hundreds of articles in regional, national, and international publications, including the *New York Times*, *Atlantic Monthly*, *Reader's Digest*, and *The Writer* magazine. He contributed six chapters for a *Guide to Mexico*.

Greenhaw, who was a Nieman Fellow at Harvard, has published about fifteen books of fiction and nonfiction. He has worked on prize-winning TV productions, and two plays he wrote have been produced. He has taught journalism and creative writing at the college level.

Greenhaw lives in Montgomery with his wife, Sally, where he spends as much time writing as his busy schedule will allow. He has several new projects in the works.